Towards an Improper Politics

Towards an Improper Politics

MARK DEVENNEY

EDINBURGH
University Press

Edinburgh University Press is one of the leading university presses in the UK. We publish academic books and journals in our selected subject areas across the humanities and social sciences, combining cutting-edge scholarship with high editorial and production values to produce academic works of lasting importance. For more information visit our website: edinburghuniversitypress.com

Edinburgh University Press Ltd
The Tun – Holyrood Road, 12(2f) Jackson's Entry, Edinburgh EH8 8PJ

First published in hardback by Edinburgh University Press 2020

Typeset in 10/13 Giovanni by
IDSUK (DataConnection) Ltd

A CIP record for this book is available from the British Library

ISBN 978 1 4744 5403 2 (hardback)
ISBN 978 1 4744 5404 9 (paperback)
ISBN 978 1 4744 5405 6 (webready PDF)
ISBN 978 1 4744 5406 3 (epub)

CONTENTS

Acknowledgements / vi

INTRODUCTION / 1

ONE / Property, Propriety and the Limits of the Proper / 6

TWO / Theorising the Improper / 33

THREE / The Performative Politics of a Brick / 67

FOUR / The Politics of Equivalence / 83

FIVE / The Improper Politics of Democracy / 103

SIX / Transnational Populist Politics / 135

CONCLUSION / 157
NOTES / 159
BIBLIOGRAPHY / 164

Index / 173

ACKNOWLEDGEMENTS

This book has taken far too long to write. Over the past six years I have presented versions of chapters to different audiences. These arguments benefited from the critical engagement generously offered by so many. In particular, my collaboration with Paula Biglieri on the British Academy funded 'Transnational Populist Politics' research project proved invaluable. Colleagues who worked on that project – Clare Woodford and German Primera – forced me to clarify my arguments in the most productive academic dialogues I have yet engaged in. Many others have argued with me about these ideas. The labour of writing is time-consuming. It is time that often goes unacknowledged in the British higher education system. Thank you to Justine who has encouraged me throughout this process, often at the expense of time we should have had together.

I dedicate the book to my brothers Darren and Michael. Michael died unexpectedly, and far too young. I miss him every day. Darren made it back from the other side.

INTRODUCTION

Why have political theorists given up on the critique of property? What has happened to our understanding of inequality as centred on the politics of property? Might we rescue this critique of inequality, without resorting to the prescriptive politics of propriety so characteristic of Marxism? Property is central to every aspect of contemporary politics. The financial crisis of 2008 had its root in sub-prime mortgages. The demands of indigenous peoples reject the logics of property established through colonial violence. The damage caused to our environment and climate has its origins in a very particular notion of land and cattle as property. In these, and many other instances, a failure to think the politics of property limits our ability to imagine better ways of living together. The wager of this book is that thinking improperly about property and propriety allows for an original critique of inequality. Theoretical and political debates of the past half century have circled around different notions of the improper – *différance*, the real, the 'other', antagonism, excess. They all allude to an impossibility that disturbs, yet concurrently lends coherence to, what is deemed proper, what can be rendered a property in itself. However, the play between the proper, propriety and the improper is ignored in post-foundationalist debates about the political. In introducing an improper politics I develop a conceptual vocabulary to engage with the politics of property and inequality from a post-foundational perspective. I characterise property, propriety and the proper as central to hegemonic order and rethink hegemony in proprietary terms. This critique of the politics of the proper also requires a rethinking of democracy. I characterise democratic politics as improper, one way to reanimate the proper bounds of reason, dominant ontologies and the policing of property, propriety and subjectivity. Thinking democracy as an improper practice of equality accords a dignity to forms of politics often deemed marginal in democratic theories. I argue that theorists of democracy have confused democratic politics with the forms taken by the state and political regimes. The text responds to two related problems of critical thought and practice. First, many argue that post-foundationalist theories of the political undermine a politics committed to material equality. The charge is patently false. However, such theories often take for granted existing forms of property. They fail to rethink property as a contingent intervention in and unequal articulation of life chances – a key to understanding the distribution of precarity. Second, the politics of the left too quickly invokes the proper – the claim to know what is right justified with recourse to a philosophy of history, to an ethics, or to a politics with prior ontological warrant. Such certainties too often generate disciplinary forms of politics. In the past century these ranged from the worst forms of violence deployed in defence of the communist ideal to the petty policing of speech, behaviour and acts in the name of an ethics of certainty. Often such certainties justify violence as a means towards a greater end. They traduce democratic equality and abuse its promise as an end to be realised rather than as a practice to be enacted – no matter what the circumstances.

In Chapter 1, I argue that property and possession are central to the thinking of politics. I characterise property as a contingent political intervention, which in articulating 'things' as property, renders them open to appropriation. If property claims are contingent then any attempt to limit or control access to worlds recast as property is political. Second, I maintain that property is always tied in uncertain ways to forms of propriety. Proprietary orders police behaviour, norms and property through both explicit and implicit rules. I defend the bold claim that ontological judgements about what is proper to being are always articulated with forms of appropriation. The triad of inequality, impropriety and violence anchor hegemonic forms of proprietary order – and are always articulated with particular ways of being. I situate this notion of proprietary order in relation to the colonial logics of property and appropriation that haunt so called 'Western' political theory. The chapter effects a shift in the ways in which hegemony is conceptualised, placing logics of property, propriety and historical injustice at the heart of political order.

Chapter 2 sketches a politics of the improper. This entails an account of the improper that does not merely mirror the proper, as its alter ego. Agamben, writing in 1973, rejected the notion of politics as improper for this very reason (Agamben 1973: 141–2). He later characterises as authentic a politics that would render inoperative the anthropological machine of the West. I am unconvinced by this argument. My account of the improper assumes that there is no proper way of being, living or organising life with

prior warrant. Ethics is always implicated in hegemonic struggles to determine what should be the case, rather than an abstract, ahistorical version
of what should be the case. Ethical arguments do not stand above the fray
lending justification to particular forms of politics. An improper politics
begins *in media res* so to speak and cannot simply step out of the order it
rejects. It destabilises relations of property, propriety and inequality and
aims to enact equality as an ongoing demand and lived practice. I contrast
this argument with the invocation of the common, developed by among
others Hardt and Negri (2009). Likewise, while political resistance may take
counter-hegemonic or populist form – along the lines developed by Laclau
and Mouffe – improper forms of politics are often marginal to political and
institutional order, as well as to counter-hegemonies. An improper politics
may include withdrawal from dominant regimes; the breaking of bounds
through occupation, hacktivism, trespass and theft; alternative forms of
hegemony such as populism; and transnational forms of political organisation. In contrast with the emphasis on political regimes and the seizure of
sovereign power, the improper is in excess of all forms of proprietary order.
These arguments anticipate my reading of democracy and populism in the
following chapters. These opening chapters establish the conceptual contours of this work.

The following chapters advance this theoretical trajectory through engagement with a range of key concepts in critical political theory: performativity;
equivalence; democracy; and populism. In Chapter 3 I argue that political
theorists have too often mistaken their own object, collaborating in the
depoliticising of proprietary order. I develop a suggestion from Judith Butler
that political theorists, in disavowing the economy, have performatively
secured their own domain of study. I misread her 'insurrectionary ontology'
as an improper intervention against dominant forms of the proper. Butler
puts the foreclosed to work in unpicking the violence intrinsic to proper
ways of being. I reconstruct her account of the performative, emphasising
those moments when it touches on questions of the proper. This extends her
account of assembly and performative politics in relation to the politics of
property and propriety. A politics of assembly, in its enactment of equality,
renegotiates bodies and their properties; how we conceptualise the demos;
and the performativity of property as a way of regulating what Butler terms
the space of appearance.

This reframing of the notion of performativity insists upon the materiality of all political struggles and of discourse. In Chapter 4, I extend this
argument in relation to post-Marxist accounts of hegemony. I contend,
with Laclau and Mouffe, that contingency is central to an improper politics.
However, their works elide key questions about contemporary capitalism

and ignore the role of both property and financial equivalence in securing hegemony. I start with a close reading of *Hegemony and Socialist Strategy* (1985). The authors reject the Marxist account of equivalence and the money form. They argue that there is no underlying positive content – for Marx socially necessary labour time and surplus value – to monetary forms of equivalence. Having rejected Marx's notion of equivalence they turn from the discussion of the value form in Marxist theory to thinking equivalence in linguistic and discursive terms. Hegemony, they argue, depends on the articulation of different political identities as equivalent in opposition to a common antagonist. This is a missed opportunity. They do not carry through their critique of Marx, to rethink the role that finance plays in articulating forms of political order. The money form establishes relations of equivalence that render every element of life a unit of exchange. They might have rethought the money form as a contingent form of hegemonic articulation, emphasising the contingency of value, the contingency of the relation between abstract labour and the expression of value, and the retroactive causality necessary to the realisation of value. This suggests a different way of thinking about political economy within post-Marxist theory. The value form is a contingent means for articulating the hegemony of capital – contingent both as a form and in its attribution of value to commodities. Logics of equivalence I contend are not the same as democratic practices of equality. This argument puts in to question the notions of difference and equivalence so elemental to post-Marxist notions of the political.

Chapter 5 examines the implications of the improper for the understanding of democracy, and in particular for accounts of radical democracy. The word democracy quite literally means the power(s) of the demos: the demos, without qualification, exercises power. This says nothing about who counts as a member of the demos, nor does it determine the proper nature of its power. In contrast with radical democratic (Mouffe 2000; Norval 2007), deliberative (Gutmann and Thompson 2004) and representative (Urbinati 2006; Saward 2010) theories of democracy, I contend that the democratic subject is never proper to itself. Democratic demands challenge all forms of propriety that limit, by defining the bounds of the proper, the role, the place and the membership of a demos. Contemporary accounts of democracy deploy different principles of exclusion to determine who counts as a member of the demos. Political theorists often hint at the unqualified right to be a member of the demos but all too quickly quash this idea as an unrealistic and dangerous excess. Developing arguments drawn from Rancière (1999) and Ober (2008) I conclude that there is no principle proper to the demos. The excessive nature of democratic power means that it has no appropriate limits. This excess of power is not something beyond the demos. It is the very site for the improper enactment of equality. Democracy enacts equality in excess of proprietary order. Having made this argument the chapter proceeds to investigate the implications of this for key concepts in democratic thought – in particular representation, liberty and the political party.

Chapter 6 is more speculative than those that precede it. It imagines a democratic populist politics that improperly queers our thinking of the people. Populism is always deemed improper, a challenge to the dominant proprietary forms of order. The characterisation of the people as animalistic, voracious or unrealistic is oft deployed to discipline electoral democracies. My central concern is the relation between populism and democracy. First, I argue that populism is not in itself democratic. It is only democratic insofar as it evidences a politics that enacts equality. I distinguish the demos from the people and argue that populist logics are not equivalent to democratic logics. The demos stretches to breaking point whatever notion of the people has become hegemonic. Second, I argue that a democratic and populist politics must be transnational. When populism is articulated to an imagined national community it betrays democratic equality. I draw an analogy between contemporary debates in queer theory about trans politics and transnational populist politics. The chapter recalls too the arguments of Chapter 4 about equivalence. I argue that populist forms of politics inadequately address the hegemonic forms of equivalence that underpin logics of finance and capital.

The form of this book is somewhat different to the traditional academic text. Each chapter is prefaced with a narrative about a particular object, play, work of art or political acts. The stories trace a different trajectory to the main theoretical arguments. In each case I cast the story in light of the politics of property and the improper. This is a decidedly partial reading, one that complements the main text. The stories, taken together, allude to a political history of democracy as improper. The Conclusion of the book articulates these stories – which take us from Ireland to the Congo, from Argentina to South Africa and Slovenia – in terms of a politics of the improper.

ONE

Property, Propriety and the Limits of the Proper

So What Exactly is Communication?

There are literally billions of mobile phones in use across the world. They all require the conflict mineral coltan to enable their high-density capacitators. Much of this coltan is mined in the Democratic Republic of the Congo where it has fuelled decades of civil war. Illegally mined coltan enters the supply chains of Apple, Samsung Dell, Sony and Vodafone. Most coltan mining is 'legal'. It relies on charters granted to international mining companies by the contested sovereignty of the Congolese government. Salaries paid to mine workers are higher than the average wages paid in the Congo, though still paltry. Often mines function because of agreements (tax) with local militia to ensure that mined coltan can leave the Congo – via Rwanda. The illegal *creusers* work in disused tunnels, or on discarded rubble heaps, to extract the remaining coltan with bare hands and pick axes (Amnesty International 2016: 4–11). Workers are often children. This coltan is sold to the mines, or in the various market towns across the region, from where it finds its way back in to the supply chain, having become the legal property of the purchaser. In these 'zones of exploitation' industrial mining is deemed too costly. Illegal mining reduces the cost of extracting the coltan. It benefits the warlords and other organised groups who feed it back in to legal supply chains. Legal and illegal find a happy concordance as traders mediate the smooth integration of illegal coltan into legitimate property regimes. Possession wrought by violence becomes legally enforceable property. This overlap should not divert our gaze from the legal companies granted property rights over coltan. Legality is bought, secured all too often through bribes, and brings with it the requirement for violent exclusion. The Congolese state issues leases, or sells mines, to international companies. The selling of rights to copper and coltan mining follows a common logic. Land, or right, nominally owned by the Congolese state, is sold to offshore companies for less than their actual worth. Shell companies then sell the rights on, at a large profit, to multinational mining firms such as Glencor. Money paid to the shell company finds its way back to the Congolese state (Burgis 2015: 50–1) where it is deployed as a slush fund by dominant elites. These proprietary rights allow companies to demarcate territory, deploy private security and negotiate 'taxes' with local rebel groups. Global supply chains shuttle these minerals via Rwanda and Uganda to ports and airports in Belgium and the Netherlands. The old colonial trading routes are the well-oiled grooves delivering coltan to the global market. Communicative democracy's other face is the mineral infrastructure of every phone, the supply chain, the networked world of extractive capital.

Introduction

In 1995, Gerry Cohen characterised the liberal theory of property as an ideological fiction that justified the expropriation of resources common to all. The division of the world into privately owned property, he argued, should always be subject to the veto of co-owners (Cohen 1995: 69). His intervention was a small footnote to centuries of debate about the place of property in democratic societies. Today, however, property is a footnote to critical theoretical debates about democracy. This is extraordinary as are the bare facts about the ownership of the world. Approximately 90 per cent of the world's population own no property (neither intellectual nor physical). The legal persons that own property are often global corporations granted personhood in international law. Oxfam research shows that twenty-six individuals own as much global wealth as the poorest 50 per cent (3.4 billion individuals) of the global population. The richest 1 per cent of the population own the same amount of wealth as the other 99 per cent (Hardoon 2017). Property rights wielded by global elites, by transnational corporations and by powerful states are the infrastructural rigging of inequality. For Marxists and anarchists, property is intrinsically political – rather than an economic matter best left to the experts. Today these worldviews are barely audible echoes in the fallen statue parks of the former Soviet bloc. Contemporary theorists of radical democracy unwittingly acquiesce in Hayek's dictum that modern civilisation rests on the institution of private property (Hayek 1960: 171).

I reject this unspoken consensus and rethink the politics of property from a post-foundationalist perspective. Some will be disappointed. I do not propose a new theory of, or justification for, property. Such a theory would mistake its object. Instead, extending post-foundationalist accounts of hegemony and police, I conceptualise social order as proprietary. Proprietary orders articulate together property and propriety. These are the axes around which inequality is ordered. I give no simple definition of property but do contend that it rests on exclusion and exclusivity. First, I reprise the complexity of Marx's account of property that ties it to propriety, to violence and to legal order. The 'Marxisms' of the twentieth century rinse dried this complexity. Second, I argue that property and propriety are elemental to the thinking of hegemony, of gender politics, to the postcolonial globe and decolonial politics, and to the model of development that has destroyed the planet and its ecosystem. I turn to Schmitt's *Nomos of the Earth* to think through the relation between political order, ontology and divisions of territory and property. This is a response to repeated critiques that post-Marxism fails to address historically constituted relations of material force. Third, I return to property as one refracted lens through which to conceptualise hegemony. Property delimits access to and control over worlds. It delineates appropriate forms of behaviour and subjectivity. It articulates the world as proper and orders appropriate forms of behaviour. If this chapter has too overt a focus on property this is in part a corrective to post-Marxist accounts of the political, in part an attempt to further the deconstruction of Marx begun in the post-Marxist tradition.

Property and the Politics of Marxism

Why do contemporary theorists of the political ignore property? It was not always thus. If for two millennia property was central to debates about democratic politics it is now, as Pierson argues, 'the subject of pretty widespread neglect' (Pierson 2015: 3). The demise of property as an object of critical political inquiry coincides squarely with the end of the Cold War. In the decade following the collapse of the Soviet world, legal experts abetted these new states in drawing up legal frameworks compatible with international law. Central to these legal norms was private property and the legally incorporated corporation. The legal boundaries of post-Communist states had to first be established. In some instances, most notably in Yugoslavia, such boundary drawing was finalised after bloody civil wars.

Legally enforceable territorial boundaries went hand in glove with the establishment of a regime of enforceable property rights linked to increasingly abstract versions of property. Industries, land and assets once under the legal proprietorship of states, and nominally at least of the sovereign people, were sold or leased. A gloss of legality legitimised the enrichment of communist officials who had once managed state companies. The most egregious example was the privatisation of the oil industries in Russia. However, privatisation was not limited to communist states. Social democracies too sold off state assets, expanded the realms and objects subject to the law of property and actively encouraged individual self-valorisation. Legally enforceable global systems of property were established. The right of individuals to own private property was celebrated as the restoration of wrongs committed by Communist states. Despite this optimistic gloss, the post-communist global proprietary order established the rights of legal property holders, primarily private corporations, rather than of individual property holders. This global legal architecture includes the standardisation of land registration, a system first invented during the British colonisation of Ireland. In Australia and the United States, it was elemental to the violent dispossession of indigenous peoples. Land registration was mimicked in legal norms that established property rights over genes, information and intellectual property. The post-Cold War period in effect saw two unprecedented developments in property law. First, they became global in nature and enforceable against signatory states. Second, property regimes were extended to include genetic resources, information, codes and business practices. Ironically, even as property regimes were refined, political theorists in large part ignored the place of property in thinking about both political order and normative questions about equality.

The critique of private property was, however, central to now discredited Marxist theories of the social formation. Marx argued that private ownership of, and control over, the means of production forces those who *legally* own nothing but their labour to sell it as a commodity. Those who own property do not have to work. Once *legally redefined* as a property, the labour of the individual could be sold for a wage. In England enclosures beginning in the sixteenth century, and largely completed by the nineteenth century, rearticulated land as private property forcing those with traditional claims over common land to sell their labour. Similar processes of accumulation by dispossession continue in the present day. They returned to Britain with the privatisation of public lands and housing – 10 per cent of the total land mass of Britain, after the election of Margaret Thatcher in 1979 (Christophers 2018: 8). Similar violent processes of dispossession characterised colonial occupations across the globe following a pattern established by the British in Ireland. In the colonial context, as Greer notes, the establishment of both private and common forms of property were elemental to a politics of dispossession (Greer 2012: 365).

Marx characterised the liberal ontology of property in one's self as the ideological justification for control and ownership of the earth's resources. He conceptualised legal property as elemental to the capitalist mode of production. Private property alienates the worker from his labour and from the product of *his* labour. Marx and Engels write in the *Communist Manifesto* that 'the theory of the Communists may be summed up in the single sentence: Abolition of Private Property' (Marx and Engels 1985: 498). Post-foundational theorists of the political rejected the associated ontology. It assumes that all political antagonisms are explicable in terms of ownership and control over the means of production (Laclau and Mouffe 1985: Chapter 1). My improper reading aims to illuminate a more nuanced critique of property in Marx's texts. I find in Marx a more complex account of property as elemental to the so-called base and superstructure. He avoids abstract moralism and politicises the history of property recognising its violence. This reading forces a rethinking of the politics of hegemony.

For Marx, property is part of both the economic base and the superstructure – in fact, it undermines the distinction between the two. Although elemental to the day-to-day organisation of economic production, property requires legal definition and protection. This resulted in decades long, often futile debates between Marxist theorists about the role of property in the social order.[1] Cahan and Balibar, for example, claimed to 'resolve' the debate arguing that economic forms of possession precede their legal formulation, which merely codifies already existent facts (Axelrad Cahan 1994: 392). They find justification for this argument in Marx's works. However, their argument fails to address the real difficulty: legal and political framing are intrinsic to the very notion of property not merely reflective of another reality. Property does not exist unless it is articulated, secured and protected by legal violence. They are constitutive of any regime of property. The legal articulation of property is central to capitalist and other forms of production – and its valences are overdetermined by those complexes. Property belies any crude distinction between the economic and the political. This ambiguity already indicates the possibility of thinking capitalism without recourse to the idea that there is an ultimate economic reality to the social order.

It is striking how post-Marxist theorists forget that property undermines any easy distinction between economy and polity, and is central to the thinking of political order. This was not quite the case for Laclau and Mouffe's *Hegemony and Socialist Strategy* (1985) where property plays a marginal role in their rendering of hegemony. They refuse the idea that property serves to secure the existence of dominant relations of production, and view it as articulated within the ensemble of these relations (Laclau and Mouffe 1985: 102). If so, we cannot conceptualise property in itself. Articulation as a 'practice establish[es] a relation among elements such that their identity is modified as a result of the articulatory practice. The structured totality resulting from the articulatory practice, we will call discourse' (Laclau and Mouffe 1985: 107). This notion of discourse transcends the distinction between the linguistic and the extra-linguistic, the material and the immaterial. It allows us to think property in terms of the articulation between linguistic, legal, symbolic and material elements. As elements of an overdetermined apparatus, the legal, political and economic components of property are inseparable – other than as a methodological conceit. Property rights demarcate rights of use, the specification of abuse, forms of exclusion and inclusion, and the right to profit. To abuse Wittgenstein property forms 'have no one thing in common . . . for all that they are related to one another in many different ways' (Wittgenstein 2009: Remark 65). These authors refine Marx's analysis of property – freeing it of any positive determination – but they simultaneously underplay its significance for hegemonic order.

Marx avoided abstract moralism. The critique of property begins immanent to the logics and ideological promises that underpin it as a practice. He does not invoke a universal ontology or ethics that knows in advance what is right. The common assertion, for example, that the world is held in common by all humanity is at best a political intervention that aims to change how we live. At worst, it is no better than a biblical politics that attributes to human beings the preordained right to collective ownership of the earth. Private property does not result from a dispossession of what was *originally* held in common. This assumes that we know what is properly common. It assumes that the establishment of the common has a prior warrant. There is no prior warrant to the commons. Any assertion otherwise is the worst form of idealism – one that Marx would have rejected.

Marx thus historicises and politicises the establishment of property. His was an explicit critique of the naturalisation of property in the contract tradition. Property is deemed one element of a contingent configuration of sociopolitical relations. Property like '[human essence] is no abstraction inherent in each single individual. In its reality it is the ensemble of social relations' (Marx 1975: thesis vi). Marx made this explicit in *On the Jewish Question*:

> the political annulment of private property does not mean the abolition of private property: on the contrary it presupposes it. The state . . . abolishes distinctions based on birth, rank, education and occupation, when

it declares birth, social rank, education and occupation to be non-political distinctions, when it proclaims . . . that every member of the nation is an equal participant in national sovereignty, when it treats all elements of the real life of the nation from the standpoint of the state. Nevertheless, the state allows private property, education, occupation, to act and assert their particular nature in their own way – i.e., as private property, as education, as occupation. Far from abolishing these real distinctions, the state only exists on the presupposition of their existence; it feels itself to be a political state and asserts its universality only in opposition to these elements of its being' (Marx 1984: 219)

The standard reading of this text is well known. Representative democracies extend the franchise regardless of property and title. However, the political annulment of private property as a requirement for participation in the polity legitimates a system of economic inequality and property in civil society.[2] Representative democracies sustain the separation between the (abstractly equal) political community and the unequal private community of economic interests in civil society.[3] However, there is more to this text than the conventional reading allows. Marx contends that national sovereignty bounds and polices representation, maintaining the separation between civil and political society. It protects the property rights that structure inequality. States police both their external territorial boundaries and the internal boundaries wrought by legal property. Marx here alludes to the relationship between ontology and appropriation. The order of private property is articulated with the proprieties of nation, citizenship, gender, belonging and occupation. The state exists on the presupposition of these distinctions. The inequalities sustained by education and occupation, like those of property, give proper order to bodies, space and time. In each case, the distinction between the linguistic and the material, the base and the superstructure, makes no sense. Marx's critique of liberal democracy concerns both ownership and control over resources and lives, and the ordering of the social world, the allocation of persons and things to their proper place(s).

Marx also recognises that property originates with 'conquest, enslavement, robbery, murder, in short, force' (Marx 1976: 874). Violence haunts every account of private property. A careful deconstruction of the dry, legalistic justifications of property demonstrates their repeated attempts to veil this violence. In late eighteenth and early nineteenth-century political debate property was deemed a key right. Von Savigny's *Treatise on Possession* (2010) eloquently summarised the then dominant interpretation of ancient Roman property law. He argued that the transformation of possession into legal property takes place without the stain of violence. Possession as a fact without legal warrant presupposes detention – the ability to exclude others from enjoyment of what is possessed. Violence is the ever-present other face of possession. However, violence can 'never avail as a juridical proceeding' (Von Savigny 2010: 18). Property as the legal power to deal with a thing at one's will must have legal warrant without violence. Von Savigny identifies two solutions to this dilemma. The first, *usucaption*, is found in most civil law systems. Usucaption recognises something as legal property after a period of uninterrupted possession. However, this does not solve the problem. It maintains the link between legal property that restricts rights of access and benefit and the non-legal (violent) possession of a thing. A second legal possibility arises in instances when there is a disturbance of existing possession by the violent act(s) of a non-possessor. Legal redress in this case is an *interdict*:

> Whoever has merely the possession of a thing does not thereby obtain any right to detention, but he has the right of demanding that no one else shall use force against him; and in such case, if his possession is forcibly invaded he may protect himself by interdicts. Possession is the foundation of these interdicts. (Von Savigny 2010: 7)

In fact, neither of these legal instruments insulates law from violence. Concluding the book Von Savigny admits as much. In disputes about possession, what counts is the *factum* of possession, the physical ability to exclude others. Marx states baldly what liberal theorists of property implicitly acknowledge: property regimes presuppose either explicit or implicit recourse to violence. Reading Von Savigny carefully has its uses: liberalism assumes that private property is just. An infringement on the right of the individual to own and dispose of their time, labour and property is deemed an unwarranted imposition on, and limitation of, individual equality on the free market. Yet this freedom presupposes a violence it simultaneously denies.

Marx's critique of property is difficult to surpass. He recognises – unlike many of his interpreters – that property is explicable only in terms of the ensemble of social relations. He tracks the historical emergence of private property through land clearance, enclosure, colonial violence and commodification. He underscores the horror of these processes. There are, however, important limits to this account. Although hinted at Marx never completed a non-foundationalist account of the social formation or of property. He maintained that, in the last instance, the social formation is explicable in terms of foundational logics related to ownership and control of the means of production. He identifies privileged agents of history based on this analysis. He ties this to a philosophy of history, and to a politics of knowledge, that later Marxists used to authorise revolutionary violence. To put the point bluntly: Marx assumes that there is a proper accounting for the social formation. He articulates this proper accounting to a proper politics. In what follows I take my cue from Marx but rethink property and propriety in non-foundationalist terms.

Social Formation, Hegemony and the Politics of Property

The post-Marxist critique of Marxism does not touch, or indeed engage with, the critique of property. It is a shortcoming tantamount to giving up on the critique of material inequality. The place of property in Marx's account of capital troubles any attempt to defend economic essentialism. Laclau and Mouffe never adequately deconstruct the elements that together configure the 'economic base' in Marxist theory. They turn too quickly from a critique of essentialism to a focus on the impossibility of society and the unfixity of identity. Let them make the point themselves:

> It is not the case that the field of the economy is a self regulated space subject to endogenous laws; nor does there exist a constitutive principle for social agents which can be fixed in an ultimate class core . . . unfixity has become the condition of every social identity . . . identity is given solely by articulation within a hegemonic formation . . . (Laclau and Mouffe 1985: 85–6)

Note the rapid jumps. They begin with a rejection of the economy as a self-regulated space. They then insist upon the unfixity of class identity and finally turn to the articulation of social identity. They shift from an analysis of social formation – in terms of the relationships between production reproduction, political representation, institutions and state – to the impossibility of suturing political identity. They are aware, and earlier note, that hegemonic logics concern far more than the articulation of identity. The glues that fix socio-political orders go beyond the identification of subjects with empty signifiers. The material infrastructures that deliver broadband to some parts of the world but not others; the configuration of transport, trade and shipping networks; the infrastructural designs for new cities; and the global rules that structure the operations of multinational corporations and states are all not explicable in terms of identity and identification. If this point seems banal – which it is – it indicates the political ground sacrificed with too overt a focus on logics of identification.

However, Laclau and Mouffe's critique of Althusser makes exactly this point. Their concern is that Althusser, despite his critique of humanism, reintroduces conceptual closure in his thinking of social order (Laclau and Mouffe 1985: 97–101). This closure coincides with the argument that the economy determines in the last instance the dominant instance of the social formation – the instance that secures the extraction of surplus value. In flirting with structuralist terminology Althusser unwittingly reintroduces the abstract universal object 'the economy'. His critique of the humanist interpretation of Marx had rejected essentialism, the argument that a particular object, modality or notion of being contains the conditions of its own existence. He contended that every instance of the social formation is only explicable in terms of the concrete system of social relations, as a historically contingent object of thought. Yet he simultaneously argues that the economy determines in the last instance which element of the social formation secures the extraction of surplus value. Moreover, for Althusser and Balibar the elements that comprise a mode of production are invariants – all modes of production may be understood in terms of the configuration of these basic elements. They include the direct producer, non-producers and the means of production. By varying the relations of these elements, we can generate a comparative table of all modes of production. However, Laclau and Mouffe argue, overdetermination entails the lack of an ultimate literality to the social. They write: 'We . . . consider the openness of the social as the constitutive ground, or negative essence of the existing, and the diverse social orders as precarious and ultimately failed attempts to domesticate the field of differences' (Laclau and Mouffe 1985: 95–6). They reject the residues of essentialism in the works of Althusser. However, they do not reframe the elements central to Marxist accounts of the economy. Rather, they take as their starting point the post-Saussurian linguistic paradigm.

Their discussion of counter-hegemony focuses on the articulation of equivalence between different antagonisms thought in terms of identity. Counter-hegemonic articulation requires radical investments, with an affective dimension, in empty signifiers that link a chain of equivalences. Laclau links signification to 'affect [which] is not something that exists . . . independent of language . . . the complexes we call "discursive or hegemonic formations" . . . articulate differential and equivalential logics, [which] would be unintelligible without the affective component' (Laclau 2005: 111). Collective identifications are constitutive of the 'mode of existence of human beings' in the field of politics (Laclau 2005: 28).

This jump is far too quick. It results in them forgetting their own commitment to overdetermination. It is as if the ontological question – the need to identify – is exempt from the logics implied by their radical account of overdetermination. There is a point at which they might have done this – and it concerns the conceptualisation of property. Balibar, in distinguishing between 'the relations of production *themselves* . . . and their *"legal expression"* sharply distinguishes . . . "property" from the law of property' (my emphasis). Law expresses rather than articulates property relations. Discordance between the economic forms of property and their legal expression arise at moments of transition between modes of production. He 'look[s] for the relations of production behind the legal forms' to determine what property is as a structure that precedes law. Every element of the economic structure of capitalism presupposes 'the existence of an [abstract and universal] legal system'. The legal order distributes and distinguishes persons from things and establishes a contract system between owners, contractors and employees. Law, he contends, reflects 'in the strict sense' the universality of commodity exchange finally realised in the capitalist mode of production. However, abstract universality is contradicted by the fact that ownership of the means of production is concentrated in a small class. This dissonance allows for the appropriation of surplus value through the legal purchase of labour power in an apparently equal legal relation. Balibar thus explains the meaning of determination in the last instance: the social relations of production determine which instance of the social formation secures the appropriation of surplus value (Balibar et al. 2017: 361). Had Laclau and Mouffe focused on the importance attributed to property in *Reading Capital* (Althusser 1970) their account of hegemony might have looked rather different. They would reject the assertion that law merely expresses an underlying truth of property. Instead, property is a technology of articulation that shapes space, objects, information and relations between subjects. Thinking of property as a practice of articulation emphasises that articulation takes different forms. It is not simply about articulation in terms of logics of signification. When post-Marxists talk about the equivalence of demands in the formation of a counter-hegemonic project they forget that there are other ways of constructing relations of equivalence. I return to this point in Chapter 4.

Balibar himself points to just such an interpretation of Marx's *Poverty of Philosophy*:

> In each historical epoch [Marx writes] property has developed differently and under a set of entirely different social relations. Thus to define bourgeois property is nothing else than to give an exposition of all the social relations of bourgeois production. To try to give a definition of property as of an independent relation, a category apart, an abstract and eternal idea, can be nothing but an illusion of metaphysics or jurisprudence. (Marx quoted in Balibar et al. 2017: 173)

Property takes different forms in different proprietary orders: to understand property is to relate it to its condition of possibility as an element within a material and historical configuration. If the social is not a closed structure, defined by an underlying essence, then there is no original property, no original structure that later takes on legal form. Rather, property is performatively remade in specific contexts. We can reject economic determination yet accept these aspects of Marx's argument. To forget the articulation of worlds, things and relations as property, to emphasise the forging of a common will at the expense of materially structured inequalities is to misunderstand hegemonic politics.

In fact, Laclau and Mouffe forget property a second time. When celebrating the democratic revolutions of the eighteenth century they argue that the 'field of hegemony' is expanded after the democratic revolutions of the eighteenth century. The irradiation effects of equality renders society a contingent order. In contrast, pre-capitalist and pre-democratic societies have 'repetitive practices within a closed system of difference . . .' (Laclau and Mouffe 1985: 138). Yet these same democratic revolutions enshrined the sacrosanct right to property. Equality, liberty *and* property were central to both the American and French revolutions. In the case of the American Revolution, the Articles of Confederation counted slaves a property (Finkelman 2012: 118). Property was enshrined in the Declaration of the Rights of the Man and of the Citizen of 1789 alongside liberty, security and resistance to oppression – immediately following the declaration that all are born free and equal. The irradiation effects of equality certainly render society contingent. However, property secures forms of repetitive practice that irradiate across the globe, that configure and limit equality and liberty. They fail to consider property as elemental to these democratic revolutions.

Something is lost in the post-Marxist critique of Marxism. Laclau and Mouffe presciently argued that neoliberalism recasts positive liberty as authoritarian while institutionalising negative freedom. However, their detailed prescription of a radical democratic antidote could not anticipate the 'propertisation' of every aspect of social and political life. Wendy Brown writes, almost despairingly, of neoliberalism as 'a ubiquitous common sense . . . [which] suffuse[s] workplaces, schools, hospitals, gyms, air travel, policing, and all manner of human desire and emotions' (Brown 2018: 61). Economisation marketises every aspect of life and reinforces 'hetero-patriarchal Christian familialism' (Brown 2018: 66). Brown's (2015) *Undoing the Demos* delivers an unsparing critique of neoliberalism as a political rationality – but it lacks what we find in earlier Marxist tracts – a political account of relations of property, ownership and control over the means for the reproduction of lives. In contrast with these accounts, I view hegemonic order as a proprietary regime. This captures the complexity of social organisation: the articulation of a common sense; the forms of political identification which give subjects a place in the social order;

the silent, infrastructural processes that coordinate the movement of subjects and objects through the world. A proprietary order includes relations of propriety and property, the policing of the proper bounds of a social formation, the anonymous logistical orders that glue together these relations and the legal articulation of rights, liberties and subject positions.

Property, Territory and the Politics of Being

I use the term 'proprietary' to insist upon the intrinsic relationship between modes of being and modes of appropriation. Schmitt's *Nomos of the Earth* opens with just such an argument. Post-Marxist theorists rely on Schmitt's account of the friend–enemy relation in his *Concept of the Political* (1996). Mouffe (2013: 138), for example, argues that the political entails the drawing of distinctions between friend and enemy. The 'Political' presupposes a common identification irreducible to moral or economic imperatives. It is distinct from everyday politics. However, she never addresses Schmitt's later text *Nomos of the Earth* (2003). There he contends that European global order, the nomos prior to the First World War, articulated the world as a set of distinct sovereign, political communities with mutually recognised territorial boundaries. Europe, he suggests could have established a global political order based on these principles had it properly appropriated, and organised, the rest of the earth not yet constituted on these terms. This was what Germany attempted in the late nineteenth century imitating other colonial European powers. The colonisation of 'South West Africa' (now Namibia) resulted in the establishment of the first extermination camps on Shark Island. German colonisers, led by Goring's father, appropriated *lebensraum* from the Herero peoples, declaring that the land was the property of Germany. Schmitt's argument is racist but it was also an accurate rendering of the dominant political ethos. It goes some way toward conceptualising proprietary order. A proprietary order (my phrase) articulates a 'nomos' that for Schmitt comprises ontological, political, moral, legal and property relations. He writes: 'Every ontonomous and ontological judgment derives from the land . . . land appropriation is the primeval act in founding law' (Schmitt 2003: 45).

Political and legal orders, on this reading, require the appropriation of land. The appropriation establishes internal and external borders: *internally* the division and distribution of land establishes the order of ownership, property and title; *externally* defined borders ground legal title in international law and secure the recognition of appropriation and of property, by the state. Such divisions of territory are ontological and material. The word nomos originally meant to appropriate and divide land. Its root is *nehmen* (to take) – the Dutch word *neem*, to take, retains the residue of this etymology. The nomos of the earth is not only about norms. Rather it concerns the organisation of appropriation; the drawing and maintenance of boundaries; the forms of property, division and title – articulated to a legal order and to ways of being (Schmitt 2003: Chapter 1). Schmitt explicitly politicises ontology. He does not ask 'what is being?' Rather he associates ontology with a defined nomos of the earth, with the different regimes for the appropriation and division of the earth. Any claim about what is proper to human being is implicated in a certain nomos. This link between property, and what is proper to being, is implied in the Latin root *proprius*. *Proprius*, as that which is proper to the human being, becomes *proprete*, what is one's property. Those proper to themselves may own property. Rather than aiming to think the 'question of Being', Schmitt reads ontological questions as articulated to modes of appropriation, to territorial divisions, and to the policing which maintains these divisions. In this light, he proposes a lost link between *nehmen* as appropriation and the taking of a proper name. Personal names signify what is deemed proper to each person, allocating to each their proper place in the world – but the proper name requires this wider proprietary order for its policing.

Schmitt wrote the *Nomos of the Earth* in the dying days of the European colonial order – the conquest, occupation and articulation of the planet as a common proprietary regime. The rendering fictitious of the national borders central to this nomos marks its end. His retroactive legitimations of colonial occupation and 'occidental' rationality are repellent – but no text is limited by the author's express intention. I take from Schmitt the idea that a nomos presupposes a global vision of being: a normative vision of how things are articulated with modes of appropriation, division and production. These relate to dominant ideas about civilisation, propriety and humanity. Schmitt diagnoses the colonial nomos that after the so-called 'age of discovery' imagined the globe as a space to be demarcated and divided. This nomos legitimated appropriation, killing and genocidal horrors previously unthinkable, in the name of civilisation. Writing at the beginning of the Cold War, Schmitt contends that a new nomos will become hegemonic. He is uncertain about the form it will take. His insistence on the intrinsic relation between modes of being and modes of appropriation is what interests me. The nation state paradigm is no longer the sole or even primary site where borders are drawn, property articulated and modes of being established. Borders are now bio-political, literally marked on the bodies of subjects, mapping value, movement, rights and liabilities on terms irreducible to citizenship and territory. These questions delimit any study of the contemporary 'nomos' of the earth.

What does this reading of Schmitt add to the conceptualisation of proprietary order? I noted that Balibar links determination in the last instance to property. The legal form taken by property expresses, he argues, the prior reality of possession. However, Balibar could not explain why the material configuration of inequality requires its legal form. Schmitt, by contrast, offers no analysis of capital – yet he understands the intrinsic relationship between the European nation state, territorial ordering and division and the politics of colonial violence and race. I accept, with Balibar, that any political order articulates differential access to the resources necessary for the reproduction of lives. Property is a technology central to this articulation. However, it has no essence. Its forms shift shape in relation to the overdetermined social formation. Property articulates, and is articulated by, the sovereign delimitation of territory, boundaries and global legal orders. These orders bear a relation to possible ways of being – they are not merely formal shells. There is no essence to being – rather it finds expression in these different possible modalities of proprietary order. There are two further issues. The first concerns the category of person and its relation to property. The second concerns the relationship between state and corporate sovereignty.

First, Roberto Esposito has argued that the fundamental division of what he terms 'Western' legal orders is that between persons and things. Only things can become property. Persons deemed rational cannot become property (Esposito 2015). The category person was a malleable conceit deployed historically to render some not properly human. Locke's rendering of the individual proper to itself mirrors his casting of indigenous Americans as uncivilised and incapable of owning land as nomadic pastoralists. It was deployed to justify the ownership of some human beings as slaves and the dispossession and mass killing of others. In the twentieth century, the legal category of personhood was extended to reframe corporations as legal persons capable of owning and disposing of property. When one asks the question of what is proper to the person we are implicated in the distribution of properties – of who can, or does, own property; of whose labour can be bought as a commodity; of centuries old practices of violent dispossession which scar the present; and of properties deemed proper to the human. The original link between the question of being and those things which are deemed incapable of 'being' proper to themselves – and thus open to appropriation – is not neutral. Legal orders cannot legitimate property without the stain of violent dispossession. What is proper to human beings is integral to these modes of appropriation, to apparatuses of propriety, which police order. Rancière terms the police 'an order of bodies that defines the allocation of ways of doing, of being, and of saying, and sees that those bodies are assigned by name to a particular place and task' (Rancière 1999: 28–9). As Cheryl Harris notes, property is related to the properties we attributed to different bodies. Whiteness becomes a form of property when social norms overlap with legal orders to give to those deemed white a property status in law (Harris 1993: 1723). The ordering of property distributes subjects and subject positions, and the specific proprieties attributed to subjects. I use the term proprietary regime to describe these overdetermined orders. For Esposito what is distinct about the current conjuncture is the disarticulation of the distinction between persons and things, a disarticulation whose primary site is the body. The body never fitted neatly into this legal division, and 'was left to vacillate between one and the other' until the present day when 'protruding into both categories of person and thing' (Esposito 2015: 103) it undermines the great distinction. We will have cause to return to this discussion, but we should note the key claim Esposito makes: legal orders have had to recognise the provenance of the body in the realm of an emergent common (whether this be through the circulation of organs or its remaking in terms of a common genetic heritage.) This entails a gradual remaking of the distinction between person and thing that, for so long, was central to the rendering of worlds as property. It is indicative of an emerging proprietary order that regulates not individual persons or things, but information, codes, disembodied bodies. I disagree with Esposito on one point only. He views this disarticulation as the site of an emergent common. It is rather a contested site in which new forms of property and propriety aim to police and appropriate what others insist is the common heritage of humanity.

Second, in focusing on the territorial nation state Schmitt misses the historical interlacing of state and corporate sovereignty. Barkan has traced the emergence of sovereign nation state regimes in parallel with the exceptions granted to corporate powers. Corporate and state power in the modern period were mutually constitutive. Corporations exercised sovereign powers over territory and resources through the granting of immunities by nation states. This was as true of the seventeenth-century Dutch East India Corporation as it is for those multinational corporations granted exceptions by sovereign powers in the twenty-first century. The multinational corporations residing in the City of London, or those companies acting to extract resources through mining concessions, deploy sovereign powers over territory and subjects (Barkan 2013: 5–9). These powers extend to the right to police territory and deploy violence in the name of order. Barkan's argument helps us to make sense of the transmogrification of the neoliberal state. The marketised state participates in the market, commissioning and providing services in direct competition with private sector corporations. States secure the conditions for market competition and act in the market they preserve.

The liberal ideal of the state as a neutral arbiter, above the fray of contestation, no longer holds, if it ever did. As stakeholders, states are no longer the sovereign representatives of the people they claim to represent. They are competitors in the market, offering contracts to other parts of the state in direct competition with private providers. Decisions such as Brexit hark back to the primordial myth of a unified body politic that can exercise sovereign control over its self. However, there is no longer a body politic (if there ever was) able to act in this form. Nation states no longer control the acts of a body partitioned, sold, marketised and distributed like a dissected corpse across a digitised world. This shifting terrain makes explicit the key relationship between sovereignty and property. These are overlapping elements of an articulated property, state and capital complex. Democratic demands for the regulation of the excesses of the market no longer resonate. Such interventions are the acts of quasi-public/private institutions whose interests do not correspond to the legitimation functions once performed by the welfare state (Habermas 1979; O'Connor 2001).

Thinking the political in terms of a 'sovereign people' capable of acting upon itself legitimates an ancient fiction, a fiction that clads the oligarchies of today in the cloak of democracy. The other face of this imaginary is the neurotic building of walls. Wendy Brown notes that 'Nation-state walls are modern-day temples housing the ghost of political sovereignty' (Brown 2010: 133). The sovereign democratic state is a ghost, haunting the political imaginary of the left, but already superseded by forces we have yet fully to grasp. Recognising that the link between sovereign power and democratic power is broken helps to explain, for example, the deployment of ancient rules of sovereign exception during the past decade of the 'war on terror'. Sovereign power is not democratic power. An improper politics rejects the markers of certainty that inspired leftist politics for much of the twentieth century – including the confusion of sovereign with democratic power. Bidding farewell to this imaginary does not foreclose thinking an other democracy. It allows for a remaking of democratic politics and its key terms – demos and people; sovereignty and bio-power; equality and liberty.[4]

Let me draw some provisional conclusions. A proprietary order comprises a set of rules, norms and institutions. These include explicit legal demarcations such as laws of property, citizenship and crime as well as the implicit codes structuring appropriate behaviours. Such regimes structure how government(ality) is constituted and organised. This modification of the notion of police extends an argument implicit in Rancière's work. A police order, he argues, 'rests on a logic of the proper' that presupposes a certain propriety of place and function (Rancière 2010: 5). Democracy interrupts what appears as a natural order, what Adorno once termed second nature, enacting the equality on which any social order relies. Thinking hegemony in these terms shifts our focus to among other things the infrastructural constitution of our worlds. Easterling describes infrastructures as 'the shared standards and ideas that control everything from technical objects to management styles' (Easterling 2014: 6). They are the operating systems that reconfigure the world according to a set of templates that make certain things possible and others impossible (see Chapter 4). This argument forces, too, a reconsideration of the place of ontology in post-Marxist theories. I reject the argument that because 'Being' is an impossible object, it returns in the form of repeated failed identifications. Proprietary orders often prevail regardless of political identifications. Property is one of these infrastructures, almost a legal operating system, adaptable and replicable in diverse contexts – and at the same time world making. Reframing post-Marxist accounts of hegemony in terms of proprietary order does not mean that property is the material base that determines the ordering of all other properties and proprieties. There is no property *sub specie aeternitatis*. If so what is property? It is to this question that I now turn.

What 'is' Property?

A proprietary regime is an ensemble that configures relations of property, of propriety and of the proper. All such orders police and map the modes of behaviour and action that configure, and are configured by, divisions of property. Property is not then a thing, an object, possessed by a legal person. Rather it is an overdetermined set of relations demarcating and ordering space, time and subjectivity through varied apparatuses of enclosure. To capture is at the same time to define and demarcate a thing as an object of property. The simplest example is land. In order to become property, land is demarcated and parcelled out, defined as what can be owned. Colonial land surveys mapped out the basic units that were the later investment opportunities for financial capital, as I argue in relation to the 1833 survey of Ireland in Chapter 4. Such forms of capture were also practices of subjectification. They establish and police different subject positions. In the case of land, these include owner, trespasser, rentier, investor and sharecropper. No matter what the nature of the property is, its existence delineates benefit and legal offence. In being ordered and divided, land becomes a measurable asset as part of a territory, with borders, tied to a specific regime of belonging, of citizenship, and possible valuation. Contemporary forms of property echo these practices. Central to police orders is that 'property law ceaselessly runs to catch up with the intangible property linked to the new technologies' extending logics of property to ever more domains (Rancière 1999: 110). Let me set out this understanding of property.

First, property is not a thing. It is a set of relations that distributes rights, benefits and control over things now made property. These include political, economic and legal forms of articulation. Legal personhood cannot be attributed to things that may become property. What can be made property, and how things are made property, depends on, and articulates, dominant proprietary orders. This account accords with Laclau's notion of 'discourse' as 'a meaningful totality which transcends the distinction between the linguistic and the extra-linguistic . . .' (Laclau 1993: 435). Property as a discourse articulates together linguistic and extra-linguistic elements. The question of the meaning of the elements is secondary to their articulation as a relational apparatus that divides and organises the world in certain ways. Such division and organisation establishes what the object is in relation to other objects. In talking of property the distinction between words and things is blurred.

Second, property requires justification because it is not simply given in the order of things. The maintenance of property, the definition of what is proper and improper, is political from the off. In noting this, I do not find common cause with the innumerable theorists who aim to provide just such a justification. Munzer (1990) and Waldron (1988), for example, invoke principles of utility, justice and equality to abstractly justify the institution of property. These forms of moral justification become overly complex once the legal argument that property is a bundle of rights is accepted. Instead, I start with the argument of MacDonald (2009) who defines property simply as a right of exclusion *in rem*. The reason moral theorists would seek to justify property is because it requires exclusion. I would qualify MacDonald's definition in one respect: what is given *in rem* already presupposes an articulated distinction between person and thing. There is virtue in applying Occam's razor – but this should not blunt critique: property has become what it now is; property is dynamic and performative as Keenan (2014) argues and property is configured in a set of specific, though dynamic, social relations. Keenan recognises the contingency of property and on this basis argues that it may be politically and legally remade. Keenan is right – as a relational complex property may be politicised. Yet we should also recognise that property is always a relation of exclusion. To work within existing property regimes is to accept, even if through gritted teeth, a dominant regime. Property sediments certain social relations and institutionalises practices which define and distribute rights of access to resources.

Third, there is an intrinsic – though contingent – articulation of sovereign power with property. Sovereign power guarantees the order of property through both legal and violent means. A critique of property is immediately a challenge to political orders that give legal right to existing property relations. Drawing on Schmitt's account of nomos, I noted the intrinsic relation between sovereignty, the maintenance of territorial bounds and orders of property. While property regimes now extend beyond the reach of nation states, the enforcement of these regimes still falls to sovereign orders that police international conventions. As the example of coltan in relation to mobile phones demonstrates, property regimes are not limited by the territorial bounds of nation states – but they presuppose these bounds if they are to be enforced.

Fourth, property articulates together a range of subject positions. For Agamben the apparatuses that 'govern and guide' human beings also establish forms of subjectification. Contemporary social orders are governed, he contends, by a proliferation of apparatuses, 'a dissemination that pushes to the extreme the masquerade that [accompanies] every social identity' (Agamben 2009: 15). However, Agamben fails to note that certain apparatuses extend their power in disproportion to this proliferation and severely limit this dissemination. Subjectification does not only concern identity – rather it all too often establishes relations of inclusion and exclusion that operate regardless of identity. His refinement of the notion of apparatus is useful. However, I reject the argument that humans are 'unable to intervene in their own processes of subjectification any more than in their own apparatuses' (ibid.: 24). Property as an apparatus establishes subject positions with differential rights of access to, control over and profit from property. Legally recognised persons may include citizens and non-citizens, individual property owners, states, corporations or universities granted the status of legal personhood. With that comes the right to call on state violence in order to protect property.

Fifth, property structures social relations in a dynamic fashion. Property regimes are contestable sites of antagonistic struggle. If we tie together the different elements that I have called the apparatus of property – processes of articulation and justification; sovereign power; and subjectification – we can identify instances when the apparatus of property, or specific elements of that apparatus, are contested. This abstract description of property as an apparatus acknowledges that many forms of exclusion, discrimination and control are unrelated to property. There are forms of social relation to which this abstraction does not apply. It recognises, too, that the elements and their configuration are constantly in transition. It reconstructs the apparatus of property both descriptively and theoretically, recognising that the contingency of property apparatuses is itself elemental to their power effects.

Sixth, property orders presuppose the possible use of violence. Rousseau's (1987a) 'Discourse on the origins of inequality' famously equates enclosure and property with war, horror and starvation. More pertinent for my argument is that on entering the social contract (Rousseau 1987b), individuals gain not only civil liberty but also title and property over land and goods. Rousseau writes that 'in accepting the goods of private individuals, the community is far from despoiling them; rather, in so doing it merely assures them of legitimate possession changing usurpation into a true right, and enjoyment in to proprietary ownership . . .' (Rousseau 1987b: 152). Note the phrasing: usurpation becomes right.[5] Possession becomes a 'proper right' protected by a properly founded sovereign, and is more secure than in a state of nature where possession is guaranteed only by individual force. The founding of the political regime secures property for owners and magically transforms the violence of usurpation into a right. The 'general will' founds a proprietary regime: it institutionalises formal civil equality but simultaneously justifies the economic inequality and violence secured through occupation and possession in the state of nature.[6] At this point Rousseau's argument threatens to dissolve. He considers the position of a foreigner from whose point of view property 'is not legitimate . . . because [this particular] state has its possessions only through the "first come, first served" principle as applied to its members and then passed on from them to the state' (Rousseau 1987b: 153). The foreigner poses a threat to 'democratically' secured property because from their point of view it is not democratic. By what right is an order of property established which legitimates the founder's possession? By what right are boundaries drawn between those who are citizens and those who are not? The full force of the sovereign will protects what Rousseau himself terms usurpation. The foreigner may make democratic claims in the name of equality, but the sovereign secures the 'general will' against democracy and equality. The proper limits of the democratic regime limit the equality in whose name they were first introduced (see Woodford and Devenney forthcoming).[7]

Rousseau indirectly justifies the politics of eighteenth-century imperialism. In remaking land and resources as property, settler colonialism casts indigenous peoples as criminals without land title, as foreigners (Woodford and Devenney forthcoming).[8] Neither Von Savigny nor Rousseau can explain how possession becomes a legal right to property without violence. Legal property cannot escape this simple fact of possession as detention, a detention reliant on exclusion and violence. Once recognised as legal property the holders acquire the rights to protection associated with life and liberty. In this case, property, life and liberty are already articulations of law rather than the natural foundations for law. Reading possession in light of its foundational role in legal and political discourses about the right to own, and thereby exclude others, emphasises the performativity central to all forms of property – possession is the violent remainder that no legal norm can efface. The retroactive justification of violence is also the imposition of a worldview that underpins global order as we noted above in relation to Schmitt.

Seventh, democratic *politics can reactivate the bounds of the proper and property* in the name of equality. My reason for overemphasising property is because vast disparities in wealth and income linked to property are too often ignored by contemporary radical theorists of the political. Acting improperly, we transgress both a dominant modus vivendi and a legally circumscribed order of property. Property – if we are to abstract it as a practice or an apparatus – articulates together a range of elements whose meaning and operation depend on the relations they enter into. This includes the capture and appropriation of things as property; the justification for such practices; the exercise of sovereign forms of violence to secure property; the forms of subjectification; and the performative reiterations that bound property to what is proper.

Conclusion: Proprietary Order and Social Formation

This chapter has emphasised the proprietary dimensions of hegemonic order. Radical democrats have forgotten that property is the key form taken by inequality. This has meant reading post-foundationalist theories against the grain. These preliminary conclusions accept, with Chambers, that to study the social formation is always already to be implicated in the social formation (Chambers 2014: 2). There is no bird's eye view to guarantee that my account of proprietary order is even passingly objective. Rather, the claim to study proprietary order is at the same time a critical intervention in that order. A proprietary regime is an overdetermined, systematic articulation of a range of practices into a whole. It is a systematicity in process, breached and cleaved by moments of undecidability, by improper enactments of equality, by contradictory practices that never finally cohere. Proprietary orders are articulated around dominant nodal points – apparatuses that lend coherence to an otherwise incoherent sprawl.

Let me conclude by knotting together these apparatuses – filtered through the example of conflict minerals and mobile phones. The mobile phone exemplifies, according to Agamben, an apparatus that captures man in processes of desubjectification. He writes: 'He who lets himself be captured by the "cellular telephone" apparatus – whatever the intensity of the desire that has driven him – cannot acquire a new subjectivity, but only a number through which he can eventually be controlled' (Agamben 2009: 21). Modern appara-tuses of power he argues, contra Foucault, capture subjects without any pos-sibility of critical intervention. On this view an apparatus is 'anything which has in some way the capacity to capture, orient, determine, intercept, model, control, or secure the gestures, behaviours, opinions or discourses of living beings' (Agamben 2009: 14). Living beings are caught in apparatuses through processes of subjectification. Between living beings and apparatuses there is a relentless battle. He despairingly suggests that the battle has been lost. We see an echo of Heidegger's notion of inauthenticity here, and perhaps ironically the more pessimistic readings of Adorno and Horkheimer's (1985) *Dialectic of Enlightenment*.

I argue instead that all apparatuses are contingent and vulnerable to rearticulation. It is ironic that the example chosen by Agamben is the mobile phone. The example betrays the profound problem with his politics: he is committed to some notion of an authentic relation to life, to a profanation of the apparatuses. Yet he has no notion of the set of relations embedded in the mobile phone – no sense of how this universal object bears with it a range of forms of subjection, of differential positions of global power, of networks that do leave space for intervention. His becomes a conserva-tive gesture, an appeal to impossibility in the worst sense. The proprietary regime that makes the mobile phone possible includes national forms of democratic politics; of production and reproduction; of violence; of modes of subjection; the organisation of time and space as well as possible spaces for resistance. Let us study these in more detail.

Contemporary democratic theory is much concerned with deliberation and public reason. Unlike deliberative democrats, I ask how public and pri-vate forms of deliberation, communication and election police the proper limits of democracy. Contemporary liberal democracies are characterised by a twin phalanx of strategies adapted from the arsenal of the left: first, an identity-based politics that rearticulates liberal democratic rights to enact the equality of all identities; and second, an actuarial politics that polices iden-tity claims in terms of neoliberal accountability. What appears as democratic public debate places serious political questions off-limits, in particular mate-rial equality. This is obvious if one reads deliberative democrats. Economic questions are from the off deemed secondary to the basic rights which ensure deliberation.[9] The mobile phone is central to the coordination of these com-municative apparatuses. Public opinion is negotiated through electronic manipulation and stream(lin)ing of information. The material infrastructure of public opinion is marshalled using high-density capacitators that snake across space and time. The public sphere is not a space of freedom. Rather, it is marshalled and ordered with a set of exclusions and inclusions that distrib-ute belonging, propriety and access to communication.

This reference to coltan indicates, second, the centrality of productive and reproductive relations to thinking proprietary order. Such an analysis raises a range of questions. These include: the production, distribution, commodification and administration of the goods and services necessary for life; the politicisation of sex through the medicalisation and privatisation of reproductive relations; the extension of logistical forms of control over labour, goods and services; the extension of logistical and extractive technologies aligned to predatory capital and war machines; the globalisation of property, quality and trade rules regardless of difference; and the recasting of reproductive labour as a commodity. The fact that every mobile phone requires coltan means that we can tack in one metal the grossest of inequalities. The nub of such relations is the exercise of control over transport, trade, communication and territory. We cannot understand the forms that deliberation in demarcated public spheres take unless we relate them back to this distribution of power and extraction. As Timothy Mitchell argues with regard to oil in *Carbon Democracy*, there is an intrinsic not a secondary relation between the material configurations of global order and the forms taken by democratic politics (Mitchell 2013). Conceptualising these configurations allows us to think about the pressure points, the places where democrats may challenge the policing of inequality. Agamben's concern about the loss of the authentic relation to being in the apparatus barely scratches the surface of such an analysis.

Policing proprietary orders, third, requires violence. Democratic theorists tend to concentrate on the sovereign violence of states – policing within territorially defined borders and war in foreign territories. However, the distribution of legitimate violence is rather different from what the classical model allows. Contemporary proprietary order is policed by so-called humanitarian war, the gradual undermining of the Geneva Convention and the rise of militarised policing in the 'banlieues' of the world. The discussion of the uses of coltan points to more prosaic forms of violence – and indicates the risk of an analysis which thinks that a proprietary order overlaps with legal forms of ordering. One reason why the question of coltan has become a rallying cry for activists against globalisation is because it links the warlords, markets in metals, and some of the largest suppliers of technological goods across the globe including Apple, HP, Sony and Toshiba. Coltan extraction in the Eastern and Southern provinces of the Congo demonstrates that proprietary orders rely on illegal forms of trade, extraction and exploitation of subjects impoverished in war and through colonial occupations. Amnesty International's 2016 report on the Coltan trade makes this explicit. Illegal forms of coltan enter the global supply chain as mines purchase coltan from the *creusers* who work in the zones of exploitation using bare hands to mine. The zones exist because the Congolese state polices and protects international mining companies granted proprietary rights to mine. Illegal forms of extraction complement legal mining, controlled by warlords with direct ties to the markets in Rwanda. From there coltan makes its way, legally, to the world's phone and computer companies. The routes are easy to trace but ignored by many companies, despite their commitments to ensuring fairness in supply chains. This focus on supply chain management demonstrates the ways in which possession wrought by violence becomes legally enforceable property. Proprietary orders are framed as legal orders. However, the politics of global supply chains links the products that lubricate communication back to unseen forms of violence.

This reference to violence points to a fourth issue – that of sovereign power. The democratic tradition emphasises the sovereignty of the people. The exercise of violence is legitimate because it secures the lives of a sovereign people. I reject this notion of the sovereign people as the starting point for the study of democratic politics. The history of the legal form of the corporation makes this clear. Corporations, granted their status of incorporation by states, are the other face of modern state formation. This status grants police powers and property powers to the corporation – powers exempt from popular sovereignty. Barkan (2012: Chapter 2) demonstrates, for example, that the history of corporate power is co-extensive with the consolidation of state sovereignty in the nineteenth century. Corporations charged with acting in the public interest were granted eminent domain to protect their own interests – not necessarily those of a public weal. The private corporation of the late nineteenth and early twentieth centuries had its historical roots in the exemptions granted to the colonial trading companies – companies which deployed property claims over the territories they occupied in the name of the crown. Sovereignty was always a contested, divided power, and was never simply vested in the exemptions granted to a sovereign. The example of the City of London Corporation makes this all too clear, as I argue later in the book. At the centre of these concerns is property – corporations exercise property rights not only over land but over the goods they produce, the processes used in production, the labour of their employees – and as incorporated may sell shares in the corporation as a tradeable property.

The modes of subjectivation and subjectivity made possible within a proprietary order vary between different apparatuses and practices. Subjectivity is not the same as identity – we all move through, adapt to and adopt different subject positions. Agamben's user of the mobile phone, captured by the apparatus, is situated in relation to all of those implicated in its production and distribution. These include the child labourer paid two dollars for a twelve-hour day; the traders who sell the metal; the companies that manage the supply chain. She is also a consumer, paying a monthly fee, one of a network of users, doubtless assigned a profile by vendors advertising to market segments. The contract ties her to a credit agency which polices payments and evaluates her credit worthiness. This is not to say that we are caught up in false consciousness and require theoretical clarification from party theorists. Rather, it is to confirm that there is no bird's eye view. The world is not available to us as an object, either of perception or of mere use.

These different subject positions depend, fifth, upon the articulation of time and of space. Proprietary orders police appropriate uses of time and of space. They delimit who can do what, where, when and how. Different practices articulate space and time differently but increasingly their use is framed in terms of quantifiable value. In the case of coltan its extraction combines the legal demarcation and policing of areas where mining takes place with spaces deregulated yet controlled. These spaces are framed within the logics of the sovereign nation state – and its ability to grant concessions, secure territorial bounds and define property and title. Coltan production relies on supply chains that organise the time of its production and distribution within these spaces. It finds its way to ports such as Ostend or Antwerp (the port from which colonial Belgium coordinated its murderous extraction of rubber from the Congo) and from there to the factories that manufacture the communicative infrastructures of our world. It becomes part of just-in-time production lines and is subject to new forms of valuation.

A proprietary regime then is an ensemble that configures relations of property, of propriety and of the proper. All such orders police and map the modes of behaviour and action supported by divisions of property. Property is not a thing, nor an object, possessed by a legal person. Rather it is a set of relations that demarcates and orders space, time and subjectivity. In its many different forms, property requires enclosure. Enclosure both excludes and, in the act of exclusion, establishes something as property. Understanding a proprietary regime requires that we unpick the overlapping forms of property which deliver coltan to our phones; the violent takings of possession and the exclusions which complement this making of legal property; the subject positions and proprieties associated with these property regimes; and the proprieties linked to the use and distribution of the phone and its global networks. Contemporary proprietary regimes anticipate and cater for protest. Adorno noted this in the period immediately following 1968. The barricades, he contends, are ridiculous against 'those who administer the bomb . . . a game and the lords of the manor let the gamesters go on playing for the time being' (Adorno 1969: 261). Adorno defends thinking as a compromised practice of freedom. In contrast, I argue that democracy is an improper form of political intervention pointing beyond the bounds of existing order. Proprietary regimes are always antagonistic. The deployment of violence is indicative of their weakness. However 'antagonism [also] constitutes the limits of every objectivity' (Laclau and Mouffe 1985: 127). There is always space – no matter how limited – for intervention. In the case of coltan extraction, political challenges may occur at any point in the supply chain – from production through to consumption. There are key nodal points which if interrupted would halt the reproduction of the globe's communicative infrastructure. If in analysing a proprietary order we map the modes of behaviour and action that both configure, and are configured by, divisions of property then we also identify moments of risk, spaces for hegemonic intervention and disruption. This notion of the proper marks a break with accounts of hegemony or police order which focus on the politics of identification. I ask how proprietary regimes secure and manage their borders, their populations and the proper bounds linked to property and proprietorial order. Political regimes are secured through the ordering and configuration of space and the regulation of access to the means for the reproduction and production of lives. Any attempted description of a proprietary regime is itself political. This focus on the policing of the social formation through a politics of the proper, of propriety, allows us to grasp more concretely the hegemonic formation that has been termed neoliberalism.

TWO

Theorising the Improper

The Sovereign Exception: Occupying St Paul's Cross

On 15 and 16 October 2011 a space adjoined to St Paul's Churchyard in London was occupied. The occupation comprised approximately 200 tents, a few hundred participants at any one time, medical supplies, a library, cooking facilities and toilets. The occupiers networked with other camps around the world. They established procedures for making decisions about life in, and the future of, the camp including how to respond to the local authority and the police. The camp was coordinated by meetings of a general assembly and different working groups in a spoke-like system of decision making. The occupiers answered to no authority other than that of the assembly. It suspended the political authority of the state and of the City of London Corporation.

The social scientific literature focuses on a set of particular questions about Occupy. These include its global reach; its decision making and democratic structures; its rejection of conventional politics in favour of an anarchist inspired recipe of collective decision making by all present (what Lorey (2015) termed a presentist form of democracy); its challenge to the political and financial institutions responsible for the 2008 crash epitomised by the slogan 'We are the 99%'; and its relation to and differences from more conventional social movements.

Surprisingly there is little focus on the antagonistic confrontations with those deemed to have legal, propriety authority over the occupied space. St Paul's Cross is land owned by the Corporation of London, although a small part is owned by the Church of England. Nor has any author focused on the laws invoked to justify the removal of the occupants. These superseded the legal right to lawful protest under articles 10 and 11 of the European Convention. At stake were rights over property and propriety, and the claim made by the Corporation of London to lawful possession of the highway. The legal judgement in favour of the City of London Corporation combined a straightforward verification of the corporation's claim to possession, with a set of statements about the inappropriate nature of the occupation. The occupiers, the judge concluded, violated health and safety standards, caused crime, spread noise pollution, housed abusive drinkers, encouraged the spread of vermin and made others feel unsafe in their lawful use of the highway. He ruled that there had been a violation of rights to possession, and that the occupiers constituted a public nuisance and undermined health and safety. He granted an order for possession to the City, combined with injunctive and declaratory relief providing legal remedy to remove the protest. The judge concluded that

> [T]he harm caused by this protest camp, in this place, is materially greater than the harm that would be likely if the protest were conducted by the same protestors, assembling every day but without the tents and all the other impedimenta they have brought.

The camp he said had resulted in a 'loss of open space that the public can get to . . . has strained the local drainage system beyond capacity . . . has caused nuisance by the generation of noise and smell . . . and has made a material change in the use of the land for which planning permission would not be granted (*City of London* v *Samede* [2012] EWHC 34 (QB) Case no: HQ11X04327).

The protestors were improper in two senses: first, they refused to recognise, indeed contested, the sovereign authority of the City of London over this land; second, they put in to question the appropriate rules of behaviour associated with the land. They forced the City authorities to negotiate with their impropriety. However, it was not only the immediately visible that is of import. The 'City of London' is ruled by its own council. It has proprietary rights over its own territory. The British sovereign must request permission before entering the square mile of the City. The City is also exempt from many of the laws that apply in the rest of the United Kingdom. This includes, for example, the Freedom of Information Act of 2000, which would require full disclosure of the financial dealings of the City and its occupants. The City has the only unelected representative to the House of Commons – known as the *Remembrancer*. The *Remembrancer* can object to laws passed by Parliament that undermine the legal exemptions granted to the City. She has a private parliamentary office of six lawyers that scrutinise legislation. If you doubt the power of this obscure functionary note that the Word grammar tool does not recognise the word unless it is capitalised. He is supported by a powerful advocacy organisation, the City of London Council. Exemption from the normal tax laws mean that, within the square mile, tax havens for the wealthy are managed. Money passes through various investment vehicles loosely regulated, if at all, by the state. The occupation then took place in an area deemed exceptional to the rule of law in the UK. Every Chancellor of the Exchequer in post-war Britain has promised the protection of these ancient rights. Tony Blair quietly dropped a 1996 manifesto pledge to subject the City to British law before his election to office in 1997.

What is the origin of these ancient rights? The City of London claims that its rights of exception extend back to time immemorial, before Magna Carta, before the Saxon invasion, to unrecorded time preceding parliamentary democracy (Shaxson 2011: 264). The occupation took temporary control over the one place where this ancient freedom was concentrated: St Paul's Cross. In the words of the Corporation itself the freedoms of the City are 'rooted in the ancient rights and privileges enjoyed by citizens before the Norman conquest' (https://www.cityoflondon.gov.uk/about-the-city/history/Pages/city-government.aspx). St Paul's Cross was the one location where the monarch could exercise no sovereign power against those who protested or publically refused allegiance to the king. The same rights of exception were, over centuries, transformed into the current rights of financial exception and exemption. The irony extends beyond the fact that this was once a place of protest against the monarch. The City was, Glasman writes, one of the longest standing democratic communes with a 2,000-year history. The Romans established the area that is now the City as a self-governing commune. These practices continued in the folk moots of Medieval times (when all citizens would gather at St Paul's Cross to debate and vote on regulation of the commune) and in the 1191 declaration by the City declaring its status as an independent commune. It had become in Glasman's words 'the custodian of the ancient liberties of the English people and the champion of common law against state encroachment' (Glasman 2014: 1). The second charter of the 1690 Revolution enshrined these rights:

> the Mayor, commonality and citizens of London shall for ever here-
> after remain, continue and be, and prescribe to be, a body politic, in
> re, facto, et nomine and enjoy all their rights, gifts, charters, grants,
> liberties, privileges, franchises, customs, usages, constitutions, prescrip-
> tions, immunities, markets, duties, tolls, lands, tenements, estates and
> hereditaments whatsoever.

Already democratic rights are framed as rights of exemption from national taxation, tariffs, trade agreements and the like.

Occupy challenged the privileges enjoyed by the City. It high-lighted the arbitrary demarcation of the City from the rest of London in physical terms, a demarcation that stands in for a more fundamen-tal protection from the laws delimiting the demos. The occupation reset the terms of the proper and returned to political debate a set of issues long sidelined. It challenged the state to exercise violence in the name of property, against protestors using their rights under articles 10 and 11 of the European Convention, and more impor-tantly under the ancient rights extended to all citizens in this space of freedom. It opened up the question of the relation between the right to private property and those other rights of liberty and life compro-mised by this right. The derogation of proprietary rights to the City by Parliament is a parsing off of sovereign powers to a private corpo-ration central to iniquitous property relations on a global scale. This parsing of sovereignty is not new – as noted in the previous chapter, sovereign and corporate powers have evolved side by side. The occu-pation unwittingly asked the question of why this space of exception is no longer a democratic space, a space of experiment, of testing where sovereignty is contested.

Proprietary regimes order inequalities. Improper forms of politics challenge these orders. My assumption is that there is nothing proper to (human) being together. 'Unwarranted assurance as to the relation between politics and truth' (Bennington 2016: 2) forestalls improper forms of political inter-vention. Dissensus begins with those who break the bounds of the proper. It fashions other worlds and reanimates lost histories yet cannot be coded in advance. It might include trespass, transgression of accepted norms, withdrawal from or resistance against, dominant regimes, the articulation

of counter-hegemonies, blockage, hacktivism, occupation, theft or riot.
Rather than emphasise a politics aimed at the seizure of sovereign power
I think the improper in excess of sovereign order. And rather than offer a
taxonomy of such acts – a futile gesture *par excellence* – I think the improper
in three dimensions: first, as more than the negative of an existing proprietary regime; second, without ontological warrant; and third in terms of
some possible declensions.

The Improper Politics of Antagonism

Derrida's 1966 lecture, 'Structure, Sign and Play in the Discourse of the Human
Sciences', developed the nucleus of an improper politics. Derrida writes:

> The event I called a rupture would presumably have come about when the
> structurality of structure had to begin to be thought . . . it became necessary
> to think . . . the desire for the centre in the constitution of structure and the
> process of signification . . . a central presence which was never itself, which
> has always already been transported outside itself in its surrogate . . . From
> then on it was probably necessary to begin to think that . . . the centre could
> not be thought in the form of a being-present, that the centre had no natu-
> ral locus, that it was not a fixed locus . . . The absence of the transcendental
> signified extends the domain and the interplay of signification *ad infinitu.*
> (Derrida 1978: 280)

The proper of the structure is a surrogate 'constantly transported outside of
itself'. Philosophy presents a series of metaphorical and metonymical sub-
stitutions for this absent centre: 'eidos, arché, telos, energeia, ousia (essence,
existence, substance, subject) aletheia, transcendentality, consciousness, or
conscience, God, man, and so forth' (Derrida 1978). They all aim to quell
the play of difference. Derrida asks why is it that the centre returns as an
object of desire. He does not assume that this desire is necessary. Moreover,
if this essay assays the moment when 'language invades the universal problematic' it does so by radically decentring language. Generalised discursivity
on Derrida's count indicates that language cannot properly signify its own
limits. If so, it cannot 'properly' grasp objects of thought – because subject,
object and language are mutually constitutive. The proper is not Derrida's
primary concern but it is a recurrent leitmotif in his work. In 'Force of law'
he notes that deconstruction destabilises paradoxes of value like the proper
and property, right and law. It troubles the systems of property and propriety
that 'govern today's dominant juridical discourse' (Derrida 2002: 255). In
Specters of Marx he imagines the New International as without organisation,

nation, state or property. The improper *arrivant*, unexpected, undermines domestic contracts of state, family, territory and property (Derrida 1994: 81–2). The new international destabilises any properly delimited polis.

Derrida's essay was pivotal to the development of post-Marxist theories of the political, in particular in the work of Laclau and Mouffe (1985). However, these authors argue that the absence of any ultimate foundation has to be signified. Laclau and Mouffe argue that social order is an impossible object requiring identifications that temporarily fix the infinite play of signification. The impossibility of society is represented by props, which cover for this lack. Hegemonic politics concerns an ongoing war of position over the limits of the proper (Laclau and Mouffe 1985: 112). Their reading of Derrida reaches its conceptual apogee in the concept of antagonism. Here, however, the infrastructure of their argument frays as the question Derrida poses concerning the taken for granted desire for a centre returns. At this point, an improper politics becomes thinkable. How did they conceptualise antagonism and how does this point to the improper?

Laclau first considered the inability of Marxism to explain political antagonisms in the context of Argentinian politics in the 1960s and 1970s. The Argentinian crisis of May 1969 began with a joint student–trade union demonstration in Córdoba. Why, Laclau asks, did middle class students unite with trade unionists to oppose the Ongania dictatorship? Following the anti-Peronist coup of 1955, the military had exercised indirect power through control over economic policy and the exclusion of Peronists from government. It propped up agricultural capital and secured ideological hegemony by incorporating the middle classes, trade unions and key officials of the socialist and communist parties. The liberalisation of the economy, however, allowed international capital to increase profit with the development of constant capital and economies of scale. These policies impoverished the middle classes and 'creat[ed] the conditions for a new pole of popular regrouping which was eventually to allow the antagonism between the middle class and the proletariat to be bypassed' (Laclau 1970: 13).

Political antagonism in this case did not correspond with class position. While the possibility of antagonism arises in the context of a structural crisis, it requires ideological signifiers such as Peronism to unify different classes into a common oppositional project. Strangely, Laclau still concludes that the working class will smash the bourgeois state and replace it with popular institutions of mass power. It is as if he cannot yet reject the Marxist assumption that class identity precedes and determines political organisation. His reliance on Marxist explanatory tools reaches breaking point in *Politics and Ideology in Marxist Theory* (1977). On the one hand, he argues, classes are antagonistic because of their position in a mode of production:

'surplus-value . . . constitutes simultaneously the relation between capitalists and workers and the antagonism between them; or rather, it constitutes that relation as an antagonistic one' (Laclau 1977: 104). However, in political struggle dominated sectors must work together in antagonistic opposition. The people exists at the political and ideological level. Classes struggle to

> articulate popular democratic interpellations in the ideological discourse of antagonistic classes . . . Every class struggles at the ideological level simulta-
> neously as a class and as the people . . . [it] gives coherence to its ideological
> discourse by presenting its class objectives as the consummation of popular
> objectives. (Laclau 1977: 109)

Popular struggles then are the terrain on which antagonistic classes operate to win their objectives. Once again, Laclau assumes that classes are the agents of political organisation, but are not themselves the result of political artic-ulation. They exist simply by virtue of the structure of capitalist society. In political struggle, however, antagonism never follows class lines. It is this argument that wins out in later texts where the source and the locus of political antagonism becomes a problem for Laclau. These conceptual difficulties originate in response to determinate political circumstances – in this case debates about capitalism, neo-imperialism and political strug-gle in the Argentinian context. Laclau is struggling with political struggles that clearly do not conform to any Marxist account of class. He resolves this failure by arguing that popular struggles are the cladding of more real economic struggles.

The force of such theoretical tensions is fully realised in *Hegemony and Socialist Strategy* (Laclau and Mouffe 1985). Laclau and Mouffe categorically reject the assumption that class position is automatically antagonistic. A popular will, antagonistic to a dominant order, results from the articula-tion of different emancipatory demands against neoliberal hegemony. This may seem obvious but it requires that they rethink political antagonism. Marxist theorists interpreted antagonism as either 'real' opposition or as 'logical' opposition. Real oppositions occur in the natural world. In a physi-cal collision, for example, one or both of the objects may break. Yet physi-cal collisions are not antagonistic in the political sense. Physical force may play a role in political struggle – but the politics does not lie in the use of physical violence. Class struggle is not antagonistic because a police officer hits a worker (Laclau and Mouffe, 1985: 124). Antagonism, they conclude, cannot be real opposition in this sense. What about logical opposition? Logical contradictions are conceptual. The relation of the terms to each other exhausts their reality – logic presupposes the proper identity of its constituent units and deductively determines what must be the case given these prior assumptions. Yet logic is inadequate when describing political antagonisms. Political struggles are not the workings out of rational choice or game theoretic fantasies. The assumption that political scientists in appealing to the facts or to reason can explain antagonism misses something about political struggle that exceeds logic and empirical fact. At stake in antagonistic struggles is the integrity of the objects or subjects of struggle. Political antagonisms then put in to question the objectivity of the forces in conflict. They write:

> I cannot be a full presence for myself. Nor is the force that antagonises me such a full presence; its objective being is a symbol of my non-being . . . Antagonism constitutes the limits of every objectivity . . . Societies are constituted as a repression of the consciousness of the impossibility that penetrates them. (Laclau and Mouffe 1985: 127)

Antagonism indicates the failure of objectivity, rationality, being, identity and language. Note the path of this argument. It begins with a pressing political concern – how to understand political struggles in 1960s Argentina inexplicable in class terms. Antagonism names a political and a theoretical problem. Their response is political and theoretical. Particular antagonisms operate across two overlapping dimensions – the ontic (everyday politics) and the ontological (the Political) – distinct only in theoretical terms. The ontological refers to the failure of all objectivity, to the impossibility of being, the absence of a transcendental signified. Particular ontic contents stand in for this impossibility.

This version of antagonism trespasses boundaries. It suggests that there are no objects proper to politics. However, in reading this failure of objectivity in ontological terms they assume an ontological need, now framed in terms of the distinction between politics (the ontic) and the Political (the ontological). Properly political acts concern the symbolic institution of the social as such. Democratic regimes may address day-to-day demands, but counter-hegemonic opposition puts in to question the very institution of society. Mouffe writes:

> by the Political I mean the dimension of antagonism which I take to be constitutive of human societies, while by politics I mean the set of practices and institutions through which an order is created organising human coexistence in the context of conflictuality provided by the political. (Mouffe 2005: 9)

On this reading antagonism has 'as one of its defining features a dimension of deficient being of failed unicity . . . which shows itself through its absence' (Laclau 2005: 223). Note the use of words: deficient being implies that there is something missing; failed unicity implies that universality is experienced as a failure. Once antagonism is interpreted as pointing to a deficiency of being, the story of hegemonic politics follows. Hegemonic politics, politics proper, concerns the attempt to lay 'penultimate foundations' because there are no ultimate foundations. Politics requires ideological closure. Ethics attempts to keep this openness always present. 'Politics conceals the abyss on which it is built' but an ethics committed to radical democracy always keeps this abyss in view (Marchart 2017: 510).

Should we not pause? These authors assume an ontological need (the desire for closure) but this itself requires explanation. Politics proper articulates a counter-hegemony that answers the call of this ontological need. In so doing, it secures the penultimate foundations for society. Forms of politics that do not take on this task are deemed inadequate. Mouffe (2013), for example, contends that the Occupy movement did not engage on properly political terms because it rejected institutional solutions, and did not articulate a counter-hegemonic political project. On my reading, these were improper enactments of equality. They were political. They did not aim to transform and re-establish the 'proper' place of politics. Rather they enacted new spaces, practices and ways of living together and in so doing animated histories long forgotten. The post-Marxist account cannot but view these as 'merely' ontic interventions. I accept with these authors that antagonism indicates a certain impossibility. However, this impossibility, lack, gap, excess – or whatever name we might give to it – does not presuppose that political interventions should take a specific form. Having opened the possibility of thinking politics in improper terms the authors return it to its proper place. What if 'Being' does not return as an impossible object of desire? Does not such a 'negative' ontology have as its other face the insistent return of what had been rejected (Adorno 1973: 136)? The proper returns as a desire for centre – but why take this desire for granted?

Marxists had insisted on an intrinsic link between antagonism and the material conditions of inequality. We can agree with Mouffe that such inequalities do not determine either the form, or the necessity, of a counter-hegemonic politics. However, once the notion of antagonism is rescued from its positive ontological valence Laclau and Mouffe do not rethink the associated terms of property, ownership and production. In Chapter 1 I noted the abstract forms of property ownership and control, the various forms of measurement and quantification, the 'economisation' of political relations and the proliferation of discourses of quality, all of which negate political participation in the name of value neutrality and accountability. I developed a discursive account of property – a discursive account that is materialist in refusing both idealism and realism. The post-Marxist account of hegemony does not address these logics. Antagonism indicates the contingency of all such relations, the possibility of their rearticulation. Yet many of these logics do not rely on the ontological assumptions guiding Laclau and Mouffe. Thinking the improper and its relation to the proper allows us to consider a wider range of political interventions and extend our conceptualisation of antagonism.

Žižek has developed a related critique of post-Marxist theories. His solution is a 'withheld' Marxism that leaves us waiting for capitalism to engender its own revolutionary downfall. In the capitalist social formation the real of the economy, the imaginary of democratic ideology and the symbolic of political hegemony are knotted together (Žižek 2004: 6). This knotting has the consequence that:

> the relationship between economy and politics is ultimately that of the well-known visual paradox of 'two faces of a vase', never both – one has to make a choice. In the same way, one either focuses on the political, and the domain of economy is reduced to the 'servicing of goods' or one focuses on economy, and politics is reduced to a theatre of appearances, to a passing phenomenon which will disappear with the arrival of the developed communist economy. (Žižek 2006: 56)

Post-Marxists on his reading cannot see that capitalist economic relations structure political contingency. They address the symptoms of capitalism (contingency, multiculturalism, new social movements) but not capitalism itself. Žižek argues, recalling Althusser, that the economy determines the production and appropriation of surplus value and appoints one element of the social formation to secure this exploitation. It has retroactively established itself as the unquestioned horizon of our time. With Badiou, he characterises democratic politics as the ideological form of capitalism. Democratic ideology creates an irrecoverable political deficit (Badiou 2018: 27) which cannot be the starting point for a politics of the left. Instead, they demand a politics of the authentic act. Žižek characterises the authentic act (as opposed to mere action) as that which 'subverts the very structuring principle of a field . . . redefining the very contours of what is possible and in so doing creating retroactively the conditions of its own possibility' (Žižek 2004: 121). Such acts of pure expenditure change the very coordinates of what is possible within a historical constellation (Žižek 2004: 81). An act of such radical expenditure is required because capitalism is premised on the revolutionary logic of the not all, a process of continual transformation, which renders everything contingent. Capital includes in its logic all critique, which contributes to the reform of capitalism rather than its transformation. Critique is grist to the capitalist mill. Žižek mirrors those on the academic left who in seeking a truly revolutionary act reduce all forms of resistance to mere 'action'. They demand a 'proper' politics centred on political axioms, party organisation and communist politics. Bennington writes of such postulation:

> The loudest denouncers of 'so-called liberal democracy,' from left and right, thrive on all it makes possible and become the stars of an entertainment business that still sometimes calls itself philosophy. Their complacency . . . stems from an unwarranted assurance as to the relation between politics and truth (or even Truth) and more especially from an assumption of being in possession of the latter, or at least of being able to call us all sternly back to it from our supposedly sceptical and irresponsibly complicit postmodern play and revelry. (Bennington 2016: 2)

Žižek is right that economic questions are a footnote to post-Marxist work. Yet he assumes that he is in possession of the proper truth. Rethinking democratic politics in terms of the improper forces a change in emphasis. We can think improper forms of politics as challenges to the hegemonic organisation of property, propriety and inequality. We can simultaneously refuse the ontological need structuring post-Marxist accounts. The primary question of politics is not a fundamental lack of being. Economic categories are political technologies that articulate the world in certain ways. The political and the economic are inseparable, other than through a performative policing of the distinction. Žižek polices the distinction between the political and the economic in a perverse echo of the dominant consensus. We should interrogate his tacit depoliticisation of economic categories. I begin this work in reframing performativity and materiality (Chapter 3); equivalence, finance and hegemony (Chapter 4); and inequality and democracy (Chapter 5). I take from this reading one key concern though. A politics of the improper does not mirror existing forms of order. This is alluded to by Žižek's notion of an act of pure expenditure – an act that is not grist to the mill of existing order. To think improperly is to imagine and enact what might seem impossible – to act as 'impossibilists' in the name of democratic equality. One last step is to rethink contingency in terms of equality, drawing on arguments developed by Rancière.

Disagreement and Equality

Mouffe and Laclau rightly note that political order cannot be naturalised. However, they simultaneously reintroduce a proper notion of the 'Political'. Rancière rejects the ontological refuge of such theories. Political theory, in turning to ontology, polices what counts as politics (Rancière 1999: 6–7). For Rancière, disagreement cannot be resolved through an appeal to the objective facts, logic or communicative rationality. Rather, disagreement is the space of the possible enactment of equality by the demos. In this respect, Rancière rejects the hegemonic account of the political. Hegemony is a form of police order. Such ordering is distinct from a politics of equality. Policing allots subjects to their proper place and has, *throughout history*, ordered the social world unequally. Politics as disagreement stages conflict over the subjects, objects and the places of politics. It does not assume a negative ontology that requires repeated political identifications.[1] Rancière's reading of contingency refuses the conceptualisation of antagonism as a *prima philosophia* (Marchart 2017: 149).

For Laclau the impossibility of final closure is not a regional ontology. It is characteristic of 'Being' as such, whereas for Rancière this claim is precisely how 'philosophy rids itself of politics' expelling disagreement to 'achieve the true essence of what politics talks about' (Rancière 1999: xiii). Knowing what is properly political authorises judgements about what counts as a political intervention. It is perhaps wilfully perverse to suggest an essentialist core to Laclau's post-Marxism. As Žižek noted three decades ago now 'Laclau's anti-essentialism compels us to conclude that it is impossible to define any . . . essence, any cluster of positive properties which would remain the same in all possible worlds' (Žižek 1989: 98). However, for Laclau the impossibility of defining any essence returns as the demand that we find props that represent this impossibility. Rancière develops a different understanding of disagreement. Rather than valorise an ontological need he links contingency to an equality that no hegemonic order can recognise. He reads the texts of political philosophy against the grain, finding moments of improper equality. For example, he reads Kant's notion of the unconditional thus:

> Democratic politics opposes the meta-political play of appearance and its denial with this practice of the 'as if' that constitutes a subject's forms of materialization and that opens up an aesthetic community, in Kantian fashion, a community that demands the consent of the very person who does not acknowledge it. (Rancière 1999: 90)

Note the improper rendering of the 'as if' here. Democratic politics opposes the play of appearances – the shadow play found in various Marxist accounts of ideology. Despite his critique of the Marxist account of false consciousness, Laclau relies on a form of ideology critique. He rejects an objectivist account of ideology. Nonetheless, the political logic of hegemony means that 'the creation of the illusion of closure is indispensable to the constitution of the social link. It is the study of the mechanisms making this illusion possible that constitutes the field of a contemporary theory of ideology' (Laclau 2014: 35).

Note the word illusion. The social theorist retains his privileges as interpreter of the real. His role is to study the mechanisms that make closure possible. Rancière fixes on the equality implicit in the practice of the 'as if'. The categorical imperative stipulates that one acts *as if* all humans are equal. Rather than limit this to the unconditional he imagines it 'opening onto the emergence of an aesthetic community' enacting equal freedom here and now. The unconditional does not indicate the impossibility of freedom – and thus a politics of delay, of failed promises, of infinite deferral. Rather the unconditional is the *an'arkhe* that founds the community of equals. All rule, he contends, relies on this unconditioned freedom even as it articulates a regime of inequality. The anarchic equality of all opens every regime to challenge. For Rancière *an'arkhe* is the improper basis of any community. It disturbs the attempts of communities to immunise themselves against equality. If so then democracy is not a regime founded and secured through hegemonic articulation and political identification. Rather, on terms I develop more fully in Chapter 5 the demos is both unaccountable and uncountable. It is not proper to rule and 'disjoins entitlements to govern' (Rancière, 2007b: 39). This argument improperly rethinks two key planks of post-Marxism: first the reliance on (post-) structural linguistics, and second the relationship between property, wealth and inequality. I briefly discuss each in turn.

Laclau developed the most consistent political critique, and development, of the structural linguistic model. His argument follows three steps. He accepts with Saussure that language is a relational system of differences in which the 'totality of language is involved in every single act of signification' (Laclau 2007: 36). However, the system of language cannot secure its own limits. This results in an apparent paradox: if 'the differences do not constitute a system then no signification at all would be possible' (Laclau 2007: 36). The limits of the system cannot be signified. If difference is not to collapse into indifference then these limits must be signified. Laclau concludes that the impossible being of the system can only be signified by an empty signifier, a particular signifier which acts as a stand-in for the constitutive lack of the system (Laclau 2007: 39–40). Yet as noted above this argument relies on certain unfounded assumptions. Why would we assume that language is a system? Why assume that there is a totality called language? If there is no closed system then why should this impossibility require signification? Why is closure necessary? Laclau frees language from the assumption that there is any easy correlation between sense and reference – but insists that signification is only possible if there is an attempt to close the gap. There are other alternatives. What if there is no system of language? Surely signification is labile, subject to performative error and remaking, uncontrollable? Rancière points toward a different account. He finds in writing the 'availability of a series of words lacking a legitimate speaker' that interrupts any logic of the proper (Panagia 2000: 115). This excess of words he terms literarity. He identifies an excess of 'words . . . in relation to the things named; [an] excess relating to the requirements for the production of life; . . . and [an] excess of words vis-à-vis the modes of communication that function to legitimate "the proper" itself' (Panagia 2000: 115). This bears no relation to systemic questions about the limits of language. The 'fundamental ability to proliferate words is unceasingly contested by those who claim to speak correctly'. A poetics of politics 'affirms that politics is an activity of reconfiguration of that which is given in the sensible' (Panagia 2000: 115; Woodford 2017). At stake in the staging of political disagreement is the status of objects, of subjects, of the forms of reproduction and communication. Such an excess is unaccountable. The terms proper to police order are open to abuse. There is an echo here – though the argument is distinct – of Deleuze's reading of Foucault on discourse. Laclau presupposes the impossible homogeneity of the linguistic system as the programmatic element of repeated identifications. In contrast, Foucault's notion of discourse recognises that 'statements of a discursive formation . . . use several systems of languages' simultaneously. A discursive formation on this count is 'formed by rules of change or variation . . . found on the same level and these rules make the family a medium for dispersion and heterogeneity, the very opposite of homogeneity' (Deleuze 1988: 5). If this is right then there is no point in beginning with the presupposition of a homogenous linguistic system – for there is no such system.

Second, Rancière links impropriety to the critique of inequality and property. He writes of Aristotle's *Politics*:

> [democracy] meant the unavoidability of conflict, the war of the poor against the rich. The forms of good, peaceful government are, in fact, a form of that war . . . the government of the poor does not mean . . . the government of the lower class; it means the government of those who are nothing – the government of those who have no title, no qualification for ruling. There are a number of powers, based on birth, knowledge, virtue, wealth, and there is the last form, the government based on nothing, nothing but the lack of basis, the lack of an entitlement or qualification for ruling. This means, properly, anarchy – the absence of any *arche*, meaning any principle leading from the essence of the common to the forms of the community. (Rancière 2003)

There is no essence to the common, no final justification for one or other form of rule – the government of the poor indicates precisely that democracy is premised on the rule of those with no property. Yet, he stops short of giving an account of the social formation, of proprietary order, of the relationship between such improper acts of equality and orders of wealth and property. An improper politics breaks with proprietary regimes. It takes inspiration from moments of trespass and transgression that simultaneously illuminate the forms taken by the proper. Democracy is *improper*. What might this mean? It names, on Rancière's terms, those who have no right to rule, those deemed not proper to rule. The constitution of a people, premised on the drawing of antagonistic boundaries, qualifies those deemed proper to rule, to represent the people. Democracy, I suggest, knows no people insofar as a people require identity papers, the drawing of limits, the establishment of what is proper, the taking of a proper name. The unconditional is the improper *abgrund* for politics but it is not the negative of a ground. There simply is no ground. To act improperly is to trespass,[2] to steal, to take equality against its policing.

Let me summarise. The concept of antagonism as developed by Laclau and Mouffe is central to thinking an improper politics. However, in delinking their conceptualisation of antagonism from Marx they fail to deconstruct property, capital and monetary equivalence. They develop a conceptual reworking of antagonism indicating the limits of any proper order. Yet in linking this to an ever-receding ontology, they reinstate a *proper* account of the political. Rancière takes a step closer to an improper politics. There is no good reason why some rule, why some have wealth, as opposed to others. There is no ground to justify a particular ordering of bodies. The enactment of equality improperly undermines any privileged claim to rule and all forms of proprietary order.

Objections to an Improper Politics

Let me now address two objections to this notion of politics as improper. The first, raised by Agamben, holds that the improper merely shadows the proper – it mimics in negative form the metaphysical presuppositions of proprietary order. He first raised this argument as a challenge to deconstruction (Agamben 1973: 141). A second objection holds that without ontology any account of the political is lost in a dangerous relativism. This argument replays the Lacanian critique of historicism. It is best represented by Copjec's (1996) *Read My Desire*.

The Improper and the Proper

Agamben dismisses a politics of the improper while establishing the premise of his own promised deactivation of 'the anthropological machine of the West' (Agamben 2015: 265). Deconstruction, he contends, is merely the other face of this anthropological machine. His argument hinges, in part, on the status we attribute to this machine. It matters little to Agamben that the very notion of the West is a nineteenth-century construct, nor that his genealogy of the secret nucleus of the West repeats the ideologemes that lend succour to the myth of 'Western reason' (see, for example, Appiah 2016). Appiah notes that the very idea of the West as an object of study only arose in the 1890s, the age of high imperialism. It was a novel concept to readers of Spengler's (1991) racist text *The Decline of the West*, and was politically rearticulated during the Cold War years. The narrative linking the West back to Athens and Rome is of recent invention. It does violence to historical fact and ignores a polyglot history that puts paid to any notion of a unified West. Agamben writes:

> The originary doubleness of the metaphysical conception of signifying manifests itself in European culture as the opposition of the proper and the improper . . . The impossibility, for our culture, of mastering this antinomy is witnessed by the constant alternation of epochs of the improper, in which the symbolic-emblematic occupies the central place in culture, and epochs of the proper, in which the improper is pushed to the margins, without either of the two discourses succeeding in entirely reducing its own double. (Agamben 1973: 141)

The deconstruction of metaphysics then is but the new garb of an ancient story that is Western metaphysics *and* politics. The 'originary doubleness' of the signifying intrinsic to 'European culture' is epitomised in the Catholic argument that congruence through discrepancy (the improper) is the best way to represent the almighty, rather than to make false images. The history of the 'West' is characterised by an alternation of epochs between the proper (the literal) and the improper (the figurative). Neither is able to reduce its double (ibid.: 141) and both are elemental to the metaphysical signature of the 'West'. The paradigmatic way of signifying by improper means is met-aphor. Read in this light deconstruction repeats the metaphysical project. These limits characterise Derrida's interpretation of Saussure: 'The metaphys-ics of writing and of the signifier [what Derrida will term grammatology] is but the reverse face of the metaphysics of the signified and the voice and not surely its transcendence' (Agamben 1973: 156). Derrida repeats the meta-physical gesture par excellence affirming the impossibility of getting beyond a 'being in force without significance' (Agamben 1998: 54).

Agamben's account is deeply problematic. Who counts as the 'our' in the quote above? What counts as European and as of the West? This fictional nar-rative of a Western tradition, even when deployed by the left, is politically damaging in skewing our vision of the many threads that feed into the present. Moreover, the reading of Derrida is too quick. In 'Tympan', the introductory essay to his 1982 collection *Margins of Philosophy*, Derrida notes that philosophy has always attempted to 'think *its other*: its proper other, the proper of its other, an other proper . . . In thinking it as such, in recognising it, one misses it. One re-appropriates it for oneself . . .' (Derrida 1982: xi). At stake for Derrida is 'an other which is no longer its [philosophy's] other', that avoids symmetrical and frontal protest, and cannot 'infinitely be reappropriated . . . engendering and interning the process of it expropriation' (Derrida 1982: xiv–xv).

The improper seems to propagate just what philosophy requires – a limit appropriable back into the metaphysical inventory. The improper thought in this way presupposes the order it simultaneously rejects. Derrida's elliptical text, marked by a margin, resists inclusion in the conventional philosophical roster. Deconstruction neither forecloses the neutralising of metaphysics nor takes for granted the originary formation of the political. Rather, a direct confrontation confirms what it opposes, and is always already anticipated by philosophical thought. Hegel's rendering of dialectic, for example, tracks different stages in the development of rational freedom: a path from primitive unity through internal division and struggle until at the end of history undifferentiated unity emerges. Deconstruction in contrast is an oblique, improper, challenge to philosophy. It poses the right question: can we imagine an improper not already anticipated by existing forms of order?

In a similar vein, Agamben reads democratic politics as just another version of this same metaphysical signature. In effect, he suspends politics and celebrates what amounts to a recipe for melancholic refusal. These arguments only makes sense if we assume that there is an originary metaphysical signature of the West that a true politics would render inoperative. Agamben's notion of inoperativity and his rethinking of property and poverty are both central to the thinking of an improper politics. However, their objects of intervention are not the metaphysical ballast of a fictional unity called the West. One last note on Derrida. In concluding 'Tympan' he writes

> that what resists here is the unthought, the suppressed, the repressed of philosophy. In order no longer to be taken in, as one so often is today, by the confused equivalence of these three notions, a conceptual elaboration must introduce into them a new play of opposition, or articulation, of difference. (Derrida 1982: xxviii)

In thinking a politics of the improper I return to these differences – to their possible articulation – but in an altogether more mundane register than the deconstruction of the onto-theological destiny of the West. Rather I am concerned to think a politics that puts in to question existing proprietary regimes – the articulation of property, propriety and the proper outlined in Chapter 1.

Politics without Ontology

A second objection to an improper politics might be termed the ontological rebuke to historicism. Rather than invoke an ontology – whether it be a Spinozist version of infinity, a new materialism, a Lacanian notion of the real – an improper politics probes the exclusions that constitute dominant ways of being. It does not assume a proper way to be, nor is it tempted to turn this impossibility into a negative theology. Rather, being is always articulated to particular forms of proprietary order. The Greek term *'ousia'* is variously translated as being, substance or as property. Fundamental ontology aims to determine what exists in and of itself without further need of predicates, what is proper to itself. The hierarchy of *Being* moves from the particular ontologies, to a general ontology and then to a fundamental ontology. Post-Marxist theorists, despite themselves, replay this classical account of the hierarchy of Being. They distinguish ontic particularity from the question of Being in general – even as they put in to question all positive ontologies. In keeping with the etymology of *ousia* I ask how what is proper to being comes to be accepted as such, and what are its effects.

Copjec characterises this argument as a form of 'Foucaultian' historicism. Historicists, she writes, reject any transcendental meta-principle irreducible to particular configurations of power. For her there is one transcendent principle: there is no meta-language. Because there is no meta-language society 'never stops realising itself' (Copjec 1996: 9). Against this argument, I accept Adorno's immanent critique of what he terms the ontological need, the assumption that the Being question requires an answer from beings. Adorno attributed a conceptual violence to this argument. He notes that for Heidegger the copula 'is' refers both to any particular judgement and to the general category of 'isness' – Being. Adorno's rebuke is pointed: 'the meaning of is just is the constant grammatical token for the synthesis of each particular judgment' (Adorno 1973: 65). While every judgement assumes the existence of a subject, 'is' does not have its own additional predicate, 'isness'. Heidegger transforms the copula into an object – 'Being' – and does conceptual violence to the constellation intrinsic to every judgement. He abstracts 'Being' from its entwinement in a constellation – and then treats such entwinement as inauthentic. The turn to the *Seinsfrage* as a search for authenticity in a commodified world is a mute tautology. Its banality indexes that something is wrong in an antagonistic social order organised around principles of equivalence, identity and abstraction. Even when posed in negative terms (as impossibility, as being towards death, as inexpressible other than in the language of the poet) Adorno refuses the question. It implicates the questioner in the search for a missing (negative) essence that does violence to the constellation of actual judgements. It abets violence in the world in the name of the recovery of the question of Being. As Derrida later writes 'Being is always understood as proper to itself' (Derrida 1982: xvi).

Adorno's critique of Heidegger is contestable but is not my concern here. However, it does apply to the ontological account of the political outlined above. There the political is distinguished from politics as the realm of the everyday (the ontic) – mere existence – where the regulated administration of everyday life takes place. The Political (always capitalised) alludes to an impossibility characteristic of being as such. It is experienced as a lack. Everyday politics is deemed ideological insofar as it covers over this contingency. Being shows itself in entities as that which they lack. This argument is dressed up as quasi-transcendental. In fact, it is both ahistorical and universal. It disguises two distinct claims. The first suggests that there is nothing essential to human beings. What the human is, what the human becomes, is a matter of work, of articulation. The second is that this impossibility returns as an ontological need. This does not follow. To pose it as such is to make a decision. Rather, what it is to be is always already articulated in relation. It has no significance outside this inexhaustible constellation. It is an overdetermined ensemble with no proper centre, no essence. Having cleared certain of the conceptual questions let me finally turn to a politics of the improper.

Politics as Improper

Improper forms of politics refuse the established terms of proprietary order. Yet the improper is not the other face of the proper. Certainly all forms of politics are contoured by what existing conditions make possible. Democratic politics must address the 'burdens of our time' – a global proprietary system that engenders precarity. However, I think the improper as both a breach of established inequalities, and as the envisioning of worlds unimaginable in terms of those inequalities. In even the darkest of moments human beings act against fascism, domination and violence. Practices of equality and democracy have a deep and rich vein but the improper has no proper bounds. It is not *an* impossibility or a lack. It intervenes in existing forms of order and reconfigures the life-world in unexpected ways but does not aim to establish a proper order. As Esposito writes 'What is properly one's own does not reside anywhere except in the knowledge of our own impropriety' (Esposito 2010: 96). In thinking the declensions of the improper as political, I do not assume that this account is exhaustive. Such a thinking begins with the account of proprietary order I developed in the previous chapter. There I insisted that hegemony concerns the articulation of property and propriety. Here I consider the improper in relation to such propriety ordering.

Politicising Property

The improper immediately politicises property. State and extra-state orders secure property. They rely on violence to defend the current and the historical enclosures essential to legal regimes of property. I began this chapter with the occupation of St Paul's. The removal of protestors was justified with reference to property laws that regulate the appropriate use of space. The occupiers reanimated ancient histories of resistance. This same space, exempt from crown law, was a contested space at the heart of the City. Naysayers dismiss such protests. Reading them improperly reconstructs and preserves the impropriety they put into play. The occupation of property, theft in its different forms, hacktivism targeted against the proprietary protection of ideas both tangible and intangible, trespass, forgery of currency or of art – these are improper acts against dominant ordering of the proper. They politicise the proper organisation of the economy, of 'oikonomos', the dominant ways in which norms structure lives and their reproduction. They challenge the independence of central banks and politicise the legal frameworks that order global proprietary regimes. Challenges to property – whether material or immaterial – make explicit the violence needed to secure enclosure. The improper raises the question of who has the right to use spaces, places and forms of knowledge. Property laws distribute and organise such access. When these laws are challenged, a world taken for granted is reanimated and rendered contingent. Democracy is *improper*. Enclosure requires the drawing and the maintenance of boundaries of exclusion and inclusion. The sovereign determination of the proper, as well as of the exception to the proper, defines trespass. Trespass as democratic enactment destabilises enclosure. However, enclosure is not simply the putting up of fences around that which is ontologically prior to the enclosure. Enclosure defines space, things, objects, properties in the very act of enclosing. To posit the commons as an alternative is to miss the point (Hardt and Negri 2000). This claim operates on the same terrain. It presumes that there are forms of the proper which have simply to be reclaimed. Instead, to engage in a politics of property is to redefine both ourselves and our world, requiring leaps of faith and of passion which redraw and remake the bounds of the given. An improper politics begins with the regime of property dominant now. As a structured totality, always contingent, it reifies certain behaviours and delimits the forms of the proper. Dissensus begins with those who break the bounds of the proper, and is often located at the margins where those bounds are maintained. The delineation of a regime of property as a critical theoretical exercise both specifies its borders, and indicates the moments of trespass and transgression which enact other ways of being, while fashioning other worlds. Such an improper account of democratic theory is no longer Marxist in any strict sense, but it begins with the question bequeathed to us by Marx: the question of who owns and controls the means whereby we reproduce our lives, and how might we transform this order.

Crime and Property

The occupation of St Paul's Cross was ruled a crime against property. The Office for National Statistics of the United Kingdom records that in the year up to March 2016 two thirds of all prosecuted crimes were property related. The offences ranged from petty theft to crimes against intellectual property. We might revisit a now familiar argument proposed by Ambrose, fourth-century Bishop of Milan, who argued forcefully that it is the rich who are the thieves, that law in demarcating the world as private dispossesses the multitude. Ambrose takes his distance from Cicero's *De Officiis* on this issue. Both agree that private property has no basis in nature. However, Cicero expresses no concern about the emergence of private property through war, treaty or law. Ambrose, in contrast, insists that nothing like private property exists in nature, *and* that the rearticulation of the world as private is a form of unjust usurpation contrary to God's will. Ambrose adapts the stoic insistence that God created the earth for the use of human beings, and that humans are created for each other, to Christian ends (Swift 1979: 181–5). Ambrose is right. There is a direct relationship between these histories of enclosure and the crime of theft. Hardt, in rather prosaic terms, notes that 'Pirates have a noble vocation: they steal property. The corporations instead steal the common and transform it in to property' (Hardt 2010: 350). The reference to piracy is apposite. Piracy in the seventeenth and eighteenth centuries was an improper response to mercantile capitalism. The pirates were in some sense symptomatic responses to their era (Bobbit 2008). However, their acts pointed beyond the limits of that era. The communities they established were often premised on communal practices of freedom and equality. Crime is the excuse deployed by states to securitise life. It is also an improper reaction against proprietary ways of organising and distributing life chances. We might interpret the most awful forms of crime in the contemporary era in just such terms. Explicitly at stake in suicide bombing, for example, is the value of lives, the means for determining this value, and the meaning of value itself. Suicide bombers reject a dominant worldview committed to secular reason, the celebration of freedom and individual innovation, the extension of both quality of life and length of life, and the primacy of the value of life on this earth. Such acts must be condemned. However, they are only explicable as the indirect expression of dominant forms of proprietary order. At stake is how each body is accounted for, accorded value and disciplined. Contemporary forms of political order rely upon an ideological and phantasmatic commitment to the rationality of the market. Such order valorises the self-interest of individuals, the extension of actuarial forms of valuation to all areas of life, the marketisation of human relationships and the use of information technologies to exercise control over the distribution of bodies in space and in time. This actuarial politics, like the insurance technologies of old, depends upon the valuing of subjects as embodied in a variety of monetised social relationships. Each of these determinants has its underside: self-interested individuals undermine the implicit moral framework required to maintain a balanced market; information technologies, rendered actuarial, rationalise discrimination against those who score badly against the calculus; and new technologies require appropriate forms of legal ownership and control, notably the ability to patent information. At stake is each body as a bearer of messages, the body as engraved with different signs and values, signs which distribute property and properties. The hacktivist and the suicide bomber, like the pirates of old, are explicable against the backdrop of these proprietorial orders.

My point is not one of justification. Nor would I invoke the notion of the common as the moral basis for a critique of privation. There is nothing common to humanity prior to the articulation of things as common. There is nothing proper to humanity that founds a political notion of the common. The improper assumption guiding this book is that wealth is violent even when this is not immediately apparent – but so too is any attempt to establish a common. The genealogy of wealth underscores its barbarity. So too does any genealogy of what it is to be human. Hardt has contended that the common is produced by the labour of the multitude, the immaterial and material work that (re)makes the world. He relies on two notions of the common – the earth as common to all; and human labour, language and affects as the production of the common. We can reject the first account as a quasi-theological fiction useful only as a political argument. What about the second? His analogy is Marx's description of how immobile property acted as a fetter on moveable property with the emergence of industrial capitalism. Today, he contends intellectual property is a fetter on the immaterial production of the common. Patent law, however, cannot police the immaterial production of common wealth. The productivity of the multitude is constrained by laws that fetter these new forces of production. Hardt asserts, on this basis, that the future is with the multitude who produce the common (Hardt 2010: 349). I concur with Hardt in one respect. Property is an apparatus of enclosure that has extended to ever more areas of knowledge, processes, information, the genetic bases of all life, the land and its products. However, history shows no favour to a multitude without existence, identity or political agency. There is no subject proper to politics, no proper order that if realised will restore to the multitude its rightful common wealth. Any form of political order will inscribe new forms of inequality that are impossible to anticipate in advance.

Animals and Humans

The relationship between property, the human and the criminal raises a related issue. What distinguishes the human from the animal? Is the drawing of this distinction a technology that secures what is proper to human beings? Introducing his final seminar, *The Beast and the Sovereign*, Derrida notes that his central questions concern: 'force and right, right and justice, of what is "proper to mankind," and the philosophical interpretation of the limits between what is called man and what is improperly and in the generic singular called the animal' (Derrida 2009: xiv). Note this linking of the proper to the question of 'mankind' and to the role that the generic word animal – a word without an appropriate referent – plays in securing 'man'. The protagonist of Coetzee's (1999) *The Lives of Animals* performatively tests these proper bounds. While delivering a set of invited lectures to academics she refuses the invocation of reason to justify the incarceration, butchery and eating of 'animals' (Coetzee, improperly, delivered the lectures in the person of Costello). Their concluding lecture finishes with this (improper) response from Costello to her interlocutors:

> When opponents are at loggerheads, we say: 'Let them reason together, and by reasoning clarify what their differences are, and thus inch closer. They may seem to share nothing else, but at least they share reason. On the present occasion, however, I am not sure I want to concede that I share reason with my opponent . . . If the last common ground that I have with him is reason, and if reason is what sets me apart from the veal calf, then thank you but no thank you, I'll talk to someone else. (Coetzee 1999: 116)

What links crime, reason and the 'animal' is the categorical drawing of the distinction between persons and things, premised on the determination of what is proper to humans – the ability to reason. Animals are not subjects of law and thus not persons. The animal cannot commit a crime nor bring a case against human beings for murder, despite some rare exceptions. Yet the concept 'animal' refers to everything and nothing. Antelopes, flies, lions, sharks, birds, ants . . . an ever-expansive list of creatures other than one exception – the human – may be made property, be killed without sanction or be produced as food. On such props is the proper order of man's being maintained – reason, subject and object, human and animal, persons and things – property. What Derrida terms 'carnophallogocentrism' articulates together in one neologism the co-implication of reason, meat eating and masculinity. Carnophallogocentrism relies on an abyssal divide between the human and the animal, a distinction undergoing profound challenge: 'The multiple and heterogeneous border of this abyssal rupture has a history. Both macroscopic and microscopic and far from being closed, that history is now passing through the most unusual phase . . . for which we have no scale' (Derrida 2008: 31). A key terrain of that challenge concerns the place of the body – which as I noted earlier enjoys the strange legal status as neither person nor thing. The body that endures, that suffers, that expresses pain, that changes and ages – what place does it hold in relation to reason? Some philosophers go so far as to suggest that a body without reason cannot experience pain – and that there is thus no moral basis to treat other species on terms equivalent to the human. The proper order of man is bound on two sides – first, by what distinguishes humans from other creatures as proper subjects, able to secure things as property; and second by the determination of things as subject to the sovereign will of these proper beings. An improper politics tests the bounds of the properly human and confronts this figure with its constitutive exclusions and violences.

Violence is central to the drawing of this bound between the animal and the properly human. For many political theorists the founding justification of political order concerns the exclusion of animalistic violence, in the name of reason. However, the animalistic violence supposedly excluded is immediately included as the reasoned violence necessary to protect the community against its own dissolution. This inclusion takes the form of the exception. In order for the rule of community to be enforced, an exception to the rule allows that some may use violence. The right to determine who can use this violence is reserved for the sovereign, a principle best encapsulated by Hobbes's description of that Great Leviathan who maintains order precisely in being exempt from the social contract (Agamben 1998: Chapter 1).

Hobbes's sovereign lives in the state of nature, and can still exercise the very violence that the founding of the polity sought to exclude. Violence is re-inscribed as the very principle of the polis. The reasonable polity requires the violence it initially sets out to exclude.

But this founding myth of political theory misses its object precisely because it constitutes, and is constituted by, the object it claims to reject. Violence is established in human community. We do not say of animals that they commit violence for which they are responsible. A lion does not set up a torture chamber to extract information, or plant land mines to kill buck, or hunt in order merely to kill. Violence is not excluded from political community. It is constituted by the drawing of the bounds that establish and maintain community. Reason in Plato's (2007) *Republic* is directly linked to the reason of state, to the justification of a specific distribution of parts within the state, which is then said to correspond to *Eudemonia*, to the form of the good, which only very few humans are capable of comprehending. The reiteration of violence within the state is not only a reiteration. Rather, it is constituted as inherent to the establishment of this order. Political community is justified on the premise that it excludes irrational, animalistic violence. In fact, such justification is constitutive of violence. Violence is intrinsic to the definition of reason, to the reason of state, and to the drawing of the line between the human and the animal.

Colonial Properties

These questions allude to the origins of the dominant configuration of property and wealth – colonial occupation, violent dispossession and centuries long practices of enclosure as the historical groundwork for global inequality. Political theorists of colonialism deployed animality as a technology and a practice of reason to justify occupation. Locke's depiction of indigenous peoples as animalistic, as incapable of exercising reason, as nomads with little interest in industry justified the seizure of land, wars of extermination and settler colonialism. It is no exaggeration to argue that the streets of London or Brussels are literally paved with the blood and the labour of those dispossessed during the enclosure movements, colonial conquest and slavery that made Europe. The proper of property is 'conquest, enslavement, robbery, murder, in short force . . .' (Marx 1976: 874).

When the era of territorial decolonisation reached its nominal end with the defeat of internal colonialism in South Africa in 1994 the outline of a postcolonial proprietary order was already emergent. The global economy restructured as informational, networked and service oriented supports excess consumption for a small minority. It relies on technologies of debt, poverty and war economies across the globe. What Montag terms necro-economics, or market death, engenders precarity and exclusion in the name of the market. He writes that

> alongside the figure of *Homo Sacer* . . . is another figure, whose death is no doubt less spectacular than the first . . . he who with impunity may be allowed to die, slowly or quickly, in the name of the rationality and equilibrium of the market. (Montag 2005: 17)

Necro-economics is allied with a politics of postcolonial forgetting. In fact, existing supply chains and forms of property in lands and resources map closely on to that history. Although property rights are increasingly immaterial and 'organised labour is a factional interest rather than the bearer of the universal interests of mankind' (Unger 2005: viii) the networked world is lubricated by oil, by minerals such as coltan, by fruit, vegetables and meat, by water all secured through leasing or property agreements across the globe (Liberti 2013). The irrelevance of Marxist political parties should not blind us to the role these primary commodities play in dominant versions of proprietary order. The resources necessary to the reproduction of life are private assets, managed through global supply chains and legal orders without respect for national borders.

What does this mean for a decolonial politics today? The revolutionary movements against European empires were framed as nationalist and socialist. National democratic struggles were committed to a two-stage theory of revolution: the end of colonialism would inevitably give way to socialism. 'Race' was interpreted as the form taken by class in the colonial state. These revolutions against colonialism and racism reached their terminus with structural adjustment programmes, loans to corrupt leaders, the privatisation of state assets, the opening of markets to international firms, the selling of agricultural lands and forests and the extension of mining rights to multinational corporations granted quasi-sovereign status over large tracts of territory. One legacy of the colonial state allowed this: land is held, in the final instance, as the property of the state. Liberti, Sassen and others have traced the gradual selling off of land and resources by postcolonial states often left with no option in response to debt. The claims of indigenous peoples were largely ignored by postcolonial nation states and the logics of property established in the colonial period were extended. Logistical technologies, supply chain management and outsourcing became the keystones of mobile global capital.

Thinking an improper, decolonial politics of property requires both a renewal of thought, and a reconstruction of earlier attempts to extend equality. We too quickly forget that – despite their limitations – welfare policies were not primarily the domain of Europe. Nasser in Egypt, the post-British Raj socialism of successive Indian governments and the redistributive policies pursued by early postcolonial governments across Africa all indicate that the privatisation of the state is not the only option (Sassen 2014: 212). Yet an improper and democratic politics today is not national democratic, populist or indeed socialist. One exemplar is the revolts in the Niger oil Delta during the past decade. Activists from the Movement for the Emancipation of the Niger Delta (MEND) deploy a range of methods including armed revolutionary struggle, kidnapping and naked occupations, and the destruction of critical pipeline infrastructure that passes through swamplands polluting the crops and the water of local communities. Such strategies may appear local. However, they impact on global stock markets, damage the revenue of multinational corporations such as Shell and Chevron and generate transnational campaigns.[3] Campaigners target the property of these corporations and the proprietary orders linking the Nigerian state, oil companies and the former colonial powers. In attacking production sites, transport by rail and by ship, the refineries and the points of consumption, activists put in to question global proprietary order.

My point is, to recall the discussion of the mobile phone in the previous chapter, that the distinction between material and immaterial production is fallacious. It misses the articulation between complex forms of financial extraction and more directly brutal forms of extraction – though the outcomes are often the same. The foreclosures carried out against 13 million households after the financial crisis are mired in similar calculative and actuarial techniques that secure the delivery of coltan to factories around the globe. What Deleuze wrote of the strike applies equally to revolutionary violence, to Leninist style vanguards and to seizures of sovereign power. The ineptitude of the unions, Deleuze writes, is linked to their 'history of struggle against the disciplines and the spaces of enclosure' (Deleuze 1992: 6). The failure of the old left to grasp 'the progressive and dispersed installation of a new system of domination' is manifest in the failure to grasp the promise of the post-2008 financial crisis. None of the old figures of resistance – national democratic struggle, hegemonic articulation, class struggle, or hybridity – is an adequate response to a system which feeds on difference as a specific property while concentrating the ownership of property. The anti-colonial resistance movements once deemed improper now implement the vision of a global market unbridled. The end of direct colonial political control never addressed the concentration of property ownership. Any account of contemporary political agency must address the abstract forms that property now takes, debt bondage, and the exercise of hegemony on terms that extend beyond national borders.

Deactivation, Inoperativity and the Politics of Property

I suggested above that notions such as the multitude are inadequate political responses to the political cartography that Hardt and Negri outline in *Empire* (Hardt and Negri 2000). No political ontology determines what counts as properly political struggle. The old figures of revolt all presumed to identify both a proper subject of politics and the proper outcome of political struggles. Political resistance too often reinstitutes the forms of order it simultaneously rejects. With Agamben, I accept that the invocation of constituent forms of revolutionary power merely echoes existing forms of order: 'A power that was only just overthrown by violence will rise again in another form in the incessant but inevitable dialectic between constituent power and constituted power' (Agamben 2014: 70). Rather than 'criticise or correct this or that concept, this or that institution of Western politics', Agamben seeks to 'shift the very site of politics itself' which has for two millennia been in the same place (Agamben 2014: 65). The key referent he argues is bare life, the inclusive exclusion of life as the bio-political basis of all politics. Agamben contends that this originary structure – which has its origins in the Greek metaphysical account of Being – must be addressed if political acts are not to repeat the logics they reject. A proper politics renders inoperative this originary structure. I have already rejected Agamben's notion of the West. His assumption that an originary structure orients the Western ontological, metaphysical and political episteme is on my view simply wrong. He wields the weapon of the 'truly political' to cut a swathe through different forms of resistance deemed inauthentic.

However, his conceptualisation of inoperativity does contribute to the thinking of an improper politics. In this regard, his discussion of property is instructive. The Franciscan commitment to poverty aimed to make use of the world without rendering it as an object, as property. This is a form of use in which the subject is constituted by and 'affected in relation with another body or with one's own body as other' (Agamben 2014: 69). This refusal of property is not a renunciation. Rather it enacts a different state of being in the world rendering it as inappropriable, but open to potential uses that are not utilitarian (Agamben 2015: 80–90). Such a deactivation of the apparatus of property realises 'man as a being of a pure potentiality that no identity and no work [can] exhaust' (Agamben 2014: 70). It opens humans to a new possible use. Destituent power thus realises freedom in the act of deactivating the proper. It is an arduous task but one in which 'classless society is already present in capitalist society' (Agamben 2015: 94). This is important for my argument. Agamben holds that the improper is already present in capitalist society. As Primera (2019) argues, inoperativity is radically anti-teleological. It presupposes a modal ontology in which there is no distinction between Being and its modes. What the human is, is constituted in the process of its modifications (Primera 2019: 136). The agent of politics presupposed in this account is an agent in the middle voice – one affected by the acts in which they engage. I mentioned Coetzee's *Lives of Animals* above. Coetzee's novels are rendered in the middle voice. The narrator is implicated in, and affected by, the narrative. She has no God's eye view to justify the making of judgements about characters. In being affected the narrator is implicated in, and responsible for, their views. This is in part Coetzee's response to the demands of history, the very particular context of apartheid. He refuses to write as one who claims to know, refuses to make fiction the agitprop of a political movement. To do so would be to reproduce the authority of the colonial settler, rather than to suspend this power, to open it to affects that cannot be determined in advance (Macaskill 1994: 470). Such practices of deactivation are possible without committing to the suspension of a metaphysics of Being. This argument is remarkably close to Rancière's account of equality. It assumes that equality is enacted here and now, rather than as an ever-deferred promise. The enactment of equality transforms the agents who act. The distinction between subject and object, between person and thing, begins to fray.

The attempted enactment of equality – always difficult, always arduous – by the Occupy camps were attempts to render inoperative orders of propriety. They never successfully deactivated dominant proprietary regimes. Rather, as critical laboratories of the future they enacted the possibility of living otherwise. The critic retroactively reconstructs the promise realised in these improper acts, yet is wary of the new forms of policing that accompany every political movement. Think, for example, of a classic demand made by these activist movements – 'Nothing about us, without us.' This slogan replays the democratic demands against monarchs during the enlightenment revolutions. It insists, correctly, that no policies or decisions that affect a group should be enacted without the consent of those affected. However, some go further and argue that a movement or its demands not be spoken about without the presence of those who engaged in the acts. This assumes the ability to control the performative reiteration of such acts in future. It closes down their possible remaking. Critical, distanced, reflection is deemed illegitimate. Activists replay the belief that they possess the proper, that they have privileged access to truth. Such a politics ends up replicating the form of the policing it simultaneously rejects.

Agamben identifies other more mundane examples of such deactivation. During a feast, the making of food and the gathering of families exceeds all utilitarian calculation. The food is prepared as part of the feast, not simply to be eaten. In the poem, language is no longer a means of communicating content – rather it enacts a potentiality of language beyond communication. Our bodies escape any attempt to make them proper to the possessive self as they age, become ill, in their need for sustenance and ablution. The proper subject (ab)uses a language which escapes him; harnesses a body over which he cannot exercise proper control; and remakes the external world as an appropriable object which he then destroys. The notion of the improper I have developed is compatible with these logics – but it refuses their link to a metaphysics of the West. It thinks deactivation as a response to forms of property and propriety that limit the enactment of equality. It encourages us to think about forms of deactivation that are mundane, but also those that might deactivate the exclusive forms of inclusion that structure precarity.

An Improper Politics of the Common

Agamben thinks a politics of inoperativity in terms of the common. 'What is common', he writes, 'is never a property but only the inappropriable' (Agamben 2015: 80). Language, the body, the landscape are inappropriable and thus common. He envisages a community-to-come in which singularities act in common without a common property. This 'inessential commonality, [is] a solidarity that in no way concerns an essence' (Agamben 1993: 18). It requires 'deactivating every juridical and social property without establishing a new identity' (Agamben 2014: 71). The improper property of the community is nothing (see Kioupkiolis 2018: 290). Everything depends, as I noted above, on how we interpret this 'nothing'. An improper politics never invokes an originary form to the common whether thought of as a positive being-in-common, a non-being-in-common or an original potentiality. I see no merit in invoking 'the very notion of things' as the basis for an improper politics. There is no secret nucleus of the 'West' to be deactivated before real politics becomes possible. However, with Agamben there is another notion of the common that I can work with – providing it is adapted. Dardot and Laval (2018) think the common as a political alternative to neoliberalism. However, unlike other theorists they do not invoke any ontology as the basis for their politics. They recognise that the 'passage from ontology to politics is always a leap of faith' (Dardot and Laval 2018: 190). No ethical, political or moral obligations follow from the supposed nature of being. Not only are there competing ontologies, competing versions of the essence of the human; there are competing accounts of what follows from such prior assumptions. Instead, an improper politics assumes that 'Being' is from the first political and overdetermined. The common is made in contingent praxis. What is made common, however, is always open to reactivation. There is no common proper to itself. Dardot and Laval work with similar assumptions: 'the common is a principle of political activity constituted by the specific activity of deliberation, judgement, decision, and the implementation of decisions' that takes historically distinct forms (Dardot and Laval 2018: 1). As a principle of political practice, the common is thought in plurality. I would only add that this is an essential rather than an empirical pluralism. It presupposes an openness that cannot be rendered proper. The establishment of a plurality of commons, of shared forms of co-activity and organisation, includes a range of practices, struggles, forms of institution, duties and sharing.

Dardot and Laval renovate and imagine alternative ways of organising the world against the state and private forms of property. I noted in the previous chapter that at the centre of legal orders of property is the distinction between person and thing. In Roman law 'res', a thing, was not a natural object. It was a legally constituted category determining what could be owned. The notion of a thing cannot be referred back to a prior ontology, or indeed to the prior existence of a thing as an object. It is constituted as a thing in the drawing of political distinctions between persons and things. Yet Roman law also articulated some sacred and public things as inappropriable. The key distinction for our purposes is that between public property (which may later be alienated by the state) and things deemed inappropriable in perpetuity and open to public use. In the postcolonial era the public property of the state has time and again been sold to private corporations. Today, there is barely anything that is inappropriable. This ancient precedent inspires Dardot and Laval to imagine a world made as common and cared for in common. Unlike this Roman precedent, the authors envisage the common as made in collective praxis (rather than through designation by the few); and contend that the subject of the common is articulated through this collective praxis (Dardot and Laval 2018: 179–83). There is then no original distinction between subject and object – rather subject and object are co-implicated in the praxis of their making. The implications of this are compatible with my account of the improper. The common is articulated in struggle. It is the site of antagonistic contestation given that both its nature and mode of organisation have no prior warrant. The common is not the expression of a pre-existing essence, but is articulated in conflict, and maintained only through performative reiteration.

Conclusion: Thinking Politics Improperly

Improper forms of politics breach established proprietary regimes. They enact an equality that is never proper. Improper knowledge breaches the dominant ordering of knowledge as intellectual property. It is knowledge without value in a system that consumes knowledge as profit. Even critical theoretical research contorts itself to the proprietary ordering of knowledge – the publishing industry, the evaluation and measurement of knowledge, the demand to generate intellectual capital through networking, research funding and publication. Knowledge as improper is unaccountable. However, it must account for its own positioning and privileges within the university system, while rejecting its terms. The identification of apparently neutral mechanisms of proprietary power feeds debates about improper forms of politics. The validity of this knowledge is not found in the institutionalised research assessment that commodifies knowledge. Improper knowledge informs and responds to demands for equality, dignity and recognition beyond and within the academy. The enactment of new ways of living is a painful process in which the proper bounds of the subject are at stake. It is not reducible to a matter of knowing. Knowledge informs transformative practices but in itself does not change the world. Political intervention requires this overlap of and clash between knowledge and subjectivity. It recognises that there is no prior order ensuring the conformity of knowledge with the world. It instigates further breaches within the dominant order, recreating an alternative relation between knowledge and political practice.

An improper politics engages in hegemonic struggle to determine how the world is both interpreted and constituted. It aims to enact equality in the world. This means that it identifies antagonists – those who oppose equality, protect privilege or exercise unjustifiable power. The assumption that all are equal includes even those who oppose equality. However, any attempt to act equally will generate antagonism aimed at protecting inequality. The resigned sigh, which invokes the rules of the system, the knowing shrug that implicitly justifies its rules, must be abjured. The characterisation of certain institutions, governments and persons as the antagonist is a prerequisite for political intervention. The abstract logics described in Chapter 1 must be held to account. What Sloterdijk (1988) a long time ago termed cynical reason must be rejected. The lines dividing property laws from theft are hard to draw. Democracy remains a mere shell when bereft of content and complicit in inequality. The logics discussed above point to spaces for intervention. In the spaces where political authority has failed; in the continued reliance of the wealthy on the consumption of the lives of others; in the arithmetic which when applied equitably violates equality; in the lives of those who cannot identify with a neutrality that evacuates all spirit from the earth; on an earth that resists its articulation as property we find the constant promise of an improper equality.

An improper account of politics then rejects idealisms that postulate about class, the multitude, the subaltern, the indiscernible event or some other such agent of revolt. Such postulation forgets the richness and variety of improper struggles against proprietary order. We have already seen that the abstract borders of the emergent order have to be patrolled, that equality is often enacted yet violated, that hegemony is contingent, differential and potentially revocable. Such a politics does not confirm Marx's hope of a revolutionary class emerging triumphant from the ashes of capitalism. It does not result in an event that treats the 'impossible real' of capitalism as certain new age communists would have it. Rather it will be the result of patient, sometimes unseen, constructions of a political order that do not depend on the privatisation of the commons, do not view politics as deliberation and that reconstitutes the reproduction of political life.

I began this chapter with the occupation of St Paul's Cathedral. This, and other occupations, challenged the proper configuration of space and the properties associated with particular spaces. The laws applied to St Paul's differed from those applicable in Tahrir, Taksim and Zucotti Park, and the many other sites occupied in 2011 across eighty countries. All of these spaces were pre-configured in terms of what was deemed a proper use. Laws of property establish rights of use, responsibility and profit. They allocate to legal persons a set of rights and obligations and delimit appropriate behaviours. These included the regulation of health and safety, sanitation, behaviour, trade and residence, and laws concerning public safety and policing and appropriate uses of violence by police. The laws appear neutral but rely on a set of presuppositions about the bounds of the proper. The occupation of spaces that seemed to be public cast the complex knots of law and property in a different light. The occupiers remade these spaces. They established new forms of use in temporary communities of mutual support.

The regulation of these properties has, as its final referent, the sovereign claims of the state. Law views violence in the hands of individuals as threatening. This is not simply because these are criminal acts against property, liberty and life. Rather law has an interest in safeguarding itself. Unsanctioned violence threatens that claim to legitimacy. The refusal of occupiers to recognise the authority of the state was deemed a form of violence. This was so even when the occupiers explicitly disavowed physical violence. The best example, according to Benjamin, is what Sorel termed the General Strike. It takes as its object the legitimacy of the system itself. Rather than protest in line with the legally demarcated space for such actions, the General Strike establishes another way of living. In this case the means – the strike – is evaluated on its own terms without reference to a different end. It enacts the equality it aims to live. While some have argued that the occupiers suffered the narcissistic delusion that they represented a profound challenge to the system, they did force a recognition that 'legitimate' property is contingent, and secured with violence. They claimed to establish their own forms of authority. The sovereign authority of the state was dispensed with in the name of a different form of democratic decision making.

Reading protest from the perspective of the improper refuses too easy a critique of Occupy. In concluding her 2015 text *Agonistics* Mouffe writes: '[In these movements] we find a common refusal of the political in its antagonistic dimension and of the constitutive role of power' (Mouffe 2013: 119). The Occupy movements, she argues, mimic neoliberal forms of order in their rejection of the state. They are reformist. However, Mouffe cannot see their radical impropriety. The retroactive reconstruction of the politics implicit, and sometimes explicit, in these movements takes due account of the overdetermined structures within which they occur – and it reconstructs their democratic potential as improper, anarchic moments, which cannot be disciplined according to the proper politics advocated by these and other critics. The occupiers in effect put history to work in destabilising the prosaic everydayness off the coiffured space of the City. This improper politics took place in the overlapping space between propriety and property, while at the same time committing those engaged in occupation to new forms of subjectivity, and new ways of living together. These were violent acts which did not lead to bloodshed, but which for a short period experimented with new forms of living at the heart of global cities.

THREE

The Performative Politics of a Brick

This is Not a Brick

A 1993 exhibition at the Johannesburg Art Gallery displayed a mounted brick titled 'THIS IS NOT A BRICK'. On the wall behind it was a blown-up photograph of a young man, arm behind his shoulder, poised to launch this same brick at police officers pointing rifles at anti-apartheid protestors.[1] The brick was, most likely, manufactured by Corobrik, the oldest private brick manufacturer in South Africa. Founded in 1902 the company supplied building materials to the pre-apartheid, apartheid and post-apartheid governments. The company describes its current mission thus:

> Corobrik believes that every citizen of our country deserves a home they can call their own. As a market leader, it is our responsibility to help provide social infrastructure, from schools and hospitals, to libraries and community centres, to build a better tomorrow together. (Company brochure, http://www.corobrik.com/company-profile)

Embodied in that brick, in that company, is the brutal history of apartheid and colonial occupation. Founded in the early years of Johannesburg's expansion on the back of gold mining, its bricks built the apartheid city with its separate development and zoning, its violent processes of dispossession, the registration of land as property, and the remaking of earth into standard sized bricks. The young man doubtless picked up the brick in anger. Did he consider what it embodied as he remade it in to a weapon to hurl at the apartheid police? Even before he refashioned its physical properties to different ends, the brick was a constellation of relations including politically engendered property rights, the economic and racial divisions constitutive of apartheid, the labour of men and women forced off the land by colonial violence and the legal order that legitimised expropriation and violence. Stolen from a building site, launched into the air as a weapon, the brick may have injured a police officer. It most likely ended up on the dusty road, after the gathered bodies were dispersed with tear gas, rubber bullets, dogs and sjamboks. The artist picked up this piece of rubble, this relic of protest – like the bricks from the Berlin Wall sold online in the very earliest days of the internet – and framed it with a photograph and that title, 'THIS IS NOT A BRICK' – echoing Magritte, but painfully so. And – the ironic destiny of resistance art – it was purchased by a gallery, categorised, doubtless insured, a commodity on the market, a relic embodying history, an artwork and a testimony, before its iteration here, remade to drive home my point about the improper.

What then is a brick? What is proper to a brick? What maintains its properties as proper? This brief description of its distinct embodiments, of the different lives led by this 'not brick' indicates its performative remaking in unpredictable contexts. None of these altered its physical existence. It is still a solid object, rectangular, three-dimensional – but these physical qualities tell us little about its properties. Indeed property is at the centre of its story, as is the improper. The brick was first property bought and sold by a company with its origins in colonial exploitation. It became the property of the developer or house builder from whom it was appropriated, and then a weapon in a demonstration where its properties took on altogether more lethal proportions. In different circumstances, it may have served as evidence of theft, of violence, of illegal protest, of injury or murder in a legal trial. Still later, it was a property sold on the art market. It was one element of the material environment – overdetermined by a set of competing discursive practices. Yet it is not what it is – its different trajectories do not relate back to an underlying essence. The same is true of all of the infrastructural conditions that secure or threaten the reproduction of our planet and our lives. The misappropriation of these conditions is often the first target for acts of collective protest. I return to the politics of bricks in the chapter that follows.

Introduction

Writing in 2010 Judith Butler posed these questions to political theorists:

> What if it has become a salient characteristic of performative processes in recent years to separate the economic from the political in order, alas, to make political theory? And have we yet begun to consider the process of performativity that makes that distinction with apparent forcefulness time and again? Where and how do we find and promote the conditions of its undoing? (Butler 2010: 160)

Butler is right. Political theorists have actively collaborated in depoliticising proprietary orders by failing to think property as political. I have argued that this is also the case in post-Marxist discourse theory. Chapter 1 reframed theories of hegemony to address the sedimentation of related forms of the proper – appropriate behaviours, proprietary bounds, property and ordering. Although Butler uses a different vocabulary, her insurrectionary ontology deploys performativity against dominant forms of the proper. She puts the foreclosed to work in unpicking the normative violence intrinsic to proper ways of being. Here I extend Butler's own arguments in order to rethink property. I suggest that she has fallen foul of her own injunction. I rethink the performative, emphasising those moments when it touches on questions of the proper. This allows me to reconceive her account of assembly and performative politics in relation to propriety and the proper. Radical challenges to the proper place of politics refigure the relations of bodies to themselves, to others and to their world. I extend the politics of assembly to think about the public enactment of equality as a renegotiation of the body and its 'properties' as well as the material property that makes, and is made, in our common world.

Performativity, Impropriety and Ontology

Butler's account of performativity was from the first improper. She has consistently put in to question established forms of propriety and has challenged the rendering of some lives as precarious. Her texts track the foreclosures, erasures and exclusions constitutive of the proper and develop what might be termed a negative capability against established hierarchies and orders. Keats first uses the term negative capability in a letter to his brothers on 21 December 1817. For Keats it indicated the capability of resting in uncertainties without the irritable reaching towards final fact and reason, a trait he attributes to Coleridge's late works. Butler too refuses to rest critique on proper foundations. At the heart of this refusal is her reading of the concept of performativity. She takes seriously Austin's claim in *How to do Things with Words* that the concept of performativity has resulted in a 'revolution in philosophy' (Austin 1962: 3). Searle and Habermas, in different ways, limited the revolutionary implications of 'performativity' delimiting it within proper and reasonable bounds. Searle refers performativity back to the intention of the speaking subject (Searle 1989: 556) despite Austin's explicit insistence that to rely on intentionality is to miss the performative power of words. Habermas reinterprets performativity as the 'illocutionary force of speech acts connected to cognitively testable validity claims with a rational basis' (Habermas 1979: 62–3). When communicating, he contends, we also *perform the act* of making validity claims about the truth, truthfulness and legitimacy of our utterance. Speakers are implicated in a virtual ideal that transcends the locality of context specific speech acts. This implicit universality is not equivalent to a form of life. Rather it is an orienting ideal for critique, a thorn in the side of reality, pointing to the limits of the given. Yet Habermas's thorn is blunted – its proper limits predetermined by the ideal of a perfectly commensurate communication. Derrida's wonderfully pithy comment about communication indicates the problems with this account. It is polite, but firm, and marks an irreducible divergence in their respective interpretations of the performative:

> Wherever there is the performative, whatever the form of communication, there is a context of legitimate, legitimising or legitimised convention that permits it to neutralise what happens, that is, the brute eventness of the *arrivant*. Performativity . . . in a certain way . . . neutralises the eventness of the event. (Derrida 2006: 112)

Communicative rationality immunises speech against the possibility of an event it cannot anticipate. It neutralises the potentiality unleashed by a possibility it 'always already' has anticipated and disciplined. Indeed Austin had struggled to discipline the insurrectionary potential of the performative. It participates in various linguistic categories and unsettles any easy distinction between illocutionary, locutionary and perlocutionary speech acts. Austin refuses easy answers – every chapter of the text reworks arguments presented in the previous chapter, liberated from that irritable reaching after certainty spurned by Keats. Butler's account of performativity pushes at an open door. In a close reading of Derrida on context and iterability she disturbs any attempt to fix the proper of both sex and gender. Butler materially remakes performativity unleashing its improper potential.

Butler's inaugural act, so to speak, is to ask if there is a proper form to speech. Here she more or less follows Derrida by rote. Derrida asks us to consider where context begins and ends – if there is a context that might finally delimit the meaning of an act. For Derrida the play of signification is subject to a permanent deferral that undermines the apparent integrity of any act. The possibility of reiteration in other contexts indicates for Butler 'a discursive performativity, a chain of resignifications without end or beginning' (Butler 1997: 27). This disjoins speech acts from sovereign control. The attribution of sovereign power over speaking to subjects relies on an unseen infrastructure, a belated metalepsis that occludes the genealogy of the subject and performatively naturalises the terms of politics. The proper name, for example, denotes singularity. It marks the entry of a new subject into the world. However, others confer it on one who cannot, yet, refuse this conferral. The proper name requires an institutional structure, a state that registers every birth and records the name that will haunt the subject through its life. As Senhor José, the unobtrusive registrar of births and deaths in Saramago's (1997) *All the Names*, realises, the search for a final sense of the proper name listed in the archive leaves the searcher stranded in a garden path of significations, a thicket in which the self is lost. For Butler performativity is a condition of possibility and impossibility of any felicitous speech act (Butler 1997: 27). It indicates the limits of any model of divine or proper performativity.

Butler takes seriously Derrida's infamous dictum '*il n'y a pas de hors-texte*' that there is no outside-text (Derrida 1976: 158).[2] We should read text here as the impossibility of a final referent. Idealism, in its different forms, aims to arrest this play, avows that it knows the object. In his 1969 essay 'Marxism and humanism', Althusser had rejected humanism precisely because it assumes that there is a universal essence to the human, and that this essence is the attribute of every single individual, as its real subject. In this view the empiricism of the concept and the idealism of the subject form part of the same problematic (Althusser 1969: 221–7). Butler, in refusing to treat sex as the real beneath gender, or gender merely as the complex mediations of an original sex, sees the body as a 'performative accomplishment which we come to believe and perform' tenuously established in time (Butler 1988a: 1). As the legacy of these sedimented acts its future is not foreclosed: 'Gender is not the expression of an essential sexuality but a regulated form of essence fabrication' (Butler 1988a). Note this radical extension of the original idea of linguistic performativity. If the linguistic act is never self-enclosed, if this is the only possible way it can get a grasp on bodies – so to speak – then so too are bodies never simply given: there is more to the body than the ways in which we signify it to ourselves. Bodies perform in ways that go beyond their signification. There is, Butler contends, a chiasmatic relation between language and the body: neither term exhausts the other which it nonetheless presupposes. For Butler there is no a priori, no proper objects, as she argues in 'Against proper objects' (Butler 1994). Laying claim to a domain proper to language, or to the body, neutralises the performative politics of the claim (Butler 1997: 13). Language has a formative power that is never finally constitutive, and politics often takes the form of improper acts against normative orders. It is thus that Butler's *Gender Trouble* traces the taboos constitutive of the fiction of gender identity as stable. She terms identity an enacted fantasy of incorporation, which presupposes that coherence is desired. It produces the illusion that the effect is the cause: 'the gendered body is performative . . . it has no ontological status apart from the various acts which constitute its reality' (Butler 1988a: 185). This production of an 'ostensibly coherent gender,' of its psychological unity, 'precludes an analysis of the political constitution of the gendered subject' (ibid.: 186). Butler famously celebrates the performativity of drag. The point is that drag is not the imitation of an original sex. Rather, the parody lies in the simple fact that the notion of original sex is already a parodic fiction. Butler ends this discussion of performativity and gender with a moment of improper promise. The power of performativity is the potential to render gender radically incredible (Butler 1988a: 192). I will return to the possibility of the radically incredible a little later in the text but I want to note here just how close these arguments are to the notion of the improper. Butler does not invoke ontological negativity as the substratum of acts of identification. Performativity goes all the way down without reference to an original. If so, what has become the regulative norm is open to reactivation. Butler characterises gender certainty as a form of 'border control' that institutes the integrity of the subject. She hints here at key elements of my argument. Citizenship too is a form of border control. It polices and constitutes identities. Property is a form of border control. Butler extends the material performativity of the body to the so-called material world – in line with my discussion of what it is to be a brick.

Butler in effect proposes a rethinking of materialism. She rejects two related forms of idealism – the first presumes that the world simply is our representations; the second assumes a real world which our significations aim to truly signify. Both assume that there is a proper order to the world. For Butler, in contrast, the real is not an objective order awaiting its correct representation, and discourse is never merely language or linguistic signs. As Laclau writes every discourse 'consists of some elements which do have material existence and others which do not' (Laclau 1990: 218). In terms of the performative operations that secure proprietary orders this raises a series of questions. How do apparently objective facts (such as sex) come to be constituted as natural? How does a thing come to be delineated as a coherent object? How is subjectivity established in relation to these supposedly neutral objects? What possibilities are reactivated when these relations are contested? What forms of iteration police and secure these orders? Butler explicitly thematises 'material existence' when turning her attention to materialisation as: 'a return to the notion of matter, not as a site or surface, but as a process of materialisation that stabilizes over time to produce the effect of boundary, of fixity, and surface we call matter' (Butler 1993: 9). We might think of this in relation to the brick with which I began this chapter. It becomes stabilised as a building material after complex processes of extraction, production and distribution. This stabilisation is subject to performative remaking and is not predetermined by the brick as a substance. Butler's words are noteworthy – the effect of a boundary is produced. We might use precisely the same words to describe the making of property. If there are no proper objects – either in language or denoted by language – then no ontology founds politics. Writing in *Precarious Life* Butler characterised her work as an insurrection at the level of ontology (Butler 2004a: 33) rather than the presentation of a new ontology. This is one way to think an improper politics. The proper requires a reiteration that simultaneously destabilises its proper bounds. It is vulnerable to performative failure. She refuses the trap of proposing a new ontology, even a negative ontology, and takes her distance from Laclau and Žižek on exactly this point. Performative failure cannot be characterised as a structural invariant of all symbolic order:

> Why should we conceive of universality as an empty place which awaits its content in an anterior and subsequent event? Is it empty only because it has already disavowed or suppressed the content from which it emerges, and where is the trace of the disavowed in the formal structure that emerges? (Butler et al. 2000: 34)

Butler asks how the stately robes of ontology occlude vision. She unpicks the performative policing of these proper limits and simultaneously demonstrates the vulnerability of these limits. Subversion plays on this performative potentiality, rendering languages, bodies, ontologies and subjects open to wounding and political challenge. I have deliberately read Butler side on, demonstrating the relevance of performativity to an improper politics. How, if at all, does this argument complement my insistence that property is central to any consideration of politics? After all property is hardly central to Butler's arguments. Or is it? In what follows I argue that property is one of the unspoken presuppositions that sediments, and fixes, forms of materialisation. I do so through a reading of certain ellipses in her performative account of assembly and dispossession.

Performativity and Politics: Possession, Property and Propriety

Butler's initial work on the politics of gender demonstrates the performativity intrinsic to the beings that we become. Her later works extend this to think about the role of performativity in political protest, assembly and in the material spaces where lives are configured. My wager is that she presupposes, but does not engage with, a politics of property falling foul of her own critique of the performative maintenance of the boundary between *oikos* and polis. This may seem an odd claim given the centrality to her work of dispossession. Butler and Athanasiou's dialogic text *Dispossession* (2013) concerns two related forms of dispossession. The first echoes Marx's account of accumulation by dispossession. It concerns the many processes and ideologies of abjection, subjection and dispossession constitutive of our worlds. This account is not unique. Sassen, for example, has studied how global rules designed to support corporate economic growth support processes of economic cleansing and expulsion (Sassen 2014: 214). The 'complex instruments [of financial capital] have brutally elementary outcomes' (ibid.: 219). In these cases, the term dispossession is apposite: the word combines two Latin verbs, *posse*, to be able; and *sedere*, to sit. Dispossession literally means the removal of that which makes it possible to remain in place. Contemporary forms of accumulation by dispossession, debt, the destruction of natural habitats and war violently dispossess and displace human beings.

However, they also link material dispossession to the foreclosures constitutive of subjectivity, the 'pre-emptive losses and inaugural submission' during which 'one is moved by others, and constituted in relation to these others' (Butler and Athanasiou 2013: 1). The term dispossession thus politicises avowedly neutral economic processes and articulates these to forms of subjection and subjectivation. Yet this argument requires more nuance. To characterise the identifications through which subjects 'come to be' as dispossession assumes an inaugural loss, a theft of something. How are the inaugural foreclosures that make subjectivity possible forms of dispossession? There is no original possession of which the subject might be dispossessed. Being able to sit in one's place does depend on constitutive relations with others – processes of identification – the complexity, uncertainty and unpredictability of which are the object of psychoanalytic thought. However, the word dispossession suggests that identity is constituted via an original lack that originates in practices of foreclosure and loss. Yet it is precisely those arguments that Butler rejects in relation to the oedipal account of subject formation. The word dispossession is appropriate only because subjects are interpellated into social relations already constituted by violent forms of dispossession – and by this I mean the constellation of relations that make it impossible for one to sit comfortably. This same point is made by Derrida for whom there is no original proper of which one might be dispossessed. He begins with the recognition that the proper name is never proper to itself. Its propriety depends upon a system of differences without proper limit. If we come to be in contexts overdetermined by inequality, then any genealogy of the self will track back to the wounds that constitute the self as relational. It will not track back to an original loss. This may seem a quibble. However, this way of framing dispossession displaces an original ontology of loss. Instead, we can focus on the role that possession plays in the theorisation of the proper, and on the place of the proper name that one inherits from within an already constituted order of inequality.

I previously traced a secret history of the concept of possession in political theory – a history that performatively refutes the disciplinary boundaries protected by political theorists. This reading is compatible with Butler's understanding of vulnerability in *Precarious Life* (Butler 2004a). There she proposes to find in our 'exposure to violence and our complicity in it, with our vulnerability to loss . . . the basis for community' (Butler 2004a: 19). Being in relation exposes us to the possibility of dispossession:

> The body implies mortality, vulnerability, agency: the skin and the flesh expose it to the gaze of others, but also to touch, and to violence and bodies put us at risk of becoming the agency and the instrument of these as well' (Butler 2004a: 26)

Vulnerability signifies a primary helplessness and need to which any society must attend. Or, in slightly more prosaic terms, 'The "I" is from the outset enthralled' (Butler 2004a: 44) but this does not presuppose a primary loss or lack. Exposure is not a lack – it is an opening to possibility. To note that the body is vulnerable, that the infant is exposed to others as it comes to be, that 'being is relation' is to recognise that the improper is the only proper to which the human may lay claim. Butler then destabilises the idea of a subject comfortably sitting in its own place. In her account of gender performativity we see a subject whose sense of place is disturbed by uncanny reminders. In thinking about the primacy of relationality she puts paid to illusions of the possessive individual. Yet this argument does not have to presuppose an original dispossession. Rather, possession is always already an act of seizure and exclusion. We should read Butler's account of naming and performativity as putting in to question any relation between the self and the possessive subject. Self-possession extends outwards to a world of things – a world classified, organised and divided into discrete entities – entities articulated as proper to themselves in an overdetermined context. This ontology of the proper – linking a conception of the self to a world of external objects, and to a set of relations to others (those who cannot be owned as property but who may sell their properties) – is what Butler's notion of performativity problematises.

It is not, then, apposite to conceptualise subject formation in terms of an original dispossession. To become a subject is to be in relation. There is no original possession of which one might be dispossessed. Such a notion of being, one which Arendt affirms in the opening pages of *The Life of the Mind* (Arendt 1981: 19–24), is not haunted by the impossible promise of an original possession that one must retrieve. We are constituted in a world of plurality. What comes to appear coincides with what is (there is no essence preceding existence) and the ego is a relational entity – constituted in and by the relations that make us. This plural world of appearance comprises 'many things, natural and artificial, living and dead, transient and sempiternal all of which have in common that they appear' (Arendt 1981: 19). The dead, matter, the environment all participate in the complex that is the overdetermined plural world of appearance. Arendt's account of plurality is material through and through. Relationality is both subjective and objective, or rather it constitutes each in terms of relation, as exposed in relation. We live in a material, plural, world (to abuse Madonna) and politics concerns how this plurality is rendered proper. We begin in rela- tion – not in dispossession. Questions about the place of the proper and possession are all the more pertinent in light of Butler's arguments about performativity and assembly. Consideration of the brick with which I began this chapter casts a different light on how we might understand the politics of occupation. Performativity indicates the improper premise that underpins any assertion of self-identity. The performativity of nam- ing situates the subject as always already constituted in relation. It renders the proper name improper to itself. As vulnerable beings, constituted in a web of unequal proprietary relations, we may be dispossessed. However, dispossession already presupposes proprietary ordering, the allocation of subjects to their proper place.

Performativity and Assembly

I began this chapter thinking about the performativity of a brick that was never just a brick. It is made through the expenditure of labour, the extraction of resources from the earth, the organisation of the material environment, of transport, oil, property laws and supply chains. It is remade in contexts that cannot be anticipated in advance. What a brick is depends upon the relational complexes in which it partakes, in this case a public protest, an art gallery and an art market. As a key element of the material world bricks materially configure how we might live together. Butler's responses to the global occupations of 2011 extends performativity in light of the politics of occupation, assembly and democracy. She establishes the materiality of this performative politics. Yet she fails to consider the configuration of that material environment as property – and the ways in which that sedimented configuration polices the possibility of protest and of politics.

Democracy and Popular Sovereignty

Butler's interpretation of assembly distinguishes *democracy as a political regime* from *popular sovereignty*. In demonstrations, or occupations, the dominant framing of the people is contested. Occupiers and protestors question the discursive power that constitutes the people and that limit the powers it can legitimately exercise (Butler 2015: 3). On my terms, these forms of protest contest the proper bounds of democratic order. They claim to embody the sovereign power of the people against the proprietary limits of liberal democratic regimes. They question the dominant terms of recognition, the dominant ontology, and their complicity in the production of precarity and abjection. Disputing the political regime's claim to represent the people, these protests contest the proper bounds of the sovereign people. As Butler notes, 'we the people' is always a wager for hegemony (Butler 2015: 4). However, these assemblies also pressed for more than the extension of recognition. They enacted a change to the relation between the recognisable and the unrecognisable, and challenged the frames that delineate the appearance of 'the people'. At stake in such assemblies is whether popular sovereignty is merely an instrument of state sovereignty. If so then popular sovereignty is robbed of its critical and democratic functions (Butler 2015: 163). Butler's point is that the claim 'we the people' exceeds the dominant modes of its representation. This disjunction between state and popular sovereignty is a requirement, she contends, for democratic governance. We might say, echoing her account of critique, that this difference allows for a questioning of the occlusive field established by any democratic regime. The framing of the people by the sovereign state structures a distribution of precarity and dominant modes for the valuation of lives.

Although Butler does not speak of it these occupations also enacted an equality that put in to question the distinction between peoples. The occupiers performatively remade the demos to include those unrecognised by nation states, while constituting a plural community without borders. Many occupations engaged in daily communication with others around the world. They debated and made decisions across the normal boundaries that constitute a sovereign people. They cast harsh light on the proper limits of democratic regimes, testing the lines of demarcation which delimit the demoi and its powers – borders, territory, property and citizenship – all rendered proper(ty) by sovereign and global orders which restrict the exercise of democratic power. This argument is compatible with that presented by Butler. However, Butler is wedded to bridging the distance between the sovereign people and the sovereign state, through democratic struggles. Instead, I emphasise the distance between the two. Democracy is never a regime. I concur that the occupiers rejected dominant versions of popular sovereignty. Sovereignty – as the Latin etymology of the word *superanus*, the ruler, one who is above, suggests – always entails regime and rule. Democratic theory erroneously assumes that an appropriate principle exists to determine who constitutes a people. As I argue in the concluding chapters the term demos does not specify who counts. Rather, this is the result of political struggle and contestation. Democracy accords no special privileges to any subject and does not delimit the people in terms of nation, ethnicity, class, wealth, gender or any other marker of exclusion. Democracy is improper.[3] Butler's distinction between democracy as a regime and an anarchic popular sovereignty gestures in this direction. Democratic practices destabilise the terms of the proper in the name of an improper equality. They do not seek merely to democratise the existing bounds of sovereign order. Regimes maintain these bounds in exercising powers of exception, policing bodies, populations, property and territories. A more radical reading of such occupations is that they reclaim democratic capability from regimes that appropriate the common ability of all to participate in diverse forms of self-rule. The analogy between the appropriation of democratic potentiality and the appropriation of resources is to the point. Butler terms these anarchist passages, moments when the legitimacy of the regime or its laws is questioned (Butler 2015: 75). But is it right to view them as passages? What lies at the end of such a passage? Rather, I view these as democratic moments when the equal capability of all is enacted against its limitation by the diverse forms of constraint that characterise state sovereignty.

Democracy as Embodied, Plural Performativity

Such a reading extends Butler's account of political performativity as embodied and plural. Democratic assemblies are, Butler contends, transient and critical. They signify in excess of their words, and use their bodies to collectively take over and reassign space as public in protest against privatisation (Butler 2015: 7). They improperly enact an 'other' way of living on the understanding that 'lives are equally valuable and interdependent . . .' (Butler 2015: 43). These movements enact the equality in diversity they simultaneously demand. They reject debtocracy, inequality, and precarity animating a future only apparently foreclosed. Such unaccountable protests disrupt how bodies and selves are accounted for (Butler and Athanasiou 2013: 102). Butler eloquently summarises this extension of performative politics:

> Since other lives, understood as part of life that exceeds me, are a condition of who I am, my life can make no exclusive claim on life, and my own life is not every other life and cannot be. In other words to be alive is already to be connected with what is living not only beyond myself, but beyond my humanness, and no self and human can live without this connection to a biological network of life that exceeds the domain of the human animal. (Butler 2015: 43)

Let me though interrogate this connection to a life that exceeds the human. The occupations challenge the differential distribution of precarity and demand a liveable life for all. This plural politics of bodies depends upon infrastructures that sustain our living in common. Butler recognises that the material conditions of life are discursively constituted sites of exclusion and dispute. During an occupation, the body is performed as a living set of relations and identifications. It is dependent upon others and on the infrastructural conditions that make lives liveable. I turn to this question of the material conditions of protest below, but we should note the radicality of Butler's rereading of Arendt. The occupations transgress the normal bounding of private from public. They make explicit that the claim to privacy is political from the beginning. Bodies acting in plurality rearticulate the public by 'seizing and reconfiguring the matter of material environments; at the same time those material environments are part of the action' (Butler 2015: 71). The material environment is not mute matter. It is not simply a support for the action; it is a subject of the action configuring bodies and being reconfigured by bodies. I indicated above that Butler is 'properly' materialist about this – she does not simply invoke a body as given, but studies they ways in which bodies are configured and reiterated in their articulation.

This notion of performativity is extended to include how bodies move through and use space, and how they are figured in the relations between linguistic, bodily and material relations. The assemblies 'articulate a new time and space for the popular will . . . which claims to be public in a way that is not yet codified into law' (Butler 2015: 75). Not only do these protests have no proper place – they question the relations between bodies, the relation of the body to itself, and the ways bodies are configured in the spaces that delimit their actions, movements and possibilities. Butler recognises that the material environment shapes and is shaped by these protests. The ramifications extend beyond the remaking of bodies in relational space. I noted in a previous chapter Esposito's reconstruction of the genealogy of the distinction between persons and things, a distinction pivotal to different forms of political order since Roman times. The instauration of the body as the focus of politics reframes democratic politics. Esposito writes:

> Ever since the statement 'we, the people' was first pronounced in the founding event of the first modern democracy, it has had a performative character – it has the effect of performing what it declares. Since then every linguistic act that seeks to have an impact on the political scene requires a mouth and a throat – the breath of bodies close enough to hear what the other says and to see what everyone can see. Hannah Arendt believed that there must be a public space in order for politics to exist. But she failed to add that this space must be filled by living bodies united by the same protests or by the same demands. (Esposito 2015: 146–7)

Esposito is too quick in his reading of Arendt. However, with Butler he forces a consideration of the materiality of bodies – their breath, their senses, their movements. If, as Butler argues, our bodies are already the site of alliances then this plural performativity puts that alliance in to play, while reconfiguring the alliances that constitute a performative demos. Performativity 'describes processes of being acted on and the conditions of possibility for acting' (Butler 2015: 63). The account of performativity that Butler developed in relation to gender is here deployed in relation to the political body. If gender is performative, if as a technology it retroactively establishes dominant ideas of gender identity as if they are natural, then so too is subjectivity performative and vulnerable to remaking. Butler misses something. Bodies come to be in spaces configured by a set of relations that impound space, give order to property and that legitimate the exercise of proprietary powers over bodies. Occupied spaces are propertied places. Butler's argument presupposes this but never explicitly thematises it. This requires a conceptualisation of the body as configured by these forms of impounding, and of identity as related to property and propriety.

The Politics of the Proper

The politics of property is at the core of any occupation as I noted in relation to the St Paul's protest above. The provision of the basic infrastructural conditions for liveable lives have over the past four decades been privatised – ranging from the provision of water and food to the biological bases of all life, the mineral resources which sustain the informational and technological means for constituting the public sphere, and the global spaces where food is produced. The 2008 financial crisis had its origins in financial leverage of over-valued stocks in property. Rights to ownership are intrinsic to the contemporary human rights consensus as well as to the global trade agreements that oil the wheels of global capital. Butler does note the privatisation of the public spaces of appearance, and the infrastructural supports for life – but does not investigate how this framing of the material argument becomes part of the contestation performed by these bodies in occupation.

It may seem bloody-minded to insist on a politics of property, rather than accept the notion of infrastructural conditions central to Butler's account. However, without an account of property and the proper – and of its differential forms of deployment – her focus on the performativity of bodies and of language is inadequately articulated to overdetermined infrastructural conditions. She brings into focus how a particular articulation of material conditions engenders precarity but does not think property as performative. Recall her own argument that the separation between polity and economy is performatively produced, reiterated and maintained. Property too is performatively maintained – though we need to differentiate the forms taken by performative politics in relation to the configuration of material space. The policing of property brings markets into being. This same policing sediments the distinction between polis and *oikos*. Against her own injunction, Butler does not rethink the myriad forms taken by property in performative terms. This is not a parting from Butler. Rather, I extend the logics at work in her text. The conditions that make lives liveable are articulated as propriety orders. Property polices subject formation, access to and organisation of resources, the uses of public and private space, and the appropriate forms of behaviour in these spaces. The occupations of the past decade all had this in common – they interrupted the functioning of these proper orders, summoning distinct forms of violence and law in each case. I agree with Butler that 'Bodies belong to the pavement, the ground, the architecture, and technology by which they live move and work and desire' (Butler 2015: 182). Yet the pavement, the ground, the architecture and the technology are private property. This sedimented architecture of the proper does not determine the performative remaking of public and private spaces. It does charge that space with invisible currents before it is occupied. It distributes rights and privileges, demarcates possible uses of violence and the physical architecture limits how one might move in space. These abstract forms of property and ownership, not immediately visible, are deployed when demonstrators are moved, when squares are cleared, when law is invoked against protest.

The Performative Politics of a Brick

So what then is a brick? Do its properties as an object foreclose its uses? In what ways is it performatively reanimated, in what ways does it animate possible performative remaking? Is a brick ever merely a brick and what type of brick might we use to bring down the exceptional politics of spaces such as the City of London? The development of the concept of performativity in Butler's work, over the course of three decades, helps me to think about the performativity of this brick – its history, the parts it played, the different ways in which it was made property. However, the brick also raises a set of concerns that Butler does not fully address. The claim to represent the people in occupations, riots and demonstrations operates to performatively test the dominant frames of appearance. It opens a space of appearance for those deemed improper, those who test rights of citizenship, of belonging and of ownership. Bodies, Butler argues, belong to the pavement, to the architecture and the infrastructures that make lives liveable. Yet the pavement does not belong to all. The infrastructures that sustain life are objects of private investment and control. It may be at one remove but the bodies that belong to the pavement are answerable to those who exercise property rights over these spaces. When the occupiers of St Paul's appeared before the court they in effect acknowledged this. I noted in the previous chapter the extraordinary genealogy of exception, of private right, that configured the space of St Paul's Cross during the occupation in London. In that case the City of London could exercise control over the collective body of the occupation because of its property rights. In attempting to reconfigure the material environment they directly challenged dominant relations of property. In testing these property rights they denaturalised property. Property is policed through performative reiteration, through the naturalisation of the divisions that limit what we can do, where, when and how. If a brick is never just a brick, if it is open to rearticulation in unpredictable frames, then it is never proper to itself. Neither is property.

FOUR

The Politics of Equivalence

Theatrical Props: Brian Friel's *Translations*

Brian Friel's *Translations* was the first play performed by the Field Day Theatre Company in the Guildhall of Derry on 23 September 1980. Nervous police officers patrolled the roads around the theatre, while an army helicopter hovered over Derry throughout the performance. Why did the opening of this play cause such consternation? Why did the army target later performances? Field Day was established by Stephen Rea, Brian Friel, Seamus Heaney and others. They imagined a fifth province in Ireland – a province beyond the four counties of Connacht, Leinster, Munster and Ulster – a province that opened the past to new scrutiny. The play is a subtle, but savage, deconstruction of the politics of British rule in Ireland. It takes place at a hedge school, in Baile Beag, Donegal, in August of 1833. The inhabitants of the village are Gaelic speakers but the lead characters also converse in Latin and Greek. A detachment of the British Royal Engineers camps nearby. Its task is to complete the first ordnance survey map of Ireland. Their relations with the local community are cordial – but for two characters only ever whispered about – the Donnelly twins engaged in acts of violent resistance. The ordnance survey entailed the mapping of the land using chains of 66 feet long, made up of 100 links, which when squared measured an acre. The chain measure was used across the Empire in the imperial project to map, value, name, register and 'propertise' all land. It was central to the ongoing imperial project to establish equivalent measures of monetary value and productivity. Ireland was remade as acreage. The survey renamed every village and landmark with an English name. English was deemed more precise than the Gaelic names that the British Army associates with disorder, finding it difficult to pinpoint exact locations that corresponded to the words. The survey aimed to secure words and things, to render them proper, adequate to each other. It tried to wipe Gaelic uncertainty from the map.

In contrast, the Gaelic speakers characterise English as a barbaric language more suited to accounting than to life. The English language supports the demarcation of land as property, a measurable, valued space subject to proprietary control. The play thematises the imposition of a colonial proprietary order that articulates together language; education (the introduction of a national system of 'proper' education which required the closing of the hedge schools); the education of the peasants and working classes to their proper station in life; a system for the *valuation* and exchange of property; and the *policing* of appropriate behaviours – the determination of where residents can be, how crops are grown and shared, who can exchange land, who has rights over the land. Friel dramatises a key moment in the violent history of British rule in Ireland, when the British Crown attempts to impose control over its nearest possession. The residents of Baile Beag retain the folkloric memory of the last land survey – the first carried out by the British and the forerunner of colonial practices of land registration imposed across the Empire. Humphrey Gilbert was employed in 1569 by the Royal Commission to carry out the survey. As one of the largest British plantation owners in Ireland, he brutally suppressed the rebellion against British rule in Kerry, displaying the heads of those killed – men, women and children – on the pathway leading up to his tent.

The play's dramatic development centres on the love between a British soldier, Captain Lancey, and Maire, an Irish resident desperate to leave Baile Beag. She regards the village as a backwater. Their love enacts the (im)possibility of another community, beyond the polarised languages of occupation, a love in a non-existent language – they cannot understand each other. Theirs is a desperate gesture against the remorseless march of 'progress' – the naming, the measurement and the rendering equivalent of the land, education and maps. It is one form of resistance but the play performs a range of forms of resistance. There is, first, the violence of the Donnelly brothers, forerunners of the Republican movement, and inheritors of the revolution of 1798. Second, there is the resistance performed by the play itself, its performance despite the violence and the occupation of 1980 Derry. Last, Friel includes an act of resistance both humorous and improper. Doalty (played in this first performance by Liam Neeson) moves the surveyor's chains used to measure each acre. The British Army surveyors are convinced that there is a problem with the theodolite, the machine used to measure each acre. Confused, they take the machine apart, bit by bit. The inhabitants of the village laugh. However, the villagers also collude in order to secure their place in the new order. Maire has a relationship with a soldier; Owen (played by Stephen Rea) helps the surveyors to translate the names from Gaelic into English; while Hugh, head of the hedge school, fluent in Gaelic, Greek and Latin, accepts employment as a teacher in the new imperial education system. At the heart of this play is proprietary order: the demarcation and allocation of the land; its rendering as a potential commodity; the allocation of proper names to every place; the regulation of movement, use and labour. These surveys were the precursors and preconditions of the property crisis that unfolded two centuries later in Ireland. Friel's play speaks to the past and to the future. It anticipates the property crisis that left post-2008 Ireland with empty estates, fenced off as private property, while thousands struggled to find secure homes.

Introduction

Laclau and Mouffe's *Hegemony and Socialist Strategy* (1985) was published in the last years of the Cold War. It aimed to rethink socialist politics against emergent neoliberal logics, notably the privatisation of state assets, the attack on the welfare state and bureaucracy, the articulation of neoliberalism with neoconservatism and the academic justifications for neoliberalism in the works of Friedman, Hayek, Nozick and Brzezinski (Laclau and Mouffe 1985: 171–5). The authors could not then anticipate the registers of contemporary neoliberalism: technologies of debt and finance extended to every part of the social fabric (Lazzarato 2012, 2015); the extension of infrastructural processes of equivalence through the soft law of international frameworks and processes (Easterling 2014; Brown 2015); the reframing of states as businesses evaluated and organised by the same metrics as enterprises (Brown 2015); the reframing of the self as an object of investment and of the family as a small enterprise (Cooper 2017). The theoretical categories central to that text – antagonism, hegemony, difference, equivalence and radical democracy – are inadequate to the modalities of financial capital. Worse, one of the key concepts, ontological contingency, seems compatible with predatory financial logics (see, for example, Žižek 2006; Boucher 2009). Their critique of economism and essentialism inadequately reconceptualised the political underpinnings of avowedly neutral economic logics. I demonstrated this with regard to property in the first two chapters. Here I focus on the place of equivalence in their conceptualisation of hegemony. I rethink it in relation to Marx's account of the money form (Laclau 1990, 1993, 2014). Their account of equivalence demonstrates the limits of Marx's labour theory of value. While I endorse their rejection of the labour theory of value, their rejection of Marx's notion of equivalence is too quick. They frame equivalence as the articulation of hegemonic links between diverse struggles against oppression, but forget the money form and the centrality of financial logics to neoliberal hegemony. I am aware that debates about value theory are central to contemporary Marxism – but here I engage only in passing with them. Instead, I develop a post-foundationalist account of logics of financial equivalence. This extends our conceptualisation of hegemony. It contours an account of an improper politics that is responsive to contemporary forms of financial hegemony.

Laclau on Hegemony and Equivalence

The notion of equivalence was central to Laclau and Mouffe's critique of Marxism and their reconceptualisation of socialist politics in *Hegemony and Socialist Strategy* (Laclau and Mouffe 1985). They think politics as the contingent articulation of equivalence between different demands, identities and movements. Political demands, they argue, do not arise endogenously from a regionally defined area but are always overdetermined. As I argued in Chapter 2 they deem *antagonism* constitutive of the political. It points to a heterogeneity, which cannot be subsumed within any historical narrative. They thus reject Marxist accounts which domesticate antagonism in terms of class position and contend that antagonism points to the limits of social objectivity as such (Laclau and Mouffe 1985; Laclau 2014). I discussed these arguments in some detail in Chapter 2. I failed, however, to address the limits of their account of equivalence, as the hegemonic articulation of different elements to a common project.

Their argument is straightforward. Hegemonic order is the result of contingent articulation. In a populist movement, for instance, equivalence is articulated between different demands, against a common enemy – the state, a ruling elite, the 1 per cent, capitalism – in terms of a common claim, perhaps justice. These counter-hegemonies are politically articulated forms of equivalence. They are contingent but not arbitrary. Their success depends on the sedimented political context to which they respond. The art of politics is the articulation of *equivalential relations* between different identities, subjects, social groups and demands. If successful such articulations establish a new hegemonic horizon, potentially setting the terms on which day-to-day political decision making and debate take place.

What though does it mean to say that differences are articulated as equivalent? What is equivalent across these differences? Laclau and Mouffe (1985: 129) argue that there are only two alternatives: either the differences share something positive or they are unified by reference to something external to them, something they oppose. They reject the first option. A common positive feature does not require a politics of articulation – it is immediately expressed. What then of a common relation to something external: 'the external reference cannot be to something positive' (Laclau and Mouffe 1985: 127) because then the equivalence is once again articulated with reference to another positive element within a system of differences. Instead, they conclude, that through equivalence 'something is expressed which the object is not' (Laclau and Mouffe 1985: 128).The equivalential link is expressed negatively. It unifies different demands, identities and social groups against something which all oppose. What they have in common is what they reject.

This is what Laclau terms populist reason (Laclau 1993). Any social order is confronted with a range of demands. Demands are both claims made to authorities and a request that something change. Authorities might well respond to isolated demands, thus neutralising their effects. However, if an extant order is unable to respond to isolated demands they may become equivalent. This is not because the demands overlap. Rather they share the failure of the authorities to respond. Over time, an equivalential chain may extend and unify different demands into a stable system of signification (Laclau 2005: 72–4). Each demand is divided between the particularity of its claim and its articulation with other demands. Their model for this account derives from structural linguistics. The logics of difference and equivalence interact, Laclau argues, 'just as linguistic identities are the seat of both syntagmatic relations of combination and paradigmatic relations of substitution' (Laclau 2005: 80). The value of a difference within any system is relational. The question then is how a system (social, linguistic or otherwise) might signify its own limits? We have seen already that the equivalential link is expressed negatively, unifying different demands, identities and social groups against something which all oppose. Unity is maintained because one element comes to signify what all others lack and what the authorities cannot provide. It becomes a signifier of affective investment and equivalential articulation. In Laclau's example, the word 'Solidarity' in the context of 1980's Poland expressed both the unity of those in opposition to the Communist regime and the particularity of the workers in Gdansk.

The study of hegemony concerns the play between these logics of difference and equivalence. They point to what Laclau in his last published text termed the rhetorical foundations of the social. The fullness of society is unachievable. Hegemonic politics deploys rhetorical devices to cover over this lack of objectivity, in particular metaphor and metonymy. The articulation of equivalential links in a hegemonic order may be interpreted in terms of tropes analogous to the logics of substitution and combination, which Saussure (1995) identified as central to any semiotic system. For Laclau, order is articulated between these two poles, impossible extremes on a continuum: either the dispersal of the social into different demands or the complete unification of the social around one demand, an empty signifier that subsumes all particulars under this general logic: 'Rhetoric is coterminous with the very structure of objectivity' (Laclau 2014: 65). The articulation of a populist alternative to a dominant order requires political articulation and affective identification, in securing a tendentious unity against a perceived oppressor.

Revisiting Marx on Equivalence

Reading this, we might ask 'what has happened to the critique of capitalism?' What do Laclau and Mouffe make of the analysis of the universal equivalent, the money form, so central to Marx? In their view, Marx undermined the radical potential of equivalence by reducing it, and the social formation, to one positive universal measure, abstract labour. Abstract labour is, at least in principle, measurable, and as value, is distinct from the materiality of commodities. Laclau and Mouffe, as I noted above, reject this reading of equivalence in terms of a positive value that grounds all other values. However, their critique of Marx's account of abstract labour seems to forget altogether the money form. Subsequent accounts of hegemony, as well as those of theorists who develop this work, gives little space to logics of debt, finance and credit.

They are at first blush right. Marx seems to regard labour as the underlying substance, the one element common to all commodities and coterminous with their value. The relations of equivalence analysed by Marx are on this reading not hegemonic, but instead express an underlying positive content – human labour power. However, a closer reading shows that Marx cannot sustain the claim that abstract (human) labour is the positive value underlying the general equivalent. The positive determination of exchange value, abstract labour, cannot be expressed other than as a wager. Abstract human labour is a ghostly, metaphorical, phantasm never adequately expressed in the universal equivalent. I develop the implications of this reading when rethinking the politics of equivalence below, but first let me read what Marx writes about equivalence a little more carefully.

Capital: Volume 1 (Marx 1976) begins with an account of the commodity and the transmogrification of the universal equivalent money into capital. On first reading, it seems that Marx uses the labour theory of value, derived from classical political economy, to explain the riddle of the commodity form. Use value reflects the simple fact that in order to be a commodity a thing must correspond to a human desire or want. Exchange value, in contrast, represents the value of a commodity relative to other commodities – in terms of something other than itself, the money form. Exchange value requires a common equivalent, the money form. Money *expresses* the relative value of different commodities. Each particular commodity is attributed a value which comes to appear as if it is a natural attribute of the commodity. This fiction allows for comparisons between, and exchanges of, different commodities regardless of their use. Commodities dressed in the garb of exchange values cultivate grotesque ideas about themselves, as Marx writes of tables. They transcend their mere sensuousness, their use value. Indeed the most useless of commodities may have the highest exchange value, as we know is the case for diamonds and gold (Marx 1976: Chapter 1).

But what does this universal equivalent money represent? The obvious answer is that a particular commodity incarnates a more fundamental universal, for Marx abstract human labour. Read this way the exchange value of a commodity expresses the *socially necessary labour time* required to produce the commodity. Everything depends on our interpretation of this phrase, 'socially necessary'. Human labour is for Marx the ghostly presence of the machine that is capital. One might say that we literally consume the lives of others every time we engage in exchange and make use of commodities. The commodity embodies in Marx's florid terms: 'congealed quantities of homogenous human labour . . . crystals of social substance' (Marx 1976: 128). But how might we measure the value of the human labour crystallised in the commodity? Here Marx issues a number of qualifications. First, value is only realised retroactively, at the point of exchange. The commodity has no intrinsic value before it is purchased, other than as a promissory note. This promissory note is what underpins markets in financial risk. Second, Marx notes that this is *abstract* human labour. Value does not express the actual time committed to the production of any one commodity, the congealed social substance. Rather price is contingent.

If abstract human labour is only realised as a value at the point of exchange then it may turn out that it has no value. Across time and space an equilibrium price emerges, what Marx terms the *socially necessary labour* across a global system of exchange and production (Marx 1976: 129).

How then do we measure or predict this socially necessary labour time? Is there any possible way to express it? For Marx there is no way back to an accurate measure of the value of human labour. Its value does not correspond to the actual time put in to the production of the commodity. Rather it is overdetermined by any number of factors including overproduction, political bartering, the reframing of consumer desire, runs on commodities, price fixing, changes to the production process, trade and a range of other contingencies. Actual labour may have no value. Labour in the abstract produces value, but this value is only 'recognised' in an act of exchange that transforms a commodity into money, the equivalential form which represents value. What is deemed socially necessary varies depending upon a range of political, ideological and other contingencies. The qualifiers of the word labour (abstract, socially necessary) do more work here than is generally acknowledged. Post-Marxist theorists, despite carefully deconstructing the political logics of Marx's notion of antagonism, are less scrupulous when reading Marx on equivalence. Read in this way financial equivalence is a technology, a practice, which remakes the world as equivalent. It is a shape shifting technology, one that remakes itself, wraps itself around different social circumstances, adapts adeptly to extract profit.

This notion of equivalence is the subject of dispute among Marxist theorists. The debate is easily summarised. The traditional view, summarised by Moseley, holds that

> (i) the necessity of money is derived from the necessity to present the abstract labour contained in commodities objectively; (ii) the exchange value of money is derived from the labour-time required to produce the money commodity and other commodities (as a specific case of the labour theory of value); and (iii) the quantity of money in circulation is derived from the sum of prices. (Moseley 2005: 4)

This interpretation disguises the real difficulties Marx has in justifying the labour theory of value. It is impossible to objectively present the abstract labour contained in commodities. The price theory as an expression of the 'real' exchange value of money is a fanciful fiction, designed in the final instance to legitimate a particular politics – one that privileges the working class as the producer of all value.

In contrast, Foley contends that qualitatively diverse labour cannot be reduced to a single index or measure. One consequence is that exploitation of surplus value cannot be measured. If the commodity theory of money no longer holds then the architectonic of Marx's account of exploitation is faulty. Foley notes that in contemporary capitalist societies the liabilities of the state act as a measure of value for the world of commodities. The symbiotic relation between state and capital has to be refigured – an argument I made in Chapter 1 in relation to sovereignty. On Foley's account, credit control is another means through which surplus value is extracted (Foley 1983: 14–16). This view is echoed by Milios (2009) who contends that money as the general equivalent representing socially necessary labour is merely an intermediate step toward capital–money functioning as an end in itself. While requiring the exploitation of labour power it extends the mechanisms of exploitation to include credit, debt and speculation. Profit is secured through interest rate manipulation and a range of other techniques. In my view, these rather arcane debates are of little value. However, they do point towards an account of the financial form that may be integrated with a rethinking of political hegemony. The financial form is not a universal equivalent. It is a pliable technology that coordinates social life in ways often unthought and largely unseen. Before making this argument let me return briefly to Marx.

Marx contends that commodification respects no theological limits. The 'agent' of this process, the money form, respects no boundaries. Quite literally, anything may be remade in terms of the general equivalent. Contingency is, however, at the heart of Marx's account of capital: the measure of value chases a phantom it cannot capture; socially necessary labour varies from second to second and is immeasurable. This lack of measure characterises the valences of neoliberal politics. Marx is constrained by his insistence that abstract labour is the source of value, but his text struggles against this straitjacket. What is the upshot of this reading? Money, and thus capital, are means for the articulation of diverse particulars as equivalent. These processes are so taken for granted that the power of this fiction is easy to forget. This form of equivalence differs from that found in Laclau and Mouffe's theory of hegemonic articulation. The money form establishes relations of equivalence that empty the commodity of its origins in social relations as Marx argues. However, money also functions as an apparently neutral technology of accounting, accountability and value. It allows diverse worlds to be read, interpreted and reframed in terms of this value. Money does not represent a more essential universal, labour power. Rather, as a febrile technology it resists definition in terms of one essential principle. It moulds itself to, and in the process reshapes, wholly different areas of social life. It is a mechanism of hegemonic articulation.

While then I concur with the post-Marxist critique of the labour theory of value, it too quickly forgets the money form. Marx's text undermines the labour theory of value. Laclau does recognise that the logic of the empty signifier parallels Marx's description of the transition from the general form of value to the money form (Laclau 2005: 93). Marx writes:

> The universal equivalent form is a form of value in general. It can, therefore, be assumed by any commodity. On the other hand, if a commodity be found to have assumed the universal equivalent form . . . this is only because and in so far as it has been excluded from the rest of all other commodities as their equivalent, and that by their own act. (Marx 1976: 162)

Marx argues that the universal equivalent is excluded from the world of particular commodities. It assumes the role of what Laclau terms an empty signifier. In it every commodity can find a form of expression – indeed anything at all, even human labour. However, if labour does not determine the value of commodities then neither does a standard such as gold, unless maintained by a hegemonic power deploying political and financial muscle to secure prices and control trade. As is well known, since 1973 there has been no political standard that might secure such a universal equivalent. Liberated from reference to any fixed value money no longer serves as a fixed universal equivalent. It does allow for anything to be converted into a measurable value and for value to be manipulated on stock markets. The variation in the value of the equivalent(s) is a key to understanding the dynamics of financial capital that exploits the contingency of value in currency, property, assets and stocks to extract value. This reading of Marx's account of the money form challenges the privileging of rhetorical tropes in post-Marxist theories – or at very least causes us to rethink these tropes in relation to the performative delimitation of a sphere termed the economy. Marchart writes in respect of Laclau that he

> feels justified (a) to apply metaphor and metonymy to the field of politics, and (b) to see in metaphor and metonymy not merely two figures among many, but the two fundamental matrices around which all other figures and tropes should be ordered'.

For Marchart 'such logics cannot be restricted to a particular social field' (Marchart 2018: 60).

However, the assumption that these logics apply across all fields means that discourse theory blindsides itself when considering financial logics. These notions of metaphor and metonymy require radical reworking if they are to explain the logics of equivalence outlined above. Thus far, I have developed an immanent critique of Marx's account of value. This account of the value form does not presuppose any ontology, any question of lack or indeed of failed meaning. The money form is supported by all kinds of affective investments. However, it does not depend on these. It transforms the social world through the implementation of abstract, systemic logics, which the rhetorical account of the political has failed to grasp. Although the money form is initially excluded from the realm of commodities in order to serve as the universal equivalent, it returns as a commodity and takes itself as an object, Baron Munchausen like, without recourse to so-called material commodities. The fact that debt and currency is guaranteed by nation states allows currency manipulation to become a mechanism for the valorisation of capital. In a similar vein, debt serves as a mechanism to brutally enforce structural adjustment policies. Let me develop two further examples of equivalential logics that operate without recourse to a political ontology.

Rethinking the Politics of Equivalence

The logic of the empty signifier – the requirement for a system to fix and maintain limits to signification which are its condition of possibility and impossibility – does not apply to the uses of money as a technology and practice. At least since 1973 the value of money has not been fixed against any standard. This opened the way to the securitisation of debts and credit through the invention of financial products that extended risk across the globe. Contemporary populist movements are often a direct response to these financial logics. The money form takes advantage of contingency in order to extract value. Money does not stand in for something else, another more real system. What money is, and how it is deployed, depends as much upon purely calculative logics as it does on political, phantasmatic and other logics. This is not to say that the uses of money are purely random. It is to point to an intrinsic contingency integral to the calculative logics of this equivalential form. Such contingency does not take the form of a lack demanding identification. Let me focus on two complementary discourses – debt and quality standards – as key political logics of austerity.

Debt

Key to the financial crisis of 2008 was the risky mortgage. As many critics have argued the 'liberation' of money from any guarantees (the gold standard, the dollar) made pricing and risk impossible to guarantee, especially as the currency used in exchange fluctuates in value. This led to the invention of financial and insurance products designed to securitise debts over the long term. Of particular importance was the derivative. Originally designed to insure against risk derivatives, it ironically extended systemic risk. The logic is simple. If all risk has been calculated, then further investments are justifiable. The securitisation of risk allowed banks to leverage debt. This had the effect of creating more money out of nothing. Once insured the same pot of money was lent out repeatedly. If each loan is securitised and insured the same capital can in theory be lent repeatedly. These loans, resting on an underlying asset, were also deemed safer if bundled together. A default in one or more debts was counted against other successful loans. Forms of arbitrage thus extended risk in an ever increasing circle. Banks acted as a clearinghouse for credit. They created money through the repeated circulation of the same debt and created wealth that undermined the control of central banks over money supply. Yet, in the final instance, they relied on the ability of the state to raise taxes if the risky investments failed. Let me take the example of the mortgage, so central to the financial crisis of 2007/8. I do so in light of the housing crisis in Ireland alluded to in my opening comments.

As has always been the case banks make a tidy profit over the life of a mortgage, perhaps 6 per cent compound. All potential customers are credit scored in order to evaluate risk. The credit score determines, in part, the interest rate that customers may be charged. It represents the bank's calculation of risk. Securitisation allowed banks to extend and leverage mortgaged loans, using an existing debt as if it were a credit because it was already secured against the risk of default. The key technology was the credit default swap, a simple financial mechanism. A bank loans out $100,000 at an interest rate of 4 per cent. It then purchases insurance on the debt, limiting liability in the case of a default. With insurance in place, the same money may be loaned out once again. In accounting terms, once a loan is insured against risk it remains on the books. Banks thus kept less reserve capital. Inevitably, one or other of the risks will default.

However, a set of related, financial products sought to offset these risks. One of these was to bundle mortgages. A few losses were absorbed by profit across the bundle. Every mortgage is insured as part of a bundle of mortgages. You might, for example, bundle 100 mortgages together. This credit default swap is sold to an insurer or an investor because profit is guaranteed by the spreading of the risk. The bundled loans were divided up into differently rated credit default swaps, so-called tranching. Those deemed to be high risk could be sold at higher rates of interest. Brokers purchased job lots of these mortgages to sell on to investors with little notion of the underlying asset, the mortgages. Because the lender no longer owned the risks they had an incentive to offer more loans on the same underlying asset. Banks then offered higher risk mortgages, bundled and insured these in the same way, and sold them as credit default swaps. These 'sub-prime' mortgages were bundled up with less risky mortgages and sold as highly rated assets. Credit agencies rated these bundled loans according to the perceived risk for investors, with higher profits linked to investment in lower rated products. In a further perverse turn, these insurance products too could be bundled and sold, as could the promise of profit and the likelihood of default. Risk spread through the financial system from brokers, to banks, to insurance houses, to pension funds. Speculation became an end in itself and equivalence a means of manipulating value in order to increase value. The retroactive effect of the pricing of derivatives was that the products designed to protect the so-called 'real' asset, had consequences for the pricing of mortgages.

Before analysing the consequences, consider how these deceptively simple products remake the world – taking housing as an example. I have noted the centrality of the bundling of risks and the leveraging of debt. In the case of Ireland, the supposed benefit of this was that more money could be loaned, at lower interest rates, to more and more individuals. The result was an unprecedented housing boom and a transformation of the environment – more houses were built than were needed. Many were left unused, or rarely used, as second homes or investment opportunities. The Irish landscape was remade, re-envisioned, as an opportunity for profit. With the financial crash these loans became toxic. The result is the ghost estates of present day Ireland – more people living without housing, and more houses without people. How was this possible? In the last instance, it depended upon centuries' long processes of land registration and the remaking of the land and housing as transferable commodities – an often violent process enforced by the British Army and supported by legions of surveyors.

When these mortgages became toxic banks attempted to develerage. Credit was drastically cut. The crisis was in part a result of panic, in part an appropriate response to forms of leverage which were inherently risky. What was the political response? The cost of these risks was transferred to purchasers and to taxpayers. Purchasers often had no way to escape the debt, even after default. Taxpayers on the other hand bailed out banks deemed 'too big to fail'. The individuals, the institutions and the system responsible for the crisis were, with a few exemplary exceptions, rescued with the transfer of capital from reserve banks. The denouement of this story was that the same institutions – banks, ratings agencies, accounting firms – then targeted state revenues. They argued that public debt posed a risk to the economy. Areas of the public sector previously exempt from neoliberal financialisation, such as pensions, schools, welfare, education and the military, were remade on the accounting terms common to business. The public realm was rearticulated as a financial asset, an investment opportunity for private capital, a means of raising capital for bankrupt states. The *res publica* was disarticulated. The terms of democratic accountability were remade in financial terms. The pliability of the term accountability is of particular note in this respect. It is no mistake that discourses of accountability and value are at the core of how public bodies are evaluated.

The failure of the demos was in one respect simple to understand. The same logics that structured the markets in risk, subject states to forms of accountability which curtail democratic decision making. Debt operates through the valuation and the purchasing of the future. It commits future generations to a particular ordering of life. It undermines the very principle of democratic regimes, the claim that the people are sovereign. We might adapt the language of Deleuze and Guattari (1984), and note that capital deterritorialises and rips free of its context even the future. Debt is that which will always already have been the case. It colonises the future. Resistance is foreclosed as the citizen becomes the monetised subject, a human resource, devoted to self-enhancement and investment. As Wendy Brown has argued, the anti-political language of governance introduces metrics of measure, derived from financial logics, which articulate the political subject as an economic being and model the state as a firm (Brown 2015: 108). Such metrics of self-investment and measure shape the conduct of conduct through distant yet intimate technologies, allowing for governance without government. Increasingly, Brown contends, the act of governing appears to devolve and responsibilise. It subjects individuals, organisations and local government to so called best practices, benchmarking and credit evaluation (Brown 2015: 124–30). Lazzarato goes further. Across every part of society, the same rules of credit are applied. Credit is a mobile logic – an infrastructure – infinitely flexible, adaptable and calculative (Lazzarato 2015: 7–8). The debt economy subjects and subjectivates all individuals as human capital and in so doing externalises all risk (previously collectivised) on to individual subjects who have to manage their own profiles so as not to fall foul of logics of debt. Equality is rewritten as a form of equivalence. Democratic accountability becomes a form of accounting, and the only value with value is the potential to make profit. Note the logics of equivalence at play here. Standardised accounting procedures allow for the monetisation of risk. These are applied to all individuals as well as organisations. Debt is extended according to a set of basic rules of assessment (based on the evaluation of risk), and the risks are securitised through a set of mobile derivative technologies such as credit default swaps, bundling and tranching. In the last instance, taxpaying citizens become the final insurer of risk and profit. These procedures are applicable to anything – to individuals, to property, to insurance products, to so-called natural assets – and they rearticulate the world in the seemingly neutral language of calculation. This is a form of equivalential articulation not explicable in terms of the logics of the empty signifier, of lack or indeed of political identification.

Infrastructural Logics

Let me turn to consider another set of equivalential practices which escape the logic of the empty signifier – Quality Standards in Higher Education. This seemingly innocuous statement is found on The Quality Assurance Agency for Higher Education in the UK website (http://www.qaa.ac.uk/en):

> This Evaluation Policy (EP) is part of the Monitoring and evaluation pillar of the Performance Management Framework. It has drawn on ENQA's Standards and Guidelines for Quality Assurance in the European Higher Education Area, the principles of ISO 9000, ISO9001: 2008, the EFQM Excellence Model and Strategy 2011–14. (Evaluation Policy: 1)

In developing quality standards, the Quality Assurance Agency (QAA) draws on the principles of ISO 9000 and ISO 9001. The International Organization for Standardization (ISO), a private non-governmental organisation, has since the 1940s overseen global technical standards across nation states. In his recent work on infrastructures, Easterling discusses ISO 9000, a seemingly innocuous specification of management guidelines for quality. All trading partners of the European Union are required to conform to these quality guidelines and over a million organisations worldwide now implement them (Easterling 2014). Bizarrely, so too does the QAA, although Easterling does not note this. Quality assurance standards, initially developed for businesses, now structure the 'delivery' of higher education. If on the one hand education has become a mechanism to indoctrinate a new generation into a politics of debt, the management of their education is subject to business like quality standards. What though are they? Easterling describes infrastructures as 'the shared standards and ideas that control everything from technical objects to management styles' (Easterling 2014: 6). They are the operating systems which structure worlds: for example, models for new builds in cities across the world and the quality processes implemented across institutions, schools, universities and libraries. These infrastructures reconfigure the world according to a set of templates which make certain things possible and others impossible. ISO 9000 and its various offshoots establish what appear to be formally empty, process focused quality standards. These guide the management of any organisation. The key principles are loose in the extreme: a focus on *customer* need; the creation of *unity* through leadership; consultation so that all *feel* included; implementation and management of *processes of quality assurance*; adaptation of clear standards to *measure* quality implementation; constant modification to improve quality; and the establishment of mutually beneficial supplier relationships.

Note the key words I have highlighted. The student is now a *customer*. Academics are encouraged to become leaders. Empty consultation processes aim to make everyone feel included (distinct from including everyone). All universities have administrative structures committed to quality assurance. These allow for the *measurement* of quality standards and all universities are measured against standardised ratings of research and teaching. The language of international standards is out of tune with the view that many academics hold of their own work. However, the QAA has transformed British universities, rendering their quality processes equivalent to those implemented in business. Most academics remain blissfully unaware of what has taken place under our noses. What appears neutral, bereft of content (indeed ISO 9000 is presented as content neutral) transforms the university, and in the long term transforms how staff and students understand themselves. Translated into quality standards the language of teaching and research is transformed. So too are the processes by which the quality of education is measured. It is common now to speak of markets, of customer focus and satisfaction, of benchmarking and of cost. The same processes encourage staff to view themselves as human capital. To put it more bluntly, every member of staff is now a cost to the university who should ideally pay their own way, through capitalisation of their knowledge. Staff are 'responsibilised' (Brown 2015) to manage their own capital, to recreate themselves as embodied capital through the generation of research income, business and third sector activities, partnerships with business and capitalisation of intellectual property. These activities are all measured in terms of quality assurance standards and compared both within (internal assessment) and without (external assessment).

My main interest here is not to engage in a critique of this transformation of higher education policy and practice – many have already done so (Collini 2012). Rather, it is to note that the mantra of quality is an infrastructural form utilised in different spaces, places and organisations. It is like an open source system, an adaptable but consistent process of management of the quality of products. Its effect is to reframe these spaces according to calculable and measurable logics, compatible with accounting and financial forms, but nonetheless distinct from them. Whether in universities or other once public institutions, the language of quality transforms what we commonly mean by the terms of democracy: accounting stands in for accountability; equivalence stands in for equality; and a feeling of consultation for democracy. The 'quality process' establishes an equivalence between distinct institutions. It allows them to be compared in terms of markers such as customer satisfaction, value for money, speed of response to complaints and the like. These processes of measurable equivalence bypass the political, phantasmatic and symbolic logics at the core of post-Marxist accounts of the political. They do not depend upon subjective identification, lack, identity or affectivity. Yet they hegemonise the social field. I argued above that money is constantly reinvented, and made other, adapted to the particular environments and practices that are monetised. However, the money form does not simply monetise areas newly commodified – for example higher education. Rather, monetisation works with a set of other practices, other mechanisms of rendering the practice of education measurable, equivalent and thus subject to valuation. Quality assurance is the equivalent of the theodolite of old – and it transforms the acreage of higher education in similar fashion.

Conclusion

In their critique of Marx's notion of equivalence Laclau and Mouffe correctly reject the argument that labour is the source of value. However, they then recast equivalence without reference to money, or to capital. They open themselves to the charge that their 'political' reading of hegemony is unable to conceptualise financialisation and commodification. Mouffe's 2013 text *Agonistics*, for example, emphasises the importance of agonistic confrontation for a politics of the left in Europe, and revisits her critique of deliberative and consensual approaches. However, her discussion of neoliberal policies fails to address the logics of financialisation. She contends that neoliberal policies must be challenged with new economic principles but, *more importantly*, with an alternative political vision. She thus distinguishes economic models from political vision: 'The economic model is . . . crucial but to create a Europe of citizens requires more than economic measures, and my main concern is the kind of political vision that needs to inform the economic proposals' (Mouffe 2013: 60). Contemporary financialisation is distinguished by the 'economisation' of political relations, and the recasting of the state, of individuals and of all other activity in terms of capitalisation and investment. If anything, we need to begin with a problematisation of the distinction between the economic and the political. Our political vision should already entail a particular organisation of social and reproductive life. This is not simply a difference of emphasis. The hegemony of neoliberalism is secured through forms of equivalence which have little to do with the articulation of a popular will. I have indicated some of these logics above – the proliferation of standards of quality, the abstract forms of property ownership and control, the forms of measurement and quantification which rearticulate the place of politics threatening to render democratic accountability irrelevant. The left must perforce challenge and reframe these apparently neutral infrastructural logics that recast worlds as calculable assets. Laclau and Mouffe's account of populism, of the articulation of counter-hegemonic equivalence, and of the logics of identification, subjectification and ontology remain a powerful rendering of how unity is engendered in the name of a democratic politics. However, such oppositional logics miss their target if they fail to account for the technologies of financial and calculative equivalence. These technologies, once deployed, cement particular ways of acting, thinking and being. They enact forms of governmentality which radically alter perceptions of, and attitudes to, space, money and to the very terms that constitute the democratic heritage. Thus far, discourse theorists have failed to come to terms with these logics.

So what does this mean for the development of a counter-hegemonic politics? The first thing to note, echoing Gramsci (2007) in the *Prison Notebooks*, is that hegemony is more than the articulation of equivalential relations organised around an empty signifier. It involves the ongoing production of consent through complex forms of inclusion – the plethora of organisations and practices that cut across the distinction between state and civil society (Gramsci 2007). However, we need to go further than this. Hegemony is secured through other complex forms of equivalence which have little to do with the articulation of a common will. I have examined two of these forms above – the monetisation of all social relation, and the introduction of international forms of standardisation. The accounting mechanisms that structure almost all our relations to the world – which delimit how we can properly move through the world – escape logics of identification. The implications are two-fold. The conceptualisation of hegemony must include the articulation of equivalential relations on terms beyond identification and antagonism. Too much of what maintains neo-liberal hegemony is the taken for granted, the unspoken forms that organise and secure our living in the world. Second, any counter-hegemony has to establish alternatives to these forms of equivalence or at the very least understand how they work to secure hegemony. This means thinking forms of resistance that challenge these logics. Let me conclude by thinking about these improper forms of resistance.

Our inspiration is Doalty in Friel's play *Translations*, with which I began this chapter. Doalty inspires the oppressors to take apart their own machine of domination, by simply moving the markers of measurement. Is this possible today? Two examples are of interest – the first is an American group 'The Debt Collective'. The group published a journal, *The Debt Resister's*

Operations Manual, and set up the rolling Jubilee debt movement. They purchase debts for very little on the secondary debt markets, and then publicly
forgive these debts – most recently 32 million dollars of US student debt.
They then went further aiming to unionise students across the USA struggling with debt. They used the collective leverage of the debt to threaten the
private banks that had made the loans. This began with 200 students whose
debts totalled around 150 million US dollars. They pushed for debt relief
and for a reduction in interest rates. But – and this is the more interesting
point – they argue that because 40 per cent of US households live on credit,
and thus survive on an ever-increasing spiral of debt, debtors' unions can
wield power over private corporations and the state. They can only do so
working in tandem. The refusal to pay debts pressurises the state to assume
public responsibility for education, health and the various other areas of
the US economy now subject to private finance. This radically reframes traditional forms of union activity. It targets debt payments, private capital,
and the responsibilities of taxpayers and the state. In these cases, resistance
targets the individualisation of debt, and collectivises responsibilisation.
Traditional unions still view the strike as an appropriate response to falling
wages, or to a worsening of terms and conditions of work. However, the
strike does not begin to address the other forms of extraction of value such
as debt. In some instances, it leaves workers in a worse position following
only marginal improvements in working conditions. Most forms of work
are tied in to the informational networks that lubricate and organise global
trade. Resistance has failed to keep up with these new logics – and inevitably misses its target.

A second form of resistance was more creative and to the point. A Chilean
artist, Francisco Tapia, collected the debt notes of students at the Universi-
dad del Mar during an occupation in May 2014. These were the only official
records – because signed by the students – of the debts owed to the university.
Chile, like the UK, has a debt-based higher education system. He burnt the
notes to the tune of 500 million US dollars, made a public video of the event
and circulated it for all to see. The point here is that all debts are recorded –
nowadays on sophisticated computer networks. However, these systems are
vulnerable to hacktivists – no matter how many times records are backed up
they can always be hacked. The system of debt depends upon the recording
of who is accountable. But the terms of accountability can be changed – as
Solon of Athens once taught us. Accounts must be preserved if they are to
remain in force.

The hegemony of the debt economy is maintained by credit agencies
that deliver risk assessments of national economies, and credit scores for
every individual. They regulate and order investment, movement of bodies

in space and time, the very building and organisation of the world that we live in. The forms of resistance outlined above take on these logics, head on. However, the question Doalty's resistance in *Translations* poses is rather different. He does not take the British Army on directly. Rather, walking back from the pub in the evening he moves the markers that allow the soldiers to measure acreage. The theodolite thus seems faulty to the army engineers. They take it apart and try to rebuild it. There are two questions posed by this act: how can we resist the measurements, assessments, information gathering and credit ratings that are the ghostly accompaniment to every body? Second, how do we take the machine apart? Doalty has the British forces take their own theodolite apart. The machinic assemblages that measure, and structure, human life have repeatedly failed, yet each failure leads to new refinements. How though might they be dismantled?

FIVE

The Improper Politics of Democracy

'We won't fuck for houses'

On 12 July 1990, South African police entered Dobsonville in Soweto, intending to raze to the ground sixty shacks, illegally erected on a strip of land dividing a high cost residential development. A mining company owned the land. The women who had built the shacks led a protest trying to stop the removals. The police arrived in casspirs and bulldozers, armed with teargas, dogs and guns. Sheila Meintjes, a South African feminist academic, interviewed participants in the protest, in the months following its end. I rely on her account in what follows. She writes:

> When the police arrived on the morning of the 12th July, with dogs and bulldozer in tow, the shacks were still intact. As the police moved to dismantle the shacks, the younger women shack-dwellers stripped off their clothes, taunted the police, ululated, shouted in anger about their plight and their pain, and sang and danced and held up printed placards demanding homes and security of tenure. (Meintjes 2007: 347)

Their main slogan was 'we won't fuck for houses'. The protest took place in the dying days of apartheid. It received particular attention because the women took off their clothes challenging their status as 'social and sexual dependents' (Meintjes 2007: 348). The press were on hand – having been invited by the protesters – to record the attempted destruction. In the twenty-four hours which followed, images of the protest were broadcast across the world. Meintjes notes that every aspect of this action was politically charged and deliberately planned. The occupation was a deliberate strategy to draw attention to the plight of the homeless in North Soweto, Johannesburg. The period before the police action saw peaceful protests, negotiations with the local council and the exploitation of legal loopholes to prevent the destruction. The naked protest was not merely a public spectacle, although the women were well aware that this act would excite outrage and fascination from the gathered media. Rather, the act lampooned the fact that women were offered housing, in exchange for sex with a prominent local councillor.

How might we interpret this act at twenty-five years remove, and why begin a chapter about democracy as improper by invoking a long forgotten moment in the struggle against racism, class inequality and sexism? The retroactive attribution of a peculiar dignity to this protest recognises a moment when the past shames us, forces us to rethink the damaged frames that shape the very possibility of political action today. There is now a growing literature about the politics of naked protest. It is characterised by a number of tropes. The first situates these protests as reiterative and transnational. They establish a transnational corporeal politics of vulnerability (Alaimo 2010; Tyler 2013). A second trope notes the importance of listening to the voices of those engaged in protest. Examples include the 2008 resistance against UK immigration law in Yarlswood (Tyler 2013); protests against the state privatisation of land in Uganda (Ebila and Tripp 2017); and the gendered corporeal politics of republican prisoners protesting British rule in 1980 and 1981. Third, critics have noted that this performative, corporeal politics is a seizure of symbolic space that puts equality to work using bio-agency (Tyler 2013; Eileraas 2014). The protest in 1990 echoed many previous acts, and is reiterated in other protests that perform vulnerability as power. It was a collective act, local, but global in its import. The protestors seemed to anticipate the neoliberal turn of the future African National Congress administration. They refused all attempts by spokespersons of the liberation movement to claim the protest. Yet they simultaneously drew on what they had learnt through political activism against apartheid. Indeed the protest cast a harsh light on its own future, even as it challenged the property order established in the colonial past. South Africa still has a housing shortage for millions of people. Many of the new houses built go to those who can afford loans, but are then subject to the vagaries of the housing market, and the quality of these houses is often very low. These protests inspire my interpretation of democracy as improper.

The protesters enacted equality against dominant forms of propriety and property. Their act broke the property laws that the apartheid police invoked when seeking permission to remove them. The land they occupied was seized through violent acts of plunder in the 1880s following the discovery of gold in the area now called Gauteng. The plunder was legitimated by legal fiat. Anglo American and other mining companies were cast as the trespassers, the thieves. The women acted against a racist history and against the effectivity of the colonial past in the present. The protest collapsed time, refusing to allow its passing to make legitimate the unaccountable violence that structured their present. The act may have appeared local but it questioned the authenticity of the sovereign power of the police, upholding the law of property. The act unravelled at its very core the territorial delimitation of the colony.

This improper occupation was also a form of impropriety, most obviously the use of naked bodies, dancing in the mud, mimicking the worst colonial fantasy but performatively enacting the long history of using the naked female body to curse the oppressor. The police did not know what to do. Their trucks stopped, the press took photographs, and the women continued to occupy the shacks and the land. They took possession of their bodies against the local councillor responsible for the allocation of houses. This was a form of possession that was not private property. Rather, in making public what conventionally is restricted to the private realm, the protest upsets the frame that orders how we see the political. Here the radical exposure of the collective body stopped the white policemen in their tracks. Their slogan, refusing to 'fuck' for a house, made clear that this apparent exposure was a reclamation. It was an act improper with regard to both the norms and the laws ordering the state. There are many aspects to this impropriety – the naked body, the loud singing and dancing, the teasing of the police, the building and the rebuilding of the shacks, the exposure to violence, the remaking of the racialised, sexualised and abjected body as the basis for resistance. I argue in what follows that the demos has no proper space. These were democratic protests breaking proprietorial bounds in the enactment of the most basic equality – an equality of the body as vulnerable, and of words as political.

After the protest, there were various attempts to narrate what had taken place – local representatives of the African National Congress claimed to have planned the protest. In interviews, representatives of the protestors contested this claim. They insisted that their protest was in the name of democratic equality beyond the official anti-apartheid opposition. Local politicians condemned the women, arguing that they had acted immorally, that although they authorised and indeed planned the protest, they would never authorise such egregious expo- sure of bodies in the dead of the South African winter. This anticipatory rejection of the patriarchal narrative of liberation, of the hegemonic articulation of the African National Congress and its allies, insists that no movement or party can own democracy, that democracy is always a demand in excess of even the most democratic of institutions, parties and practices. The demos cannot be bound I argue in what follows, but it is always the site of a contest. As Meintjes writes 'Strategically, they mobilised their vulnerability as a political tool – using their cultural and social capital of sexuality to make claims on the state' (Meintjes 2007: 366). The police left but the protest continued for months there- after. Within a year the protestors had been allocated plots in nearby Doornkop. Their network continued to operate at moments of political crisis. They demanded to be heard despite the noise of the activists, the police, the state, all of whom tried to silence their voices and dominate their bodies.

Introduction

In this chapter, I characterise democratic politics as improper. This entails three related claims: first democratic politics concerns the enactment of equality; second democracy undermines orders of property and propriety; and third democracy is not a regime (see Rancière 2007a: 71). Democratic theorists will reject this argument. Their concern is to painstakingly debate the proper form of a democratic regime. In previous chapters, I argued that democratic regimes are better conceived of as proprietary orders. All such regimes police the limits of democratic enactment and establish the proper limits of democracy – they invoke *realpolitik* to justify limits on a politics of equality. Developing post-Marxist theories of hegemony I argue that to comprehend such orders we must track the relationship between the proper, property and propriety. I begin by replaying the etymology of democ- racy. My aim is not to engage in hair splitting. Rather, I argue that the play between the two words demos and 'kratos' casts a critical light on those who assume that democracy is a regime. This argument recalls my contestation of the relationship between property and territory. Having shown the limits of democratic theory I deconstruct the key terms of the democratic common sense: property, freedom, representation, sovereignty and pluralism. In each case, I argue that an impropriety at the heart of dominant conceptual debates points to their limit. These limits are not the excuse for further analysis. Rather they are the opportunity to rethink the ancient and ongoing history of democratic politics as an improper challenge to proprietary order.

The Demos is Not a People

The first question that democratic theorists should broach, but rarely do, is who constitutes the demos. Theorists of democracy tend to take for granted the existing bounds of the demos, established nation states, even though they are historically contingent. This assumption is linked to a second, namely that in a democratic regime the people are sovereign. Dahl in a 1970 essay argued that democracy needs a legitimate principle of inclusion to determine the identity of 'the people'. He notes that the question is 'totally neglected by all the great political philosophers who wrote about democracy' (Dahl 1970: 60–1).[1] Despite Dahl's warning, many democratic theorists still assume that the question of how legitimately to bound the demos has been answered (Song 2012: 40). Admittedly, Song and other theorists of the so-called boundary problem recognise the problem. Their response, echoing Dahl, is to search for an independent moral principle to justify limiting the demos. However, such principles are not in themselves democratic. There are in fact a number of distinct positions but for the sake of argument we can distinguish those which assume that the question can be resolved in territorial terms, from those which seek to identify a relevant principle to demarcate the appropriate demos – a principle that may not be territorial. Such debates indicate a problem at the heart of democratic theory.[2] If we assume that democracy is a regime then its boundaries become a problem. Engaged in ever finer grained analytical distinctions, boundary theorists aim to make democracy proper to itself. In fact, they are finding good reason to exclude some from democratic participation – they act as the Svengalis of sovereign power.

I begin in a different place.[3] What if the boundary problem indicates a fundamental misunderstanding of democracy, if it is generated by the presupposition that democracy is a regime? The word democracy literally means the power of the people. However, there is no reason to assume that the power of the people should be associated with a sovereign regime. The word 'demos' does not specify who belongs to a people, nor that the people are equivalent to a sovereign regime. Nor, unlike other classical regimes – monarchy and oligarchy – does demos 'specify' the numbers who might comprise a people. As Ober argues:

> unlike monarchia (from the adjective monos: solitary) and oligarchia (from hoi oligoi: the few), demokratia is not in the first instance concerned with 'number.' The term demos refers to a collective body. Unlike monarchia and oligarchia, demokratia does not, therefore, answer the question: 'how many are empowered?' (Ober 2008: 4)

Ober fails to appreciate the radical implications of his own analysis. In his later book *Demopolis* he understands democracy as 'reasonably stable collective self-government by an extensive and socially diverse body of citizens . . . stable over time' (Ober 2017: 14). He briefly indicates that the question of boundaries is important, but simply assumes that existing orders resolve this question. In effect, he accepts the existing terms of boundary drawing as the basis for determining who is of the demos. This assumption simply validates the existing relationship between birth, registration of one's name, and the nation. Recognition, in the last instance, relies upon the ascription of citizenship status. However, if the demos cannot be counted, cannot give to itself a principle of self-limitation or self-legitimation, cannot finally be called to account then Ober needs an additional principle to legitimate the exclusion of some and the violent policing of territorial boundaries. In a democracy, the people, without qualification and as equal, exercise power. Yet we cannot determine a priori who belongs to the people. There are no special privileges accorded to any subject and no delimitation of the people in terms of nation, ethnicity, class, wealth, gender or any other marker of exclusion. The term 'demos' knows no borders – it is not immediately tied to one's place of birth. Were this the case then democracy itself would rely upon a moment which is wholly arbitrary. Rather democratic politics disrupts all orders according equal – not equivalent – rights and privileges to all. Democrats do not distinguish between citizens and immigrants, those who belong and those who do not. Such an understanding of democracy is improper. I assume that all regimes limit equality. They are what I termed in Chapter 1 proprietary orders, articulated regimes of the proper that police property, propriety and behaviours.

If this argument seems too quick, reflect for a moment on how Rousseau links the limitation of the demos to the question of property and possession. I detailed this in Chapter 1. Having assented to the general will, Rousseau holds, one may be forced to be free, required, for example, to sacrifice one's life in defence of the general will which knows no limit to what the demos may demand of its citizens. Yet Rousseau simultaneously establishes the proper limits of the general will by allowing that inequalities established in the state of nature become legitimate with the founding of a proprietary order. The general will, I noted, legitimises rights gained through first occupation, usurpation and enjoyment. Possession becomes a 'proper right' protected by a now democratic sovereign. In establishing a properly founded sovereign Rousseau secures an order of property. By what right is a line drawn between those who are citizens and those who are not? Rousseau invokes the full force of the sovereign will to protect what he himself terms usurpation (Rousseau 1987b). The foreigner may make democratic claims in the name of equality, but the sovereign democratic regime protects what the general will had secured, against the equality in whose name it was founded. The proper limits of democracy constrain the equality in whose name they were first introduced. In this case who comprises the demos? Is it the sovereign people, unified as a general will, or is it the single foreigner who questions the distribution of property and possession without original warrant, the violence of which cannot be wished away by sovereign fiat?[4]

The argument that there is no principle to determine the proper limits of the demos may seem counterproductive. After all, how can a subject whose definition entails the inclusion of all without borders act if it cannot properly define its own limits and identity? How can a subject in excess of itself, a people that cannot know itself without excluding others, enact the equality presupposed by democracy? It is this fear which leads democratic theorists into the futile search for origins or principles to finally determine who qualifies. Despite their best intentions, deliberative and representative democratic theories oil the wheels of undemocratic power. The quest to justify boundaries implicitly recognises this yet political theorists still obsessively try to justify these boundaries. It is a useless labour – if they are committed to democratic politics. Putting in to question these attempts to limit the demos challenges the forms of propriety which define the bounds of the proper, the borders of territory, membership of the demos and the forms of property associated with political order. To pose this problem in slightly different terms – a demos whose identity was determined in advance of democratic intervention would merely fulfil a preordained role. Democracy breaks with such pre-prepared roles. Aristotle's *Politics* already anticipates this argument. At first blush his argument is that in a democracy the poor, who are the majority, rule. He writes:

> Wherever men rule by reason of their wealth . . . that is an oligarchy, and where the poor rule, that is a democracy. But as a fact the rich are few and the poor many; for few are well to do, whereas freedom is enjoyed by all, and wealth and freedom are the grounds on which the oligarchic and the democratic parties respectively claim power in the state. (Aristotle 2000: Book 3, Chapter 8)

Aristotle draws a strange equivalence in this quote. He equates the poor with freedom, and the wealthy with oligarchy. Yet freedom is not the appropriate possession of the poor. It cannot properly be allocated to anyone but is, he goes on to write, shared by all. Wealth and freedom are not equivalent terms – yet in opposing them Aristotle suggests that wealth undermines freedom and democracy. In the case of an oligarchy, it is easy enough to determine who has wealth. Democracy, however, is rule by those who are free and in the final instance this means the rule of the poor. Later he will note that democracy is the rule of those without property. Aristotle precedes this definition of democracy with a long discussion of what principle one may use to define the citizen. He can find no satisfactory answer other than a descriptive one. He thus settles for a definition based upon who happens to be a citizen, in given circumstances. In fact, who is deemed of the demos, who counts as a citizen, is defined by legal fiat, and nothing else. On what grounds are foreigners, teenagers, prisoners or others excluded? Reasons are given but they are never exhaustive and they do not admit of a principle. It is thus, Rancière argues, that 'Democracy . . . is the product of an operation, at once inaugural and indefinitely renewed that aims to ward off an impropriety pertaining to the very principle of politics' (Rancière 2007a: 37). Democracy is improper from the point of view of the established order of politics, or, to use his term, the police. It is premised upon the simple assumption that all are equal regardless of qualification, competence or profession. The enactment of democracy 'disjoins entitlements to govern' (Rancière 2007a: 39) and is founded on disagreement rather than consensus. The unwritten rule which fashions the critique of democracy is the defence of wealth. In contrast with powers based on birth, knowledge, virtue or wealth, democracy follows from nothing but the lack of an entitlement to rule – it is anarchic in principle: 'This means, properly, anarchy—the absence of any arche, meaning any principle leading from the essence of the common to the forms of the community' (Rancière 2003). In passing it is worth noting that this is not a vindication of anarchist forms of political organisation, such as those proposed by Kropotkin. Rather, there is literally no principle that might be derived from the absence of *arche*.

Democracy was both constantly undermined, and intrinsic to, the Athenian polis. One could only be counted as a citizen of Athens if already listed as a member of the 139 demes. The democratic citizen was a divided subject defined first by their membership of a deme – and marked out as such during debates – but second the subject of the Athenian demos which required that one act in the name of the equality of all, potentially against the interests of one's deme. Demes were the locale of territorial and property questions concerning land, debt and employment. The demos stretched not only the accountability of members of the deme – it periodically put in to question the distribution of property and debt within a deme. On the terms I outlined above the demos is in excess of the forms of property and propriety that bound each deme. This tension between deme and demos might be replayed at the level of the Athenian demos. From the perspective of the city-states around it, Athens is but another deme. Democracy concerns both the proper limits of the exercise of power by the demoi and the question of how this is tied to the proper bounds of the demos. The 'demos' challenges forms of propriety that bound the proper. This is precisely the case with the representative democracies which reclaim democracy as a regime by reducing it to the rule of number. The attempt to define the demos through restrictive membership invokes a proper politics. I view the demos as always unruly, in excess of these determinations, the 'mob' disruptive of propriety and sovereignty. The demos avows one claim, repeatedly, which does not require institutional form to find an expression, which is constantly traduced by these terms of expression: we are equal.

Democratic Power is not Sovereign Power

Let me turn second to the 'kratos' of demokratia. Ober's argument is once more instructive. 'Kratos', he notes, does not mean the same as the 'archia' of monarchy and oligarchy. 'Archia' was used to denote office and magistracy. It tied power to a regime type and to sovereign order. 'Kratos' is a more general term. It signifies the capacity to act in unison. The nature of this power is underspecified as is its proper subject. After an exhaustive analysis of the distinct uses of 'kratos' and 'archia' in the classical texts Ober concludes:

> kratos, when it is used as a regime-type suffix [my emphasis], becomes power in the sense of strength, enablement, or 'capacity to do things.' This is well within the range of how the word kratos and its verb forms were used in archaic and classical Greek. Under this interpretation for isokratia, each person who stands within the ambit of 'those who were equal' (say, the citizens) would, enjoy access to public power in this 'capacity' sense. This might include, but need not be limited to, access to public offices. In sum, rather than imagining the –kratos group as sharing the –arche group's primary concern for the control of a (pre-existing) constitutional apparatus, I would suggest that the kratos-root terms originally referred to a (newly) activated political capacity. (Ober 2008: 8)

Again, Ober does not follow through on the radical implications of this reading. 'Kratos' is not only the power of a regime. It concerns activated political capacity. What is the appropriate site of this activated political capacity? Ober initially aligns it with democracy as a regime but then notes that it need not be limited to access to public office. So where then might this activated political power be exercised? Are there appropriate limits to the relations that the demos might put in to question? Is this a power which – like the demos to which it is tied – does not have an appropriate form? On this reading democracy is the improper enactment of the equal power of the demos. This rendering of democracy undermines those attempts to distinguish the multitude from the people. In their reading of modern political thought, Hardt and Negri argue that the notion of the people comes to supplant that of the multitude. The multitude is in excess of the various ways in which nation states limit the excessive potentiality of a multitude which produces our collective worlds. This notion of the multitude – central as it was to the development of Christianity – is, however, a minor figure in the history of democratic struggle and thought (Hardt and Negri 2000). Instead, we should reclaim the notion of the demos and not allow it to be confused with the idea of a people.

I noted in an earlier chapter that Butler's distinction between democracy as a regime and democratic popular sovereignty gestures in this direction (Butler 2015). However, her invocation of sovereignty presumes the possibility of establishing a democratic regime. Here we should draw a fine distinction. While it is a misnomer to assume that democracy is a regime type, we can identify moments when regimes enact equality. If we cannot determine the appropriate subject of democratic power neither can we determine in advance the issues, sites and practices which may be challenged by the power of the demos. We are already familiar with Foucault's argument that power is polymorphous, that it invests subjects criss-crossed by different discursive practices, and that it is not reducible to sovereign power. Foucault contends that 'one has to account for the constitution of the subject within a historical framework' (Foucault 1980: 117) while dispensing with the sovereign subject. His studies of the forms of exclusion constitutive of the normal, of the different regimes of truth and the variegated techniques of power indicate the multiple sites where power as capability may challenge regimes of knowledge. Power is not simply possessed by a sovereign (though it may be concentrated) but is distributed in a capillary like manner across the body politic in a variety of disciplinary, bio-political and pastoral practices. Yet these capillary networks are also sites of potential struggle. Foucault reminded us that power is exercised in the very constitution of the subjects we are, that we enact powers which are not unified but distributed and multiplied in polymorphous forms. Power inhabits the nooks and crannies of every existence.

However, Foucault ignores a key aspect of these techniques and practices. Wendy Brown notes that *'homo politicus'* is an ellipsis in his thought (Brown 2015: 74). *Homo politicus* was central to all classical theorists of democracy. This figure is anticipated by most (in the equality of the state of nature for example), even if immediately repressed by others. If we conceptualise 'kratos' as a capacity without proper place we may complicate Brown's critique of Foucault. Foucault zeros in on the complex forms of resistance to the polymorphous techniques of power. If there is no proper place for the exercise of this capacity then we might think democracy differently. This in part answers Brown who tells a pessimistic story about the eclipse of *homo politicus* not dissimilar in tone to Adorno and Horkheimer's lament to enlightenment in the *Dialectic of Enlightenment* (Adorno and Horkheimer 1985). She writes 'when liberal democracy is fully transformed into market democracy, what disappears is this capacity to limit, this platform of critique, and this sense of radical democratic inspiration and aspiration' (Brown 2015: 208). Despite her spirited critique, and critical development, of Foucault's notion of neoliberal political rationality, Brown too quickly forgets his complexification of the sites and practices of power. She equates democracy with different forms of political regime and then associates the exercise of democratic power with the powers made available to citizens. This presumption means that when state practices colonise and limit democracy, it seems to disappear.

Brown and Ober assume that political regimes are the proper site for democratic politics, even as Brown laments the degeneration of democratic institutions. Yet this assumption takes too much for granted. The demos has no proper referent. The nature of the power it exercises varies across space and time. Democracy is enacted by anyone in the name of an equality without limit. This is the peculiar power and threat of democratic agency – it questions even the most innocent forms taken by power. Are not the seventeenth-century diggers, twentieth-century feminists, contemporary eco-warriors, student protestors against debt and university fees all elemental to the history of democratic enactment, experiment and thought? None of these takes the form of a regime. Often they were systematically repressed by regimes which labelled themselves democratic. Democratic demands are often enacted despite a regime, not to a regime.

Democratic practices and demands have always put in to question the terms of the proper. Their force exceeds all forms of constitution, construction or representation in democratic communities. These are not demands that those excluded, marginalised or exploited are extended the same rights and obligations as dominant 'races' and classes. Nor is it a demand[5] for the restitution of an original state of equality. Rather the enactment of equality transforms the conditions in which lives are lived and the terms on which subjects recognise each other and themselves. Such practices cannot be recognised within the coordinates of the dominant order. Democratic politics is thus *antagonistic* not agonistic or deliberative. Democracy is not an existent order, but the processes through which such ordering is challenged. The demos respects neither authority, might, violence nor the partial will which any established sovereign state instantiates. This means, counterintuitively, that the demos does not require that all speak. It may be invoked by anyone, anywhere, in the name of equality, the axiomatic presupposition of democratic politics. To tell the story of democracy is to reconstruct those acts which come to embody, sometimes unexpectedly, the paradoxical moments when the demos speaks in excess of the bonds of identity, membership and property. This is a power beyond denomination, in the name of a universality without a concrete referent other than in the day-to-day struggles which impart to some the strange status of 'stand in for the demos'. In sum, I reject the assumption that democratic power must take the form of a regime, and that the only proper way to exercise democratic power is through official forms of politics within a clearly demarcated sovereign space. Democracy also takes its distance from a populism which presumes to identify the proper people – as I argue in the next chapter. Democratic power involves the enactment of equality against proprietary orders which police limits to equality. It may be enacted in the home against patriarchal domination, in the occupation of a factory or even (though far more rarely) by the state or transnational organisations.

This argument resembles – though is distinct from – that of Wolin in his path-breaking essay 'Fugitive democracy'. Wolin rejects the equation of democracy with political regimes and views constitutional democracies as mechanisms that bound equality. They 'curate the simulacra of democracy', he writes, securing the 'domus', the nation state, as the 'base of operations and launching pad for modern forms of power'. Constitutional democracies domesticate a people while securing a steady supply of material and human resources for imperial wars (Wolin 2016: 103–5). Wolin is rightly suspicious of the idea that democracy is a form of state. He recognises that democracy and equality have no proper form. He thus, somewhat ironically, affirms that democracy is wild, respects no boundaries, and is potentially irrational – concurring with Plato's negative characterisation of democracy. In this case, critique is replayed as affirmation. However, here I take some distance from Wolin. First, he views democracy as episodic and fugitive, a moment of rupture, often revolutionary in nature, when the wheels of normality are brought to a halt. I agree with Wolin that regimes limit democracy. However, this does not mean that democracy is episodic or ruptural. Democratic practices are ordinary – they take place every time human beings act as equals. They are often banal – but their banality should not blind us either to their occurrence, or to the fact that state and corporate powers rely on these practices. Second, if democracy is commonplace we should not dismiss all forms of state practice. This error follows from two assumptions – first, that there is a unified state which always acts against equality; second that the practices of sovereign powers are consistent. Rather, the state is a hodgepodge of apparatuses, practices, disciplines and organisations that conflict, and that rarely act in unity – again in rare instances such as war. State practices may be appropriated, and hegemonised, in the name of democracy. This argument is not an extension of Gramsci's conceptualisation of the integral state. It shares with that perspective the view that any easy distinction between state and civil society, between private and public, between economy and polity tends to reproduce dominant logics. However, political regimes sometimes act to further equality. There are many examples. Let me take one. On 24 August 2015 Germany opened its borders to all refugees from the Syrian war. At a stroke the Berlin government suspended a longstanding European convention which held that refugees should remain in the country of arrival. Merkel's government was hardly democratic – in many respects, it undermined democratic equality. For a moment, it enacted an equality without precedent in the history of the European Union. She was condemned in Germany and across Europe. Other examples include the introduction of a national health service in the United Kingdom by the post-war Labour government; the principle of equality before the law; Solon's wiping out of the debts of all Athenians. Representative regimes can act democratically – but they are not democratic. Having distinguished the power of the demos from the power exercised by sovereign states and having pluralised the possible sites where the power of the demos may be enacted against inequality, I now rethink the relations between this improper property and central concepts in democratic theory.

Property and Democracy

One of the primary apparatuses which limits democratic equality is the institution of property. I argued in the first chapter that property is a key means for the policing and securing of inequality. This was so for all the classical theorists of democracy. If regimes of property are the axes around which inequality is maintained, then democratic politics perforce challenges the unequal control of wealth and property. States secure forms of property – they render possession wrought by violent means legitimate, and concentrate violence to defend both territorial limits and the distribution of property rights – rights which specify who may benefit from what has been articulated as property. Property regimes extend beyond nation states – as I have noted about the privatisation of genetic information in previous chapters. A long tradition in political theory, however, does view property as anathema to democratic politics. Let me begin with one of the founding moments of Athenian democracy.

Plutarch's lives records that in 594 BC Solon determined that the debts of Athenian citizens should be forgiven and that debt using one's own body as security would henceforth be illegal. Solon had been elected *Archon* to end near civil war in the city. The disparities between rich and poor were extreme. Most common people were in debt to the wealthy tilling their land and pledging their bodies to secure debts. If unpaid they were sold as slaves. As Plutarch writes: 'the first thing which [Solon] settled was that what debts remained should be forgiven, and no man, for the future should engage the body of his debtor for security' (Plutarch 1998). Solon's reforms caused much anxiety among the wealthy. It is unsurprising that Aristotle later characterised democracy, with barely concealed dismay, as 'when the indigent, and not the men of property, rule' (Aristotle 2000: Book 3). Solon though was no democrat. He divided the Athenian people into four classes, distributed political power between them according to wealth – and excluded from office the poorest citizens, the *thetes*. However, his reforms established a critical link between freedom and property. He removed the 'horoi' from the bounds of indebted properties. As Finley notes these were an early form of title and land registration (echoed by the British division of land in to acres) indicating to all that the land was encumbered (Finley 1953: 251). Debt enslaved the poor, and was used as a technique to appropriate time, energy and life. Aristotle, later, explicitly ties democracy to the rule of those with no property. Solon's act echoed down the centuries. In the third century BC Phillip II, father of Alexander the Great, issued a decree making the redistribution of land and the cancellation of debt a seditious act. An earlier law of Delphi made it a crime even to propose these steps at the Assembly (Finley 1953: 253). After Solon's reforms it was still possible to take out debt against land and property – and over the centuries repeated demands for debt relief challenged the power of the ruling elites, not only in Athens.

It is Plato who most explicitly teases out the relationship between property and rule. His conception of the philosopher as Guardian requires that she has no property. Only those without property, and without personal interest, can rule in the interest of all. No philosopher writing today would tie the very possibility of their doing philosophy to having no property:

> The Guardians should be furnished with housing and a general standard of living which will not hinder them from becoming the best possible Guards, and which will give them no encouragement to do wrong in their dealings with the rest of the citizens . . . In the first place no one is to have any private property, beyond what is absolutely essential. Second, no one is to have the kind of house which cannot be entered by anyone who feels like it . . . they should impose a levy on the rest of citizens and receive an annual payment for their role which leaves them with neither profit nor a deficiency. (Plato 2007: Book 3, 416d–417b)

Property causes enmity between people. Philosophy as a lived practice, as love of wisdom, is only possible if the philosopher has no private interest. In the same way, politicians, who are for Plato philosopher kings, can only rule if they do so with a view to the universal which does not admit of private interest. The proper life can only be lived if those with private property do not rule. However Plato's text – as Rancière has argued – establishes a different inequality, that between knowledge and power. It assumes a natural order in which every human being has a proper place, in which all the parts of the social order are properly allocated. It is perhaps inevitable that Plato had already anticipated the best rejoinder to his own arguments. In his *Laws* he imagines a social order that anticipates the best utopian socialist dreams of the nineteenth century. However, he deems it not appropriate to mere mortals:

> The first and highest form of the State and of the government and of the law is that in which there prevails most widely the ancient saying, that 'Friends have all things in common.' Whether there is anywhere now, or will ever be, this communion of women and children and of property, in which the private and individual is altogether banished from life, and things which are by nature private, such as eyes and ears and hands, have become common, and in some way see and hear and act in common, and all men express praise and blame and feel joy and sorrow on the same occasions, and whatever laws there are unite the city to the utmost – whether this is possible or not, I say that no man, acting upon any other principle, will ever constitute a state which will be truer or better or more exalted in virtue. (Plato 2008: 108)

This most excellent form of state is, Plato suggests, impossible, improper we might say. Far more may be said about it but not in this context. The reference to Solon may seem arcane. Yet the relation between debt and property has always been central to the curtailment of democratic life. Solon's act reflects the widespread assumption that an active political life requires participation and time for members of the demos. Those indebted, without time, were unable to act as informed members of the polis. Moreover, these reforms were premised on the separation between the *oikos* (as the homestead) and the polis. Neither the patriachal authority of the male head of household, nor the citizens' right to exercise property over slaves, was questioned. The form that property takes today is different yet it similarly limits democratic equality. Following the struggles to end slavery, the labour performed by slaves was redefined after the industrial and political revolutions of the eighteenth and nineteenth centuries as the disposable property of the person, that is, as labour power. The legal nicety here was the distinction between labour power – which is alienable as a commodity – and the labourer, whose inherent personhood was deemed inalienable. Marx developed a critique of the function that this conception of property played in capitalist society. The idea of the free selling of labour is, he argued, a legal fiction obscuring the compulsion that underpins it. Those who own no property, and thus have no means to produce their own livelihood, are compelled to sell their labour (Marx 1976: 271).

The politics of debt today is obviously somewhat different – but it too acts to compel those in debt. While for the ancient Greeks debts against the body of the debtor were made illegal, today debt is offered against the predicted capitalisation of lives over time. It is on this basis that state debts are calculated. In the USA and the UK, graduates from higher education will begin their working lives with debts bigger than a mortgage in most parts of the world. As Lazzarato argues debt 'acts as a capture, predation and extraction machine . . . and functions as a mechanism for the production and "government" of collective and individual subjectivities' (Lazzarato 2012: 29). Debt presumes that the subject has property-in-itself. By the same token, individual property ownership is often no more than the creation of a debt obligation. This returns me to arguments in my previous chapter – debt is premised on the manipulation of relations of monetary equivalence which attack democratic and populist forms equality. Although it is not the topic of this book, debt has historically been used to leverage profit against property. It was often the excuse for colonial interventions. Rogan notes, for example, that in the last decades of the nineteenth century the extension of European political control over Turkey, Egypt and Tunisia was exacted through a politics of debt. International financial commissions exercised control over public assets, opening these economies to European states and private corporate interests (Rogan 2009: 130–1). These historical examples are reminiscent of recent events in Greece. They echo the privatisation of state assets, destruction of social democratic redistributive policies and the capture of tax by the state for financial interests in the years following the 2008 debt crisis. My point is simple – debt and property have long been the enemies of democracy. The anti-democratic pressures wielded by bond-holders against states echo practices perfected by European colonial powers over centuries. They echo the situation in Athens when Solon, acting as *Archon*, suspended debts held against the bodies of the debtor. An improper politics refuses the debtor–creditor relationships which limit equal democratic participation, in effect purchasing the time which Solon's reforms had returned to citizens. The propertied subject – the subject that owns its labour as a disposable asset – is only a step away from the indebted subject, who is preyed upon by the owner of the debt.

Locke: Liberty, Property and Protected Democracy

In 'Of property', Chapter 5, in Locke's seventeenth-century defence of a limited liberal democracy, *Two Treatises on Government*, he tethers democracy to the notional individual with an inalienable property in himself. The right to life, Locke contends, is inalienable, a God-given right which no 'man' can give up to another. No 'man' can assent to becoming a slave, although those captured in war may be made slaves. However, because men own themselves they can sell what is alienable, their labour, as if it is a commodity equivalent to all others. Locke attributes these natural rights *equally* to all men in a state of nature. They are accorded by God and distinguish men from beasts over whom humans collectively exercise proprietary rights:

> it is evident, that though the things of nature are given in common, yet man, by being master of himself, and proprietor of his own person, and the actions or labour of it, had still in himself the great foundation of property; and that, which made up the great part of what he applied to the support or comfort of his being, when invention and arts had improved the conveniences of life, was perfectly his own, and did not belong in common to others. (Locke 1988: Book 2: 5)

In a different context, I considered the way in which the very idea of man depends upon how this line between animal and human is drawn. For the present, I consider how Locke establishes a crucial nexus linking property to liberty. In so doing, he in effect justifies the caging of liberty. Locke does not treat property merely as the enumeration of things. Instead, he develops a thesis of legitimate appropriation. In Balibar's words

> to speak of a property in one's person or in oneself is not exactly to issue a contradictory proposition, pushing persons in to the order of things; it rather tries to designate the ultimate point where propriety meets with property, where 'to be' rejoins with 'to have'. (Balibar 2002: 303)

I return to this tie between property and propriety shortly. Locke holds that the mixing of individual labour with the external world renders private that which was originally given as common. In the initial justification of private property Locke limits what can be owned in two ways: no man should own so much that there is insufficient for others; and what is owned should not spoil. Money removes these limitations:

> before the desire of having more than one needed had altered the intrinsic value of things, which depends only on their usefulness to the life of man; or had agreed, that a little piece of yellow metal, which would keep without wasting or decay, should be worth a great piece of flesh, or a whole heap of corn; though men had a right to appropriate by their labour, each one of himself, as much of the things of nature, as he could use; yet this could not be much, nor to the prejudice of others, where the same plenty was left to those who would use the same industry. (Locke 1988: Book 2: 181)

The introduction of money engenders economic inequality on terms which allow men to assent to inequality in exchanging a durable measure, money. In the previous chapter, I enumerated in some detail how monetary equivalence might be deemed a form of hegemony. Locke was the first modern political theorist to link property, money and equivalence. He justifies private property on the basis that every individual has property in themselves. This notion of property in the self assumes the existence of a God who gives this property to each individual, an endowment to be cared for. This is somewhat ironic given that the *First Treatise* ridiculed Filmer's (2008) *Patriarcha* for defending the divine right of kings and appealing to scripture as the basis for political judgement. Yet God is still Locke's prop – a prop which makes property proper. His ingenious conceit is to provide a moral justification for the existence of property before it is secured by sovereign power. He simultaneously establishes property as intrinsic to democracy while magically vanquishing the violence of possession – in contrast to both Von Savigny and Rousseau who recognise the original violence of possession.

I argued in the first two chapters that democratic regimes are better conceived of as (hegemonic) proprietary regimes. Such orders distribute access too and control over different forms of the proper, police appropriate forms of behaviour, limit democratic equality and purvey a semblance of democracy. It is common to associate such orders with nation states, the apparent site of democratic contestation for at least the past two centuries. However, as recent scholarship on Locke contends, we can only understand his limited defence of democracy in relation to the colonial nomos. It is not only that Locke was involved in the writing of the *Fundamental Constitutions of Carolina*, that he owned stock in slave trading companies, that he was secretary of, and adviser to, the Lords Proprietors of the Carolinas – awful as these facts are (Armitage 2004). In themselves the facts do not of necessity mean that Locke's account of liberty and property cannot be rescued. Rather the conceptual architecture linking property and liberty severely limits democratic enactment in ways that become second nature to democratic theory. We have already seen that for Locke the self has property in its own life – and that this interiority extends outwards to justify taking possession of external things. Personhood, as property in the self, means that things which are not persons, may be made property.[6] Balibar links identity, as what is proper to one's self (propriety), to property as the possession of external things. Both propriety and property are formed through temporal processes of appropriation. Constituent property as the mode of self-constitution presumes a subject capable of sustained occupation and use of land and of things. Here property and propriety rub up against each other in ways anticipated by my arguments in Chapter 1.

There is more though: this is a subject that is racialised and gendered. Locke carefully distinguishes the man of reason proper to himself, from those he terms in his *Essay on Understanding* illiterate peoples, savages, idiots and children incapable of exercising the universal principles of knowledge. Appropriation, as Bhandar argues 'takes place via the identification of the self with property' (Bhandar 2018: 166). Those who are not proper to themselves cannot make things their property, or more precisely cannot themselves be distinguished as persons from things. Dominion requires understanding. Locke articulates property, understanding and possession seamlessly, and ties this to a particular nomos of improvement. In Bhandar's reading, there is an implicit – if not fully developed – racial anthropology of the human at play in Locke's account. Losurdo's historical reconstruction of liberalism traces its genesis to the genocides of the past four centuries, and to the slave trade – always the other face of the liberal celebration of freedom. He notes that '[alongside] black enslavement and the black slave trade, the rise of the two liberal countries either side of the Atlantic involved a process of systematic expropriation and practical genocide first of the Irish and then of the Indians' (Losurdo 2014: 20).

The point is not simply that liberal theorists were men (almost always) of their time. Rather, many of their contemporaries were deeply critical of both slavery and colonial occupation. The historical excuse is euphemistic avoidance of a rather less sanguine conclusion: liberalism was always anti-democratic, resisted democratisation, and was complicit in the worst horrors of European modernity. In Locke's case dominion of the master is extended by the work of the servant (Locke 1988: s.35, Chapter V) which he describes as 'my labour'; God gives the land to those who are reasonable and hard-working – those who improve the land through settled cultivation. When, he contends, such industrious men plant in the interior of America no one can oppose their claim to the land because, he argues, a thousand acres of the uncultivated waste of America is useless compared to ten acres of fertile cultivated land in Devonshire. An American king lives worse than an English day labourer because the 'Americans' do not improve their land by labour. Locke continually refers to America in this chapter, doubtless thinking about his own work and profit in Carolina. His defence of the absolute dominion of the self over itself – against the absolute dominion of a monarch – becomes the right of some to sell their labour and others to appropriate this labour as a commodity. The labour of slaves and servants becomes the property of the owner. As Balibar has it there is a progressive logic that links the three estates of life, liberty and property. Life is a gift of God, freely to be disposed of as one wishes. Freedom is a property of the self which means that one can commodify one's own labour as a property to be sold or lay claim to external property. Locke's account of the social contract gains traction when read in this broader context – the ongoing fall-out from the civil war in England and the broader colonial context within which the political economy of seventeenth-century England is enmeshed.

I argued in Chapter 2 that the performativity necessary to the maintenance of authority simultaneously makes that authority vulnerable. The same is true for liberalism and for the enactment of rights. However, this should not blind us to the political and material force of a liberalism now sedimented in representative institutions and so normalised as to appear neutral. This is most obvious in the case of property. The seizure of land from indigenous peoples, the genocides committed across the Americas, in Australia and New Zealand, and in every part of Africa cannot be made right – and certainly not by the representative democracies whose logics were born during the centuries of colonial expansion. This is one reason that an improper politics refuses to treat concepts such as liberty or freedom in the abstract. Such abstraction universalises what cannot be universalised. It may lead the political theorist to unwittingly replay logics which undermine rather than extend a politics of equality. Any understanding of the politics of property traces the complex relations between the historical origins of property, the forms of propriety associated therewith, and the capturing of equality performed by state apparatuses. This critique extends to recent attempts to rescue theories of democratic representation as I argue in the next section.

Democracy beyond Representation

A set of recent debates about democracy aims to rescue representation from the criticism that it undermines equality. There are two key arguments. First, they contend that the represented do not pre-exist their articulation, putting in to question the notion that the represented have pre-constituted interests. Second, they contend that representative claims are wider ranging than is normally assumed. They may 'be formal and informal, electoral and non-electoral, national and trans-national and manifest in multiple guises and spaces' (Saward 2016: 246). These arguments demand a rethinking of how representative democracy is understood and justified. However, unlike classic critics of representative democracy, constructivist theorists fail to think about the relation between property, the proper and representation. They underemphasise the disjuncture between democratic equality and representative politics. In short these attempts to radicalise representative democracy do not address the sedimented forms of inequality that structure representation (Devenney 2019). Let me take these arguments one by one.

Constructivist theorists of representation argue that the represented do not pre-exist their representation. Representation is thought of as an ongoing process of negotiation, a war of position, in which 'representative and represented [are] linked not by a static correspondence but in a dynamic process of mutual constitution' (Disch 2015: 488). For Disch democracy cannot be legitimised with reference to a pre-existing rational will or with reference to the 'real' interests of constituents. Constructivists thus extend the notion of representation to include the representative mobilisations of constituencies beyond traditional forms of electoral democracy. If representation constitutes the represented then it is possible to imagine representative claims beyond, or below, the nation state. However, this raises a set of questions about the relationship between democracy, equality and representation. Perhaps most important is how we might distinguish representative claims that are democratic from those that are discriminatory? Disch proposes that the representative process may 'be judged more or less democratic insofar as it . . . mobilise[s] both express and implicit objections from the represented' (Disch 2011: 111). This weak criterion encourages contestation, dissent and the recognition that there is no one sovereign voice. However, all sorts of contestations may be mobilised. Witness, for example, how the Trump campaign mobilised dissent, claiming to represent a squandered American greatness in the name of democracy. On this criterion, we cannot distinguish these racist forms of mobilisation from mobilisations which instantiate equality. Where Disch and Saward begin to address these normative questions they run up against a set of difficulties. Disch argues that 'the citizen standpoint opens up an option that is resolutely constructivist, democratic and enabled by empirical research' (Disch 2015: 496). Yet it is unclear why Disch invokes citizenship given the exclusionary ends to which it is often deployed. Saward attempts to escape this problem by rejecting first order judgements. Instead, he asks if representative claims enact democratic equality, an equality that is only given meaning and texture in the process of its enactment (Saward 2016: 247). For Saward equality 'is dynamic and performatively produced' (Saward 2016: 248). He acknowledges that equality is the final resting place of almost every attempt to defend democratic politics. Yet he too has questions to answer. If equality is given its meaning in practice, at what point does a claim no longer instantiate equality? He invokes equality yet gives it no content other than what it has become in practice. My point, to put it simply, is that both Disch and Saward seem to require some notion of equality if they are to argue that the extension of representative claims is democratic. If not then any representative claim whatsoever may qualify – given that on their terms such claims constitute represented communities.

In contrast to these theorists, an older critique of representative democracy contends that representation is inequality in its quintessentially political form. The constructivist turn suggests that representation activates a politics of equality. However, it fails to consider the relationship between representation and inequality. They forget the link between property, representation and civil society. Representation is presented as conceptually abstract rather than as overdetermined by the social and political conditions within which it is found. There can be no easy return to Marxist critiques of property, linked as they were to a philosophy of history, to an expressivist account of the social totality, and to a privileging of the proletariat as the subject–object of history. Yet in returning improperly to Marx's critique of representative democracy, we can rethink the relationship between inequality and representation.

Marx's critique of the extension of the franchise in 'On the Jewish question' is emblematic. He writes:

> the political annulment of private property not only fails to abolish private property but even presupposes it. The state abolishes, in its own way, distinctions of birth, social rank, education, occupation, when it declares that birth, social rank, education, occupation, are non-political distinctions, when it proclaims, without regard to these distinction, that every member of the nation is an equal participant in national sovereignty, when it treats all elements of the real life of the nation from the standpoint of the state. Nevertheless, the state allows private property, education, occupation, to

act in their way – i.e., as private property, as education, as occupation, and to exert the influence of their special nature. Far from abolishing these real distinctions, the state only exists on the presupposition of their existence; it feels itself to be a political state and asserts its universality only in opposition to these elements of its being. (Marx 1984)

The standard interpretation of this text is well known. Representative democracies are complicit in legitimising a system of economic and political inequality. Political representation, as a formal bourgeois right, betrays the substantive equality it simultaneously promises. However, like the money form, political equality is abstract. The logic of the market requires that individuals act as self-regarding actors.[7] Representative democracies thus sustain the separation between the (abstractly equal) political community and the private community of economic interests in civil society, where inequality reigns. The heterogeneous rationality of the market gives the lie to political equality.[8] Note that for Marx electoral representation is constituted as intrinsic to the reproduction of systemic inequality. Marx anticipates the constructivist turn but with a twist. He gives an account of the system of political representation, as constituted, or on some readings, determined by socio-economic conditions. He recognises that representatives may constitute new claims, but argues that such claims are constitutionally impaired by the substantive inequalities which structure socio-political order. The system of political representation separates the citizen from active participation in determining the fate of the community and belies the substantive inequalities which structure social life.

However, there is more to this quote than the traditional reading allows. For Marx the terms of equality are bounded by nation states which police the separation between civil and political society, the system of property relations which order inequality within the state and the territorial bounds of the nation. A normative and legal order is related to the organisation of appropriation, the drawing and maintenance of boundaries and the forms taken by legal property. Schmitt, as we saw in Chapter 1, contends that one can only ask ontological questions in light of their relation to legal normativity and forms of property and appropriation (Schmitt 2003: 45) The intrinsic, but contingent, links between ontology and particular modalities of appropriation suggest the terms on which any politics of representation might be conceptualised. The constructivist turn does not escape this critique, in part because it does not ask the question. Representation always concerns who counts and how political claims relate to dominant forms of appropriation, division and inequality. Saward does acknowledge that representative claims cannot be conjured out of thin air. They are made from existing terms, in his words, the 'ready mades . . . which must tap in to familiar contextual frame-works' (Saward 2006: 303) and can produce silencing effects. The constituencies evoked may be silenced as their voices are appropriated by elites (Saward 2006: 303). Representative claims are neither good nor bad – the identities constituted through representative claims may act as the basis for future dissent, or indeed as conservative restraints on the present. Yet he does not note that the very possibility of a claim becoming effective is constrained (though not determined) by hegemonic forms of order. Furthermore, the very notion of a representative claim already presupposes particular notions of hegemonic order and forms of subjectivity. While I concur with the constructivist argument that the represented are made – I insist that the terms of this making relate to particular orders of appropriation, within historically specific proprietary orders.

There is one last aspect of Marx's argument too often ignored. He equates the role of private property with those of education and occupation. These are not strictly about property, but are central to what I termed proprietary order in Chapter 1. The state exists, Marx writes, on the presupposition of the distinctions that follow from property, education and occupation. Representative democracies determine in advance the appropriate ways of being, doing and saying to use Rancière's terms (Rancière 1999: 29) and thus the types of representative claim which have resonance. They place certain issues off-limits. The representation of the democratic state as an imaginary with which all can identify relies upon general acceptance of these norms of education, occupation and nation. Marx's critique of political representation then concerns both ownership and control over resources and lives, and the ordering of the social world, the allocation of things and subjects to their proper places. The constructivist account of representation outflanks aspects of these criticisms, but not all of them.

Because they emphasise the constitutive aspects of representation, constructivists recognise the importance of mobilising and challenging different forms of political exclusion. The recognition that representation extends beyond electoral politics complements a politics aimed at making visible forms of historical exclusion, often occluded from public perception. One can envision both Disch and Saward accepting that elections are (as Charles Taylor argued in 1971) politically and culturally specific, presupposing certain notions of subject, object and reason, a certain nomos we might say. The acts which political scientists characterise as brute data are not simply given: they are institutionally bound and bound up with particularistic notions of identity and autonomy. The same is true though of representative claims: they cannot be identified independently of the language used to describe them, a language constitutive of reality. Representative claims are intersubjective practices, modes of social relation, which presuppose certain sets of logics: that claims might be heard; that the world is divided between subjects and objects; that humans can understand what is constituted in the claim made. The notions of constituency mobilisation (Disch) and representative claim (Saward) already presuppose accepted modes of social relation. These prior conditions are not thematised by scholars of the constructivist turn (Taylor 1971: 35).

Let me summarise. First, in failing to thematise the conditions which make representative claims possible, constructivists assume that the extension of representation is good for democratic politics. Democracy, however, is not the same as representation, and nor is representation its necessary prerequisite. These theorists fail to ask if representative claims, and constituency mobilisations which cut across established boundaries, are themselves overdetermined by global forms of hegemonic order. In failing to thematise these prior conditions they do not address the inequalities which relate back to established proprietary orders. Second, the very notion of representation – as establishing a relation between subject, object and voice – already presupposes certain established notions about human beings. Representation in both its constitutional and symbolic registers presupposes certain ways of being which are neither abstract nor universal. Third, representative claims always aim to establish the limits of their object. Democracy is always improper – out of time, and out of place – enacting an equality at odds with dominant modalities of the proper, with the forms of appropriation – of the self, of objects, of what is deemed proper, and thus open to becoming property. There is though one last, and fundamental, limit to these arguments.

The liberal origins of representative government are constitutive of existing practices of representation. Representative democracy was always articulated to particular regimes of property. The claims of representative democracies are undermined by contemporary regimes of property in three respects: first, the globalisation of property laws; second, the articulation of ever new realms, for example genetic information, as private assets; and last the hollowing out of the public–private distinction. Signatories to the World Trade Organization, for example, must remove 'restrictive' barriers to trade, to services (including banking, insurance, transport, communications and health) and to intellectual property (trademarks, industrial designs, genetic resources, medicines and the like.) The reframing of the public life-world as a private asset from which value may be derived radically forecloses democratic representation within national boundaries (see Honig 2016). When the demos is defined in national terms, it cannot make democratic decisions about a range of issues regulated by international treaties. The extension of representative claim making, and mobilisations, in the ways suggested by Disch and Saward presupposes this reconfiguration of the proper bounds of political and representative power. Disch and Saward have not adequately thematised the sedimented terrain on which representative claims are mounted. As a consequence, they do not adequately conceptualise democratic politics, or equality, and its relation to representation. Those constituted by prior mobilisations do not simply vanish – prior claims also have ontological effects which later exercise a centripetal weight limiting other claims. However, these effects are rarely, if ever, wholly new. They always negotiate an order configured by a set of perceived interests with residual weight. What status do we give to this materiality which constitutes the terrain on which representative claims are made? Surely they limit the forms of representative claim that may be made, constraining the language and descriptions that have a purchase on the world? Is so-called sheer materiality not already delimited and demarcated, most often as a form of property? Why is this important? Disch identifies systemic effects which privilege the wealthy. How do these structure representative democracy? Most obviously through the disproportionate financial influence that is wielded by wealthy corporate lobbyists. Perhaps more subtle is the indirect influence exerted through the material world of people and things already partitioned and apportioned. Property requires the human mapping and drawing of the world, a cartographic imaginary, in which parts of the physical world are partitioned, allocated and given value. Let me return to the example of the genetic code. Genetic sequences had no existence as property claims before they were legally recognised as entities over which property claims could be exercised. Naturalised in international property regimes such claims act as constraints on the present. When indigenous communities claim ownership of seeds developed over centuries of agricultural practice, they make the claim against companies who legally own the genetic sequence of the seeds. The existing proprietary regime requires that even counterclaims are made in terms of property. Unless framed in the language of property, they cannot be heard. Farming communities are thus forced to rearticulate the terms on which they conceptualise the means used for the reproduction of their lives and communities. Property regimes – often contested, but always invoked in the name of law and order – place severe constraints on the types of claim that may be heard. Property in this example is a form of representation and constitution. It is a performative claim maintained by violence and law. Profound inequality in the social world is founded on these legal institutions with material effects. Such relations are represented back to citizens as the natural order within which any claims they make should be framed. Disch and Saward lack a vocabulary allowing them to distinguish sedimented interests and established patterns of inequality, from the particular claims made about them.

Let me turn to the specificity of democratic equality. Inequalities have their origin in established histories of exploitation, discrimination and exclusion. Saward and Disch invoke equality but are worried that a normative stance in defence of equality in the abstract is not itself subject to agreement within political communities. It thus abstracts from interpretive disputes which are the core of representative claim making, and in so doing undermines the equality it aims to represent. Yet they simultaneously rely on an implicit or explicit commitment to political equality. I contend that they are right: democratic enactment presupposes a commitment to equality, which is verified in practice, but which is always improper. Representation is not a necessary condition for the enactment of equality. In fact, representative claims presuppose a structural inequality – they distinguish between the one making the claim, and those in whose name the claim is made. This may all too quickly result in elites taking advantage of claims made in the names of others. Democratic equality may be invoked in order to assess the limits of representative claims – but representation in itself is not a condition of democratic equality. The enactment of equality is always improper in relation to existing forms of order and their particular configurations of property and propriety. What distinguishes Rancière's account from that of Saward's is the conjunction of two elements: equality is presupposed, while its content is worked out when it is verified.[9] Democratic equality pushes beyond the established terms of representation. Representative claims constitute bounded communities of interest. Any attempt to represent the world, a polity, any attempt to give borders or number to a represented community is confronted by democratic claims which do not recognise these limits. Such practices are manifold. In liberal democracies, legitimate political involvement generally means voting for candidates, pre-approved by political parties, by those deemed citizens. Other forms of political action (assemblies, social and protest movements, riots, strikes, occupations) are cast as radical, non-conformist and marginal to the democratic consensus. In short, the organisation of space, place, time and subject positions establishes what counts as appropriate democratic behaviour in representative democracies. If representation is not entailed by democratic equality (though it may in some instances serve a politics of equality) what are we to make of political parties – the dominant form of political organisation in representative democracies?

Democracy and Political Parties

Simone Weil argued (almost a century ago) that the party-political form is incompatible with democracy. With Weil the sole question I ask is if a political party enacts democratic equality. Weil derives her idea of the good from Rousseau: the general will is true and just, and democracy, as the exercise of the freely expressed, reasoned will, is justice. Although I take exception to this reading of Rousseau, she put her finger on something important. Democracy requires that all can express their free opinion, listening to and exchanging reasons, in deciding how best to organise public life. Political parties in contrast are partisan. They are vehicles of collective passion which constrain free discussion between equals. Weil here echoes arguments with longer history (Agamben 2011). Malebranche in his *Treatise on Nature and Grace* (1992) had attempted to resolve a much older theological dispute about God's providence on earth in terms of the general will. He held that the general will accorded with God's acts. The power of providence accords perfectly with the order of the world. As Agamben argues, Malebranche's theology overlaps with the dominant scientific view of nature as discernible according to rational laws (Agamben 2011: 265). Malebranche insists upon the perfection of God's providence while recognising that men will not always act in line with providence. His text aims to reconcile longstanding disputes in Catholic theology about the government of the world, in particular the relationship between sovereign power and economic power, in this case the government of life.

The text is crucial to Rousseau's later development of his notion of the general will. It links the general will back to God's providence and the problem of how men govern each other. If the will of men cannot accord with that of God is it possible to imagine God's divine will at work in the world? If not, then there will always be plural attempts to hegemonise this will – and thus competing political parties. The question of the political party has a far longer providence one might say than political scientists might admit. For Weil, however, political parties distort the realisation of the good: they are machines to generate collective passions; they exercise collective pressure to instil conformity on members; and their goal is growth without limit (Weil 2014: 11). We need think only of the ways in which Marxist revolutionary parties – notably in their Trotskyite variations – act to discipline and educate the will of their members. Certain political theorists celebrate such discipline as the necessary correlate of revolutionary struggle. Dean can acknowledge the force exercised by the party yet argues that these excesses do not undermine its authority: 'The actuality of the Communist Party exceeds its errors and betrayals' (Dean 2016: 247). It is as if, for Dean, the Communist Party is the secular version of the Catholic Church which although it makes errors is the closest that humankind can get to the expression of God's will on earth – and thus may its excesses be excused.

In contrast, Weil argues that political parties undermine democratic politics: 'They are totalitarian in practice and in inclination.' The party name unifies a fiction dressed up as a coherent doctrine and 'kills in all souls the sense of truth and justice' dissimulating propaganda to persuade (Weil 2014: 16). Members cannot profess views distinct from those of the party nor freely consider the issues at hand – restrictions celebrated by Dean as necessary limits in the Communist struggle against capitalism. For Weil the party form quells the inner light of conscience committing individuals to a state of mendacity and inner darkness (Weil 2014: 19). Members of a political party are compelled to lie – to themselves, to the public and sometimes to the party. Parties she contends are miniature versions of a secular church. The partisan spirit induced by such intoxication induces even decent 'men' to persecute the innocent.

She proposes the abolition of parties. From the point of view of deliberative democrats, liberal and post-Marxist theorists Weil misunderstands liberal democratic pluralism. Yet there is something to Weil's arguments. Consider her alternative proposals. Weil argues that representatives should be able openly to express their views on all issues when standing for election and in parliament. Rather than conform to the discipline of a party, they can change their allegiances and views from issue to issue. She echoes those who suggest that democratic representation should take place through lot, a form of election which mirrors the anarchic premise of democratic equality. Parliaments could then allow association and disassociation on specific issues. In the public sphere, groups could coalesce around ideas. The press would never endorse candidates or parties. The abolition of parties would cause no damage to the public good but would exert a 'healthy cleansing influence well beyond the domain of public affairs . . .' (Weil 2014: 32). With Weil, we might contend that the abolition of political parties in their current form would end the intellectual leprosy which assumes that there is a true will. Political parties compete for sovereign power – the power of a regime, archia, which concentrates, orders and limits the 'kratos' of the demos. Weil's radical suggestions, ignored by political theorists, allow us to think beyond the all too easy assumption that political parties are the necessary formal expression of liberal democratic practices. Rather, parties undermine political pluralism in competing for access to the extraordinary powers concentrated in the sovereign state. The distribution of this power is what we should consider and Weil's proposals to abolish political parties are not a bad starting point. I explore this further in the chapter that follows.

Rethinking the Proper of Democracy

The current consensus assumes that democracy cannot challenge established property relations. The neoliberal worldview assumes the sanctity of a set of principles which require continued faith, despite their repeated failure. The state, in theory the bearer of sovereign democratic authority, maintains the borders that delimit land masses and imposes the laws that protect the various forms of global property against trespass. It is no longer, even *in potentia*, the bearer of a democratic will. Its claim to serve the interests of all naturalises and neutralises relations of property, which demarcate the bounds of the demos. States secure the circulation of goods, protect private property and maintain the ever-expanding balloon of financial capital. All governments insist that their primary imperative is to maintain economic stability, while preserving the current system for the ordering and distribution of life chances. What distinguishes the present neoliberal conjuncture is that the state itself participates in the market, commissioning and providing services in direct competition with the private sector. It secures the conditions for market competition and acts in the market it preserves. The liberal ideal of the state as a neutral arbiter, above the fray of contestation, no longer holds, if it ever did. This is not simply a reinvention of an argument first deployed by Poulantzas (1978), namely that fractions of capital compete for influence over state policy and law making and that the autonomous state organises the universal interest led by a dominant fraction of capital. Rather, the state acts as a fraction of capital articulating its own interests within a market against others. Moreover, the state is not an actor with one single interest. States own property, have rights and interests in property and secure conditions under which property relations are maintained. The transformation of states during the past three decades has resulted in the breaking up of the distinction between private and public. Resources once deemed public are either redirected to the private sector (as witnessed during the recent banking crises) or the state extends its own ownership of resources, especially through the varying forms of intellectual property rights. States often pursue profit on terms no different to those of the private sector. The state as stakeholder does not act as an agent of the people it represents but as a competitor in the market, offering contracts to other parts of the state in direct competition with private providers. This shifting terrain makes explicit the key relationship between sovereignty, representation and property as overlapping elements of an articulated property, state and capital complex. Democratic demands for the extension of the state, and for law to regulate the excesses of the market, no longer resonate. Such interventions are the acts of quasi-public/private institutions the interests of which no longer correspond to the legitimation functions once performed by the welfare state.

Theorising politics in terms of a sovereign demos capable of acting upon itself legitimates an ancient fiction. This fiction clads the oligarchies of today in the cloak of democracy. The sovereign democratic state does not exist. This imaginary beckons us to act in a manner that is already impossible: recognising that the link between sovereign power and democratic power is broken in part helps to explain the deployment of ancient rules of sovereign exception during the past decade of the 'war on terror'. Sovereign power is not democratic power. The improper politics I defend rejects the markers of certainty which inspired leftist politics for much of the twentieth century. The imaginary which sustains such fantasies should not foreclose all discussion of an 'other' democracy, a democracy which works through what it might mean for a people to exercise power, even as these terms ('people' and 'power') demand conceptual reworking. Democracy cannot appeal to any natural principle to justify rule. Rather, it undermines all attempts at establishing foundational principles of natural government. It is premised on the simple assumption that all are equal regardless of qualification, competence or profession. Democracy thus 'disjoins entitlements to govern' (Rancière 2007a: 39) and is founded on disagreement, rather than consensus. Rancière, as do I, ties the critique of wealth and power with the improper, that which has no place. This is not merely a weakened version of Marxism; in fact, it rejects Marxist theories of the political. The proletariat, for Marx, hold a privileged position in revolutionary struggle because they embody the very principle of capitalist society, as the becoming subject–object of history. The proletariat are the proper of democracy, because the only property they have is their labour. By contrast, the *lumpenproletariat* is deemed by Marx a class incapable of achieving class consciousness, a flotsam not engaged in production and thus marginal to any form of revolutionary struggle. Marx and Engels write in *The Communist Manifesto* of:

> The 'dangerous class,' the social scum, that passively rotting mass thrown off by the lowest layers of the old society, may, here and there, be swept into the movement by a proletarian revolution; its conditions of life, however, prepare it far more for the part of a bribed tool of reactionary intrigue. (Marx and Engels 1985: 92)

Marxist theorists are wary of the people of no property in part because they have no privileged knowledge of the dynamics of capitalist production. In contrast, I contend that democracy is an impropriety which disrupts consensus, attacking unequal wealth in all its forms, not only monetary. It begins with those who have no property, those deemed not to have properties, the social scum rejected by Marx and Engels.

Conclusion

Democracy is improper. Intrinsic to the definition of democratic politics is both the improper and impropriety. This means that democratic politics has no proper object. Democratic practices put in to question the very notion that there might be an appropriate object corresponding to the ideal of democratic equality. This includes not only the forms of propriety associated with political regimes but also the regimes of property guaranteed through the exercise of violence. For at least three decades now, democratic theorists have ignored the politics of property and taken for granted its role in preserving inequality. We must stop characterising such proprietary regimes as democratic. Instead, we should consider the state as overdetermined, criss-crossed by a multitude of practices and logics, some of which tend towards the enactment of equality. This requires that we rethink the idea of the state as a unified monolith. An improper politics begins with the regime of property dominant now. This regime is a structured totality, always contingent, which reifies certain behaviours, and delimits the forms of the proper. Dissensus begins with those who break the bounds of the proper. It is often located at the margins where those bounds are maintained. The delineation of a proprietary regime as a critical theoretical exercise specifies its borders and indicates the moments of trespass and transgression which suggest other ways of being, which fashion other worlds. Such an improper account of democratic theory is no longer Marxist in any strict sense, but it begins with the question bequeathed to us by Marx: the question of who owns and controls the means whereby we reproduce our lives, and how we might disrupt such demarcations of the proper. Democracy is enacted under only one presupposition: all are equal. This is a dangerous supposition precisely because it knows no proper limit.

SIX

Transnational Populist Politics

The People or the Demos?

1. In the early 1990s, following protracted civil war, Yugoslavia split up into the now independent states of Slovenia, Croatia, Serbia, Montenegro, Macedonia and Bosnia. Yugoslavian citizenship ended. In Slovenia, the first state to declare its independence, everyone who lived in the territory had the choice of becoming a Slovenian citizen or leaving. Citizenship status came with the award of passports, registration of birth and death, the right to work, taxation and the like. A number of Yugoslav citizens either refused to adopt Slovenian citizenship or were denied citizenship. Eventually those deemed not truly Slovenian were moved onto a Register of Aliens, a total of nearly 25,000 people. Some insisted that they were Yugoslavian; others were deemed Serb, Croat or Bosnian. These so-called aliens suffered symbolic and civic death. They were erased from the Register of Permanent Residents of Slovenia (Vezovnik 2013). They could not legally die, claim property title, could not travel or work legally. In effect they became invisible to the Slovenian state and its functionaries. They were deemed aliens despite having no residence elsewhere. The articulation of a Slovene people required these exclusions, but also these forms of registration, affiliation and symbolic identification.

2. In November 2017, Albert Thompson checked in to his local National Health Service hospital for radiotherapy treatment of prostate cancer. On leaving, he was presented with a bill for £54,000. The UK Home Office said he could not prove his citizenship. The ensuing debate concerned whether or not Mr Thompson, who had lived in the UK for forty-four years, qualified as a citizen. He arrived a few months after the so-called 'Windrush' generation. This legal dispute over his citizenship status might have resulted in his death. In March of 2018 Theresa May refused to intervene, but after much publicity he was finally offered free care six months

after the initial diagnosis. What the subsequent debate ignored is that thousands of so-called illegal immigrants – as well as those who have worked in Britain on temporary work visas – are refused care, deemed not to be of the people, unless they can afford to pay the full cost of care.

3. The election of left wing populists across Latin America in the 2000s saw the implementation of policies of national popular development. In the case of Argentina, this included the extension of social welfare programmes, investment in education and infrastructural development funded by the global sale of primary commodities, notably soya beans. The commodities consensus prioritised the 'interests' of the national people. This meant deforestation to enable the planting of soya beans and open plan mining for oil in Patagonia. The Mapuche peoples protested. They argued that these were their lands, stolen during colonial interventions. The Mapuche peoples claimed to be a nation on equal footing with the Argentine nation. Meeting with Mapuche leaders, Cristina Fernandez de Kirchner responded thus to their demands:

> you use cell phones. You are not opposing this. If I find oil in my country it is better for everyone – and maybe we have to bring those comrades who are there to another place exactly with the same characteristics and conditions . . . we cannot stop extracting petroleum because we need it for our development. (Savino 2016: 411)

In each of these cases, the articulation of a people limits the equality of some. In the first case, the very notion of the people is problematised at the moment of the 'legal' founding of the Slovene state. The contingent articulation of who is and who is not properly of the people saw 25,000 Yugoslavs rendered stateless – and improper in relation to the state. They had no legal right to own property and no place in the proprietary order regulating the passage from birth, through life to death. In the second case the figure of the illegal immigrant is deployed (wrongly as it turned out) to determine provision of health care for those deemed of the body politic. Determining who counts as a member of the people renders some bare life, *zoe*, policed as bodies included in a police order through their exclusion. In the third case the articulation of Argentinian populism is premised on attacking the worldviews, ways of life, attitude to the environment and epistemologies of indigenous peoples. The 'decolonial' claim traces an arc of continuity that links populist nationalism to colonial dispossession. The national populisms of Latin America are viewed as elemental to an ongoing process of colonial exploitation, rather than as post holders for a global left.

The examples that frame this chapter destabilise the common leftist celebration of populist politics whether in Argentina, Spain or South Africa. Despite this, I reject those critics who dismiss populism as necessarily racist, nationalist and reactionary. I make three improper arguments. First, populism is only contingently democratic. If 'the' people are made not given (Laclau 1993) then the contingent articulation of different identities, demands and movements into a common political project *may* frame the people as democratic. This is not though necessary. The thinking of a democratic populist politics refuses to equate the people and the demos. When populists articulate a proper nation, they all too quickly defend anti-democratic and racist policies. I thus distinguish the term demos from the people with their respective Greek and Latin roots. Historically they signified quite different forms of politics. I begin with the simplest question: what is meant by the word 'people'? Insisting on the importance of the generic notion of people, without qualification, allows me to rethink populism as improper, and out of step with nationally defined notions of a people. Second, I question the ontological account of populism and identification, developed by Laclau and his interlocutors. I contend that this reintroduces a politics of the proper, policing what counts as truly political. Viewing populism as one possible political logic allows us to distinguish populist logics from democratic practices – and to think a populist logic that is democratic. I draw a radical distinction between populist forms of political equivalence and the logics of financial equivalence outlined in Chapter 4. Third, I think of populism in transnational terms, abusing concepts developed by queer theorists. Only a transnational populism is democratic. Transnational logics dominate the world in which we live – whether this be in terms of global property regimes; production and distribution networks of global trade; movements of people in response to war; climate change and dispossession; or an emergent global demos that contests inequality. National populisms inadequately address these financial and political logics. I speculatively propose a transnational populist politics – a populist politics that is strategically necessary, yet has the virtue of extending the democratic logics discussed in previous chapters. I begin by contextualising the populist moment.

Contextualising the Populist Era

In December 2015, Mauricio Macri was elected President of Argentina. Global financial markets and neoliberal governments welcomed his election across the world. At the time Paula Biglieri and I had just begun a three-year research project about transnational forms of populist politics. We aimed to map the range of leftist populisms in Europe and in Latin

America, and to think a transnational people beyond 'the people'. Macri's election anticipated a radically different politics. In rapid succession Duterte in the Philippines, Trump in the USA and Bolsonaro in Brazil were elected to power. Macri's win marked a period of electoral losses for, and juridical gerrymandering against, the populist left across Latin America. At the same time, populist politics took on darker tones in Europe. If in 2015 Podemos and Syriza promised to change European politics – refusing to buckle to the pressure of global financial elites – right wing populists now reframe race, nation and masculinity against both financial elites and left wing critics of patriarchal and racist politics. Right wing populisms unite around a few core principles: nativism (a defence of the nation against interlopers, immigrants, groups deemed foreign to the imagined community, sometimes foreign capital); social conservatism (against a perceived cultural elite committed to multiculturalism, feminism, and the extension of civil liberties and rights to all); and different forms of national (welfare) chauvinism. Such populisms are easy to condemn but quick condemnation misses the political promise that the right has stitched together into a national popular will – often on transnational terms. Chantal Mouffe is right to argue that the context of these populisms is the post-democratic regimes that hollowed out popular sovereignty, public life and social democratic ideals. She is also right to argue that these right wing populisms should not be ignored – the political question is how to rearticulate precarity for a leftist project, rather than in racist terms (Mouffe 2018).

Right wing populism has as its primary antagonist the proprietary order we know as neoliberal. Neoliberalism is more than an economic logic. It has remade key demands of the post-1960s left. When consistent, neoliberal spokespersons reject discrimination based upon the contingent properties ascribed to, or claimed by, people. Instead, they insist on the inherent justice of abstract market logics – which in themselves do not discriminate. Milton Friedman famously contended that capitalism punishes racism and sexism (Friedman 2002: 111) without the need for state intervention. As has been repeatedly noted, however, neoliberals also recognise that the market is not natural (Mirowski 2013). The state is recruited to secure the flourishing of the market and protect property. This is compatible with the introduction of formal logics of measurement that appear to protect against discriminatory practices. Note as just one example the diversity and inclusion policy of Barclays Bank:

> We aim to foster a culture where individuals of all backgrounds feel confident in bringing their whole selves to work, feel included and their talents are nurtured, empowering them to contribute fully to Barclays vision and

goals. We have five global pillars of focus: Disability, Gender, LGBT (Lesbian, Gay, Bisexual & Transgender), Multicultural and Multigenerational. (https://home.barclays/who-we-are/our-strategy/diversity-and-inclusion/)

Such commitments are cast in market terms – enabling the best, developing talent, fostering competition without discrimination – in line with the anti-discriminatory policies enshrined in law. Neoliberalism also expects active intervention in markets to secure them against collapse – as happened after the 2008 financial collapse. Neoliberal practices thus extend measurable logics of valuation to every realm of life. They recast the terms inherited from our common democratic heritage: equality becomes equivalence; liberty the freedom to pursue one's goals as a self-investing subject; and democratic accountability a form of accountancy. Wendy Brown's *Undoing the Demos* (2015) sets out the logic underlying this political rationality. It entails the valuation of every possible domain in monetary terms, the interpellation of subjects as objects of self-investment, and the invention of accountancy procedures to measure everything. However, Brown, perhaps overly influenced by its US iteration, misses the nominal neoliberal rejection of explicit prejudice and discrimination. Brown is right: the logics she reconstructs entrench historic forms of discrimination, rather than address them. But Neoliberal governments give legal form to gay marriage, engage in anti-racist campaigning, account for environmental damage, protect free speech – and neoliberal spokespersons happily condemn the xenophobia of Donald Trump or Rodrigo Duterte. The European Union, for example, rearticulates gender equality as a form of measurable bio-political governmentality and measurement (Repo 2015). The commitment to gender, ethnic, race and disability rights goes hand in hand with the deployment of statistical measures to evaluate the human resource policies of all organisations. Equalities benchmarking is the leitmotif of every public and private organisation.

Inevitably, such policies betray the substantive equality they promise – but they allow organisations and governments to deploy a veil of formal equality even as they entrench existing inequalities. The logic of the market sustains the abstract equality of all in the social world while relying on the private community of property where inequality reigns. Neoliberal identity politics supports the extension of abstract civil rights to all. However, this abstract formal equality is the other face of economic inequalities sustained and deepened with the outsourcing of government, and the withdrawal of welfare support. Neoliberalism thus articulates the left's insistence on civil equality and freedom with a market logic that recognises no prejudices other than one's fitness to prevail in a competitive market. Identity politics find its denouement in the corporate training manuals that propagate the equality of all, regardless of markers of difference. I noted above that unlike classic laissez-faire liberalism the contemporary proprietary order has no problem with a strong state – a state that interpellates subjects as self-investing, views welfare as workfare, extends security and policing practices, and outsources all possible activities to the private sector in whose interests it then intervenes. Neoliberalism treats every subject as abstractly equivalent and does so clothed in the post-1968 ideal that anyone can live the life they wish, if only they work hard enough. Richard Branson is their mascot. Although rarely characterised as populist, neoliberals too articulate an image of the citizen and the people. Good citizens are responsible. They invest in their futures and do not act as a drain on the resources of the nation. They treat their bodies and minds as investment opportunities and take on the opportunity costs needed to realise their potential – ranging from yoga to paying for their funerals before death. The neoliberal 'responsibilised' subject (Brown 2015) is an abstract ideal. In a manner reminiscent of Freud's notion of the ego ideal, it punishes a subject that must constantly fail. Imprisonment and workfare are the alter ego of the subject that must look after itself, at any cost.

Viewed in this light right wing populism makes sense. It rejects both aspects of neoliberal proprietary order. First, it explicitly rejects the extension of the market to every aspect of life, insisting that states should intervene for the national people. This may take the form of welfare chauvinism, but it could mean embracing private sector investment and market politics within the borders of the nation. This entails restrictive trade barriers deemed to be in the true national interest as, for example, in Hungary. Right wing populists, second, reject the extension of civil and political liberties to immigrants, gay men and women, feminist activists, environmentalists and transgender people – the key elements of the so-called new left – in the name of the people, normality, civilisation, what is proper, 'reason'. Such policies indirectly confirm what Nancy Fraser has long insisted: the left should challenge inequalities organised around both wealth and identity (Fraser 2000). In supporting an end to all forms of prejudice – but without extending this to material equality in areas such as housing, income, wealth and property – third way political parties prepared the space for the intervention of right wing populists committed to welfare chauvinism.

Neoliberals and neoconservatives do have one thing in common: both advocate a strong state. They rely on winning sovereign power to force through their political will. Whether this takes the form of the British and American state bailing out private banks with taxpayers' wealth; or the Hungarian and Polish governments cutting state support to organisations which support refugees, and restricting news organisations with liberal or leftist leanings – the state deploys sovereign powers to reinforce inequality. The neoliberal and the neoconservative right thus adapt different aspects of the traditional left agenda for their own ends. Redistributive policies become, for neoconservatives, a form of welfare chauvinism. For neoliberals civil liberties are articulated as market freedoms. In securing these ends, sovereign power, won in elections, is reshaped – either on terms complicit with the global rules of so-called fair trade, or to police the appropriate bounds and identities of national orders. In each instance, the relationships between markets, national identity, civil freedom and state power are differently articulated. However, a set of common strategies pass between states, virus like. Neoconservatives blame refugees for taking the jobs of real citizens. They condemn political elites – both financial and cultural – for extending freedom in an immoral manner. They aim to purify the body politic of foreign elements characterised as leeches on the true body of 'the people'. They restrict the gains in equality won in environmental, gender and anti-racist struggles over decades. Let me then state the obvious. Democratic politics reclaims the language of equality from these interlopers. It commits to material equality, to equality in terms of identity and lifestyle, to the redistribution and decentralisation of sovereign powers, and recognises no borders to the people. The question I now ask is if a democratic populist politics is still possible.

Democracy and Populism

Populism raises the simplest of political questions: who is of the people? I argued in previous chapters that democratic politics has no definitive answer to this question. Any definition of the people, demarcated by what-ever principle, will undermine democracy insofar as it justifies exclusion. But what does this simplest of words, 'people', signify? The word 'people' is of Latin, rather than Greek origin. In the Roman world, the *populus* had two references: all members of the Roman people or the plebs, the poor. In the centuries long struggle, after 500 BC, termed the 'Conflict of the Orders' by Roman historians, plebs struggled against patrician power for political equality. Plebian protests included collective walks out of the city (*secessio plebis*), the insistence that plebs be permitted to stand for all official posts, and ongoing resistance to debt slavery. Livy records that in the first seces-sion of 495/494 BC the plebs retreated to the Mons Sacer refusing to work in the city (Livy 1960: 136–8). The patrician classes had refused to pass debt relief measures, overly influenced by property and debt holders. Forced to compromise the patricians agreed to the election of people's tribunes and to debt relief. Over 200 years later in 287 BC, in reforms reminiscent of those of Solon in ancient Athens, debt slavery was abolished.

These disputes are the basis of contemporary theoretical distinctions between the people as all citizens, the people as the oppressed or excluded, and the plebs as the hegemonic stand-in for the people (Rancière 1999: 9; Laclau 2005: 93–4; Agamben 2009: 31). Agamben, for example, notes a fundamental ambiguity in the term people. It oscillates between the people as a whole, unfragmented body politic, and the people as the multiplicity of needy bodies unified and simultaneously excluded within the body politic. The term 'people' on this reading includes within its conceptual architecture the *fundamental* bio-political fracture between *bios and zoe* (Agamben 2009: 32). Laclau reads this fracture as indicative of the hegemonic logic whereby the part (the plebs) claims to be the whole. In this case, a part of the 'people' presents itself as if it is the people. This division indicates for Laclau a fundamental break in the communitarian space of the people. The people is a contingent political term only stabilised through political articulation (Laclau 2005: 94 and 224). Rancière, last, reads this fracture more positively. He argues that the fracture of the communitarian space opens the possibility of an equality without qualification being put to work by the plebs. It is their 'improper property' (Rancière 1999: 8). I discussed these improper properties at some length in Chapter 2.

However, the Roman world, stretching from the Himalayas to North Africa and Britain, was riven by another clash: this concerned who counted as a citizen of the Empire. As an ever-expanding empire Rome had to address the citizenship claims of other peoples. Citizenship was variegated. Rome distinguished full citizens from those with limited citizenship rights, and from those protected under treaty obligation. Eventually in AD 212, the Edict of Caracalla extended citizenship to all free men of the Roman Empire. Overnight 30 million 'provincials became legally Roman' (Beard 2016: 527). There were then three competing registers in which the Roman term *populus* was used: first, it referred to all Romans; second, it referred to the plebs as stand in for the people; and third it extended to include all other peoples – without qualification – of the ever-expanding empire. These peoples demanded rights of citizenship. This third sense alludes to the generic meaning of the term people in all Latin languages. It can signify all of humanity, regardless of language, ethnicity, national status, age, sex, gender or any other contingent property. It is the addition of qualifiers that modifies and delimits who counts as of the people. This generic notion of the people is most compatible with the radical idea of 'demos' discussed in Chapter 5. It presupposes no natural or social distinction between human beings. In this sense people is the plural of human being – not of person or citizen. Personhood is a legal category distinguishing subjects capable of owning objects from the things that may be owned and disposed of. As the example of Slovenia makes patently obvious citizenship is a politically contingent construct. Most people will never experience this contingency – but for millions of people every year citizenship is withdrawn, contested, stolen or disavowed.

The term people is most often used today in the qualified sense to refer to a specific people, conventionally defined as a nation. In some instances, the nation may not yet exist though its recognition is demanded. This includes, for example, the cases of the Basque, the Kurds and the Palestinians. This notion of the people draws distinctions between human beings. It presupposes that there are ways of determining who and who does not belong – normally premised on contingent features about people including place of birth, religion or heritage. This must exclude some from the privileges accorded to 'proper' citizens. Within nations, it tends to be associated with specific parts of the social order – an economic, religious, gendered or racial elite. As Ernest Renan noted in 1882 such ideas of a people effect unity through brutality and forgetting. His words are worth quoting at length:

> Forgetting, I would even say historical error, is an essential factor in the creation of a nation and it is for this reason that the progress of historical studies often poses a threat to nationality. Historical inquiry, in effect, throws light on the violent acts that have taken place at the origin of every political formation, even those that have been the most benevolent in their consequences. Unity is always brutally established. The reunion of northern and southern France was the result of a campaign of terror and extermination that continued for nearly a century. (Renan 1992: 3)

Unlike contemporary theorists of populism (Laclau 2005) Renan invokes history to animate the violence of national unity – and by extension to any articulated notion of a people. When boundary theorists such as Song assert that political solidarities are impossible unless the 'demos' constituted by a set of overlapping solidarities is bounded in terms of membership and territory (Song 2012), they blithely ignore the violence constitutive of such solidarity. Laclau's account of populism as a political logic does indicate the possibility of configuring the people in terms other than nation. Unfortunately, every example he deploys concerns the articulation of a national people, an articulation that presupposes undemocratic forms of exclusion. The contingency of the elements configured to make a people is acknowledged, but the sediment of nation remains as the seedy underbelly of populist politics – even for this post-Marxist theorist (Laclau 2005). Such authors underplay the possible universality of a word which points beyond any specific denomination or articulation.

This generic notion is only ever used to draw a distinction between species. Can we imagine a populism sensitive to this excessive universality, a universality without distinction?

Laclau comes close to recognising this tension. His starting assumption is that the people is not a given: 'there is no ultimate *substratum*, no *nature naturans*, out of which existing social articulations could be explained'. Populism places us on the terrain of 'contingent political articulations' and the construction of collective (popular) wills (Laclau 2005: 169–73). Any constituted version of the people is inhabited by a certain impossibility – once articulated it can only be maintained if its boundaries are policed, or perhaps extended, in response to demands in excess of the form it now takes. I spoke above of the Mapuche peoples' struggles in Patagonia. While these may appear as sub-national they depend on acts in excess of the constituted notion of the Argentinian people. The Mapuche, in being forced to describe themselves as a people, play upon all three declensions of the term. They make demands as an oppressed group. They insist that they are a nation like any other. And they insist that they are acting as people to whom the same recognition should be extended as to every other human. I take some distance from Laclau's ontological reading of populism but this should not blind us to the central contribution of his work. He insists that a people is the result of articulation of different demands, movements and identities – into a common popular front. The limits of a people is not established in advance of political struggle, and the appeal to a people is always antagonistic – framing unity in opposition to a common enemy. For the present the only difference I would insist upon is that the notion of 'people' also contains a promissory note – imagining a transnational people without exclusion. This is a promise that national populisms attempt to contain in delineating their proper bounds.

It is in Laclau's work too that the tensions between populism and democracy are at their most acute. In *On Populist Reason* he writes:

> Empty signifiers can play their role only if they signify a chain of equivalences, and it is only if they do so that they constitute a 'people'. In other words: democracy is grounded only on the existence of a democratic subject whose emergence depends on the horizontal articulation between equivalential demands . . . So the very possibility of democracy depends on the constitution of a democratic people. (Laclau 2005: 170)

Democracy coincides with the articulation of the people – as democratic. This suggests that it is possible to articulate a people on terms that are not democratic. Earlier in the same text, Laclau argues that populism is a political logic without substantive content. On these terms then the articulation of a people as democratic requires an additional logic. Democracy is not the same as the logic of equivalence that articulates a people. What role does this supplement – democracy – play in Laclau's interpretation of populism if populism is the royal road to the Political? Laclau is uncertain. At one point, he equates democracy with institutional logics in which demands are dealt with by a regime. In other arguments he, and Mouffe, characterise democracy as the articulation of logics of equality and liberty.

Democracy presupposes the extension of equality, a substantive equality, which is not simply about the articulation of equivalent demands. To put the point differently – some demands are never democratic even if they have the signifier 'democratic' attached to them. Laclau contends that democracy requires equivalence between different demands, and that the articulation of a democratic subjectivity is contingent. However, if democracy has no proper place, if it demands an equality without equivocation, then certain demands are not democratic even when voted for by citizens – the exclusion of migrants from a territory; reductions in taxation for the wealthy; and anti-Islamic nationalist campaigns such as those carried out by Gert Wilders in the Netherlands are but three examples. It is insufficient to say that demands are democratic if articulated as such – this would render the ideal of democracy meaningless leaving democratic politics in the hands of those who hegemonise the word – regardless of how they act. Nor should we assume that the notion of 'the people' is inherently democratic. National populisms extend democracy for some at the expense of others. We know all too well the extraordinary violence that has accompanied ideas such as the 'Volk', the white race, Europeans or the true American people.

There is then no mystery: democratic populism enacts the equality of all, without qualification, here and now. As a practice, democracy cannot respect the conventional demarcations of the people in terms of nation, polis, the union of nations or even of a continent, as in a certain rendering of Bolivarism in Latin America. It will be objected that such a version of democratic populism undermines the very possibility of politics. It renders democracy a pitiful protest against domination because it is suspicious of a populist politics that draws antagonistic boundaries. I think the reverse is the case. Democracy assumes that even opponents are of the people – and it fights any attempted limitation of democratic politics. A populism committed to equality fights against those who traduce equality, but also against its own tendency to discipline equality in the name of an ideal configuration of the people. National populisms limit democratic equality. They determine, through a principle of common identity, how different lives are to be accounted for. Today not only a territorial border police draws such borders.

Rather, what we might term 'bordering' includes finely tuned algorithms to account for, value and differentiate between lives. Such algorithmic controls determine how best to enclose and regulate everybody. Democracy, however, is not accountable. It may be convoked anywhere, at any time, below, beyond and within what we think of as political regimes. It might be asserted in the family or in a neighbourhood; in a school ground or in a public square; in the United Nations General Assembly or on a university board. There is no proper people, no demos, proper to the exercise of this capability. Because there is no proper place for the exercise of democratic power its convocation unsettles the antagonistic bounds that structure the articulation of a people.

Let me draw some preliminary conclusions. Democracy marks equality without respecting the markers of identity that limit equality. Demands which are democratic convoke the equal power of the people. Demands that draw an unjustifiable limit on who constitutes the people are not democratic. In determinate circumstances, this is extraordinarily complex – the same demand might be interpreted in wholly different ways. Beginning with equality puts in to question national populisms, and the ways in which populist politics has been convoked to articulate national peoples. Acting democratically requires that we think of the people purely in the generic register of a humanity without limit. This reading represents a fundamental break with the dominant readings of populist politics – indeed it rejects populism as we have come to understand it. Before thinking a transnational populism, let me briefly indicate how this reading parts with the account developed by Laclau and his interlocutors.

Populism without Ontology

Laclau's conceptualisation of populism begins with the analyses of political struggles in Argentina during the late 1960s and culminates in his now classic 2005 text *On Populist Reason*. However, the explanation of populism in terms of a politics of identification limits democratic politics. I have already rejected the ontological fallacy that structures these arguments. This has direct implications for the discourse theoretical reading of populist politics. For Laclau heterogeneity is 'constitutive' of any social order. I read the improper as a political articulation of this argument. The Latin etymology is apposite – it links what is constituted (made to stand) to 'status'. The Latin verb *'sto'*, I stand, is the origin of the English words state and status. If the improper, or heterogeneity, is constitutive, it puts in to question that which has been made to stand – that which has status, as well as the state in its apparent unity. Heterogeneity entails that no social order is proper to itself, that no element of a social order may be conceptualised outside the set of relations that condition its possibility. However, Laclau conceptualises heterogeneity in ontological terms. Heterogeneity, he writes, has 'as one of its defining features a dimension of deficient being of failed unicity . . .' (Laclau 2005: 223) and 'unicity shows itself through its absence' (Laclau 2005: 224). There are two separate points made here although the transition is so quick that it is easy to miss. The first is that any social order is constituted as impossible. The second – which does not follow – is that this impossibility is present as an absence, as failed unicity, or as deficient being. A populist project is, on this reading, a contingent social construction in which a partial object comes to embody an impossible universality. It is thus that the people as the central category of politics become intelligible: 'a popular demand is one that embodies the absent fullness of the community' writes Laclau (2005: 225). Note this reference to absent fullness – now of the community. Populist identifications have a grip on subjects that is affective not merely conceptual. This partial object standing in for the whole becomes the object of identification for demands unfulfilled. His argument is explicitly ontological:

> whatever ontic content we decide to privilege in an ontological investment, the traces of that investment cannot be entirely concealed. The partiality we privilege will be the point that universality necessarily inhabits . . . because this ontological function can be present only when it is attached to an ontic content the latter becomes the horizon of all there is . . . the ontic and the ontological fuse into a contingent but indivisible unity. (Laclau 2005: 226)

Lacan's notion of the 'objet petit a' explains this operation: a partial object, a demand, comes to stand in for an impossible universality. When demands made to political authorities are dismissed, they may be rearticulated to a counter-hegemonic project, in which a particular object comes to stand in for an impossible universality. Thinking this in terms of the three declensions of the word people that I spoke of above might help to clarify the differences. For Laclau a partial object (let us say the plebs) comes to stand in for an impossible universality (the people), which cannot finally be signified. What Laclau terms the empty signifier is not a signifier without a signified. Rather it indicates that there is a constitutively unpresentable 'void within signification'. In a populist politics the impossible 'representation of emptiness' takes the form of the totalisation of the populist camp in which a partial content takes up the task of representing a 'universality with which it is incommensurable'. This articulation between particularity and (impossible) universality is sedimented in practices and institutions. It is not simply linguistic: 'hegemonic displacement' changes the 'configuration of the state . . . conceived of in the enlarged Gramscian sense as the ethico-political moment of the community'. All states will 'manifest the combination of particularity and universality which is inherent to the hegemonic operation' (Laclau 2005: 105–7).

The place of a generic universality here is slightly odd. On the one hand, it indicates a void in any discursive structure that requires particular forms of representation. These particulars, in order to reconfigure existing order, must draw boundaries determining who is and who is not of the people. Populism is articulated with 'the ethico-political' moments of community even as the community is in the final instance unpresentable. The idea of the people as a generic universality, a universality that puts in to question any particular version of the people is not included in this account. In part, this is because of the centrality of identification to the passionate commitments that constitute a people.[1]

The translation of this notion of identification into an account of populist politics is deeply problematic. It assumes that passionate identifications with a political cause are necessary to a hegemonic politics. It assumes that the identity of the subject is labile so that new identifications are possible, and can become the ground of political organisation. It assumes that hegemony is secured through the fixing of cathexes around a new hegemonic politics. But is the analogy between subjective and collective identification quite so easy to make? We began this account recognising the contingency of all proprietary order, a contingency cutting across all aspects of an over-determined social formation. Political identities are indeed labile but far more so than the psychoanalytic account of identification might lead one to think. The passionate attachments of the crowd are far easier to rearticulate than the fantasies that structure individual identity – and the easy confusion of the two makes for bad politics. This is a model of politics derived from the activist handbook. It presupposes the commitment of the activist – and transposes this to the social domain. It misses the banal fact that political hegemony rarely requires subjective identification. The hegemony of finance capital is secured through a range of mechanisms that the post-Marxist account of hegemony ignores. Equivalential relations are secured through the monetary form. The forms of networking and legality that secure trade do not demand identification. Participation in circuits of money, power and organisation abjures identification altogether. Transport networks configure differential forms of mobility and concentrate power in certain areas of the world. The control over space, territory and time does not require political identification. The forms of iteration that maintain institutional and bureaucratic orders are often unnoticed. The multiple ways in which life is accounted for – for example the credit scoring sys-tem – function regardless of identification. The rearticulation and reorgan-isation of these relations is the object of an improper politics. As I noted above Laclau recognises the importance of these institutional logics – but he underemphasises their importance in securing hegemony. He underesti-mates their banality and the horror of this banality.

When, then, Laclau argues that in populist forms of politics the being of the antagonists is at stake he immediately limits its scope. Antagonism can take different forms. It may be experienced as excess or as lack. It may not be noticed. It may be reconfigured in theological, ideological or political terms. Antagonism indicates that no social order can finally secure itself. This recog-nition does not require identification with empty signifiers, nor with univer-sals of any nature. It might be cause for retreat from all life in monastic form. It might, as Voltaire's (2014) *Candide* concludes, cause us to tend our gardens (if we have them) accepting the ultimate futility of any attempt to secure foundations. It may be wholly meaningless – irrelevant to the political and other decisions we make about, for example, the distribution of resources. It can, but does not have to, be rendered in ontological terms.

Laclau teaches us that the constitution of a people is a contingent pro-cess of articulation that is never complete. We must reject any confusion of this notion of populism with nationalism. National populisms ignore the equivalential mechanisms of contemporary global orders. These escape such nationalist narratives. It introduces exclusions that are undemocratic. It rearticulates and relies upon dominant forms of political order, often right wing, and the imaginaries associated therewith. It skews our vision, meaning that we cannot understand democratic challenges to national and global orders that do not take the form of collective identification.

There is, last, a particular assertion or play of power linked to the knowl-edge of the theorist of hegemony. Post-Marxist theorists engage in a form of ideology critique, despite their own protestations. Marchart, for example, relies on a politics of knowledge that is dominatory in form. He recognises that there can be no secure epistemological ground for a critical politics. Yet, he argues that all politics is ideological – it necessitates the disguise of an ontological impossibility that is nonetheless necessary. Social actors must assume ideological commitments. Marchart, the critic, is aware of this ideo-logical obfuscation. He knows that antagonism is irreducible. He can propose a radical democratic politics that is ethical not political. In Marchart's words: 'Only a saint or a Zen master . . . can float above the ideological . . . every-one else is walking knee deep in ideology . . . ideology negates the necessary category of contingency' (Marchart 2017). Ideology critique refers ideologies back to their own, ultimate groundlessness. The critic here becomes the Zen master. He knows that social order is contingent. Those poor souls knee-deep in ideology do not. Althusser relied on a distinction between science and ideology. It is hard not to see Marchart relying on a similar distinction – between those who know the ultimate contingency of all social relations, and those knee-deep in belief and ideology.

The reading of populist logics in ontological terms is politically dangerous. It replays logics of inequality in theoretical terms, vesting knowledge of what is truly the case in the master who knows that political identifications are in the last instance fallacious. It fails adequately to distinguish democratic forms of populist politics and does not distinguish equality from equivalence. Democracy is the ever-present disruption of the sediments of existing institutional forms, and of previous attempts to enact and police equality. Populism as radical and democratic breaks with the bounds of any established populous. It is transnational in impulse. This argument stretches populism to its very limits. It contrasts the people with the demos and views the demos as the counterpoint to any attempt to give an account of the people – the demos in this sense is unaccountable and uncounted. I thus accept Laclau's claim 'that the very possibility of democracy depends on the constitution of a democratic people' (Laclau 2005: 170). However, this requires that an adequate account of democratic as opposed to equivalential logics is developed. Such an account puts in to question any populist logic.

Transnational Populist Politics

A populism premised on the identification of the people, as opposed to people as a generic concept, risks undermining the democracy and the equality which it at the same time professes. Democracy is not equivalent to populism. A populism that is democratic addresses the extraordinary extension of inequality in relation to property, income and life chances across the globe. It does so in the name of a generic humanity, an equality without limit. Such a populism is transnational. It begins to imagine, as did the neoliberals in the 1950s, a different world order.[2] Let us think such an order against the dominant consensus.

Thinking the Transnational

I have argued that democratic equality requires the convocation of a people without limit. This demand may seem over the top, idealist, too ambitious. It follows from a recognition of the changed world we live in. Hegemony is exercised through global trade rules and practices, while wealth and inequality are protected outside the borders of the nation state. A democratic populist politics cannot become entangled in national logics which protect identity-based politics and insulate forms of solidarity that traduce equality. Such a notion of the demos compels us to ask if a 'transnational populism' is possible. Here I set out some initial thoughts about how this might be conceptualised. I avoid the obvious – transnational does not mean an alliance of nations (after all we cannot assume the identity of these nations), nor of different populist parties from specific nations working together. Rather, it suggests the calling in to being of the impossible – a people beyond the nation. We live in a world configured by a transnational *oikos*, by agreements that structure how we live. These accords range from climate regulations all the way down to what can count as property, what a module is at university, where humans beings can move across the planet. The threat of global environmental destruction in particular requires that we consider humanity as co-implicated in a precarious common life on this globe.

National democracies assume an accord between citizen identity ascribed at birth and the identity of the subject interpellated by that call into being. Let us take our cue from queer theorists. The 'trans' of transnationalism destabilises the easy fit between identity as citizen ascribed at birth and a transnation. This is a people struggling with translation beyond the ascriptions of nationalist politics. Jack Halberstam argues that Trans* points to an 'insufficiency of classificatory systems'. The solution is not to think in terms of ever more refined categorisations of identity. Rather it is to 'think in new and different ways about what it means to claim a body' (Halberstam 2018: 50). Halberstam rethinks the body as an architectural practice, made and remade, rather than given. This emphasises and 'represents the art of becoming, the necessity of imagining, and the fleshy insistence of transitivity' (Halberstam 2018: 136). The radical implication is a recognition of the queerness of all claims to the body, of all bodies.

A transnational populist politics, by analogy, is always in a state of becoming. It breaks with the simple ascription of citizen identity to bodies, and it thinks the body politic as a site of imagination and fleshy insistence. At the centre of Halberstam's questioning of too simple a politics of identity is naming. Naming is at the core of the state apparatus of capture undergone by every person deemed a citizen. The queering of populism undermines the proprietary control over the name now allocated to the national state. This has a number of secondary consequences. The image of populist politics is often tarnished with that of the strong man politician who comes to embody the nation. A transnational queered populism breaks the primordial articulation of nationalism to masculinity. This queering of nation accords with Laclau's basic insight concerning a radical heterogeneity at the heart of being. In queering the nation, we should remember the etymology of the word – nation originates in the Latin verb '*nasci*' – to give birth. The interpellation that bounds and binds birth to nation is what a transnational populism queers. It recognises that these institutional labels no longer attach so easily to bodies at odds with a community that can no longer secure its bounds; it begins to point to practices that disorder the no longer stable body politic, in the name of a people without proper name realised only as a presupposition. As queer studies quickly established, such processes of disordering can have extraordinary effects. We might echo questions posed by these activists. What laws apply to subjects whose sense of self no longer accords with the existing binding of the people? How do the binary distinctions between citizen and non-citizen police identity doing violence to those who do not fit the categories, and to those deemed appropriate to the categories? Is the body reducible to identities ascribed in practices that constitute and protect a people? The 'trans' of transnational focuses on the heterogeneity and multiplicity intrinsic to any notion of the people. It confuses the different declensions of the term putting an unqualified universality to work. This universality does not imagine all as the same. Rather it is open to an impossible infinity from the beginning.[3]

Rethinking Sovereignty

Neoliberals and neoconservatives are committed to the sovereignty of unified nation states; to the extension of policing and violence in the name of political order; to inequality; and to limited freedom. A transnational populism systematically challenges the extraordinary powers of exception vested in the sovereign state. The left, in all but its anarchist forms, accepts with the right that the winning of state and sovereign power is the central political question. Tax revenues, police powers, and bureaucracies of unprecedented size and scope grant to the holders of sovereignty the ability to remake the world. Nonetheless, participants in the electoral game accept democratic pluralism. They recognise that they may lose power to parties who disagree with their policies. This toothless pluralism, translated by democratic theorists into a formal ideal of constitutional pluralism, insists on a substantive neutrality about the good life. Rather than set out a substantive account of the good life, democratic theory recognises, according to Habermas, Mouffe and others, that there is no single notion of the good. Because substantive versions of the good life are contingent, authors in these traditions insist upon an irreducible pluralism, or an axiomatic pluralism, against all monism. This characterises deliberative accounts, Spinozist versions of the multitude and radical democratic accounts of hegemony. Pluralists argue that there is no common good. Any consensus about values is partial.

Democracy institutionalises pluralism, as its first principle, within a set of prior rules of the game – rules that include neutrality about what constitutes the good life.

Yet if this pluralism extends to all aspects of organised political life, including for example property, then there is a problem. There are many different accounts of a just system of property. However, the existence of a particular regime of property requires that some cannot participate on equal terms. If this is so then certain regimes of property are incompatible with democratic politics. Radical democrats respond that pluralism is axiomatic and ontological, and that while there are no a priori reasons for privileging one form of life over another, what prevails is the outcome of hegemonic political struggle. In the realm of ontological purity this may well be the case. However, any sort of radical democrat committed to pluralism must concur that regimes of property are antagonistic to a radical democratic politics. It is thus that most radical democrats insist on material redistribution.

However, there is a second problem with this liberal account of pluralism: it leaves intact the unity of sovereign power. Swallowing a toothless version of pluralism, the left has refused to redistribute sovereign power – the concentration of political authority in the executive powers of the state normally exercised by a president, prime minister and agencies of the state. This sovereign political power concentrates the collective ability of all to act. Whether of the left or right, political parties rarely question the integrity of the sovereign nation state. When, playing the game of pluralism, the right wins elections the prerogatives of the sovereign state are deployed to remake the world. In defence of democratic pluralism, leftist parties watch inert as right wing parties undo the limited forms of economic redistribution they once introduced. A radical democratic politics democratises both sovereign power and wealth. Taking pluralism to its logical conclusion requires the dilution of the sovereign power of central governments and the redistribution of these powers to local assemblies, cities and regions. Such a redistribution begins to address democratic demands that liberal, sovereign democracies can never address – to do so is to dissolve the very power that pluralists compete to control. Indigenous communities demanding restitution for historical wrongs could, on this count, take control of territory nationalised after colonial occupations; autonomist regions might have sovereign powers extended to them; and democratic powers may be exercised by the many who are normally excluded from access to power. Such redistributions of sovereign power would include the right to levy taxation in the name of wealth redistribution. Politically it would cement the democratisation of political powers that cannot be undone when right wing parties seize national power. To put this point differently: a populist politics that is democratic changes the very terrain, the rules, that structure the game of democratic politics. Neoliberal politicians have completely rewritten the rules that frame democratic politics, abusing sovereign authority and violence to secure market fundamentalism. A transnational populism then works both below and above the national state. It commits to the redistribution of wealth and political power. It rejects the concentration of the collective capability of all in the monarchical vestiges of executive power.

On these two counts, left wing populism is limited. Let me take an emblematic example. In *For a Left Populism* (2018), Mouffe celebrates the radical democratic potential immanent to the symbolic resources of the 'West'. On her reading, adapted from that of Schmitt, democratic liberalism articulates together two ultimately irreconcilable values. Liberalism emphasises the universal rights of all while '[democratic] equality requires the construction of a people and a frontier between a "we" and a "they"' (Mouffe 2018: 15). Mouffe thus links democratic equality with popular sovereignty and interprets democracy as the power of a defined people. While the people are constructed – not given in advance – such a construction recognises the libidinal investment in existing national communities (Mouffe 2018: 71). Mouffe is quick to acknowledge that national populisms are ambivalent. A leftist politics mobilises around 'patriotic identification with the best and more egalitarian aspects of the national tradition' (Mouffe 2018: 71). The key terrain of struggle is thus the sovereign national people. It is only when such a struggle is won across a range of countries that a more radically democratic politics might be envisaged.

I accept with Mouffe that any notion of a people is the result of contingent articulations. These always take place in the context of sedimented practices and identities. I am less comfortable with the all too easy equation of democratic equality with the sovereignty of a people. I am tempted to reverse her argument: democratic equality points beyond the limits of existing forms of nationally defined peoples. The commitment to liberal rights always requires recognition of citizenship in an established community. Mouffe is aware of this – but there is a tension between her insistence on the affective bonds necessary to the formation of a collective identity and the commitment to an equality without bounds. This is most pertinent when she contrasts right wing forms of national exclusivity that target immigrant communities, from left wing populism which articulates together the concerns of environmental, feminist, immigrant, working class and LGBT communities inter alia. Such a radical democratic citizenship, drawing on older traditions of civic Republicanism, is for Mouffe the basis of a leftist populism. However, this common identification with citizenship as a grammar of conduct restricts radical democratic politics. To put the same point slightly differently: the drawing of bounds around a people cannot but undermine the commitment to the equality of all. To insist that this is not problematic if similar forms of democratisation occur elsewhere is to miss the point. Inequality is not simply a matter of the relations between those within a particular nation. Rather the articulation of different national communities is simultaneously the establishment and deepening of relations of inequality with others. The maintenance of existing national communities replicates historical forms of injustice, of removals from land, of inequalities in the distribution and organisation of resource distribution. Sovereign forms of populism are not the solution – they replicate these forms of inequality.

Remaking Global Finance

If the redistribution of sovereign power is central to any future populist politics so too is a limitation on the powers of financial capital. Three immediate changes would alter the financial architecture of the globe. First, all tax havens including the City of London should be subject to global common laws regulating finance. Second, the US Federal Reserve should be nationalised. It is not commonly known that the Federal Reserve is owned by private banks who appoint six members of the nine-member board. US economic and global financial policy is controlled by private finance. Third, we should begin where Solon began: global debt as well as individual debts should end in recognition of the histories of dispossession that are the pathway to a politics of debt.

It may seem contradictory to call for the redistribution of sovereign power while insisting on a remaking of global regimes of finance. The reverse is the case. The global banking system is the other face of sovereign political power. Without existing forms of sovereign power, it would lose its institutional infrastructure. Sovereignty, finance and debt presuppose each other. Financial capital has captured the state. It relies on captive national populations to underwrite the debts that structure the global economy. National and global debts are cashed in against the lives of citizens accounted for, measured and valued. Nation states secure the property rights of private corporations and some individuals against most of humanity. As I argued in Chapter 1, nation states secure both territory and property. All nation states police these divisions – indeed this is the basis of sovereign political order. The remaking of sovereignty is simultaneously a retaking of democratic power against dominant forms of wealth and property. This form of politics begins with the political impulses of the present: demands of indigenous communities for the restitution of land; the global deregulation of borders; challenges to the sovereign prerogatives of the nation state by separatist and other movements; the growth of global cities often more powerful than nation states; and the recognition that climate change knows no borders. Democracy requires that we think of transnational democratic politics as no longer centred on the people but on the equal capability of all people.

Conclusion

Populist equivalence is not the necessary form that politics takes in response to a radical heterogeneity. It is one competing response among others. Populism is often a reaction to other forms of equivalence that dominate our everyday lives. These traduce the democratic inheritance we live with – quality regimes, financial equivalence, debt, accountancy and management. These forms of equivalence are the lifeblood of neoliberal hegemony. Those committed to democratic equality must begin to think of alternative mechanisms for the production, reproduction, distribution and organisation of our time, the spaces we occupy, the equality we presuppose. The demos stretches any notion of the people to breaking point. It extends our understanding of what power it is that a people may exercise when laying claim to be the demos. This, I have suggested, requires queering the 'trans' in transnationalism indicating the distance between the ascription of national identity and a transnational populism that redefines populism in democratic and queer terms.

CONCLUSION

Six stories animate this book. They range across time and space, linking the past to the present, thinking of the spaces we live in as haunted, improper to themselves. Each story unpicks aspects of contemporary proprietary ordering. Proprietary orders articulate together differences, differentially distribute precarity, and establish subject positions and forms of power. Hegemony is comprehensible only in light of this global distribution of precarity. The articulation of property and propriety cuts across the normal boundaries of nation and state. If we are to think the demos in terms of the enactment of equality then its reference point is this order – not the conventional bounds that define national peoples. Democracy I contend does not have a proper place. To think democracy is at the same time to challenge dominant relations of property, sovereignty and economic inequality. It requires that we consider how these sedimented orders of property and wealth articulate with other properties – the properties ascribed to human beings, or laid claim to, against these ascriptions. It requires that we think of democracy as the extension of equality to every realm. Such a politics is messy – it fits no box, does not conform to a theory, has no proper place. It reanimates the past genealogically restoring to our histories moments when equality as improper erupted. The occupiers in the City of London did exactly this. Such a politics is impatient. It does not wait for the future to come.

The stories I have told insist that democracy begins with the material organisation of property and propriety. They range from the politics of a brick, to the extraction of the coltan that makes global communication possible. In each case, bodies are at stake when democracy is enacted – the bodies of occupiers, of protesters, or of peoples whose sense of self is articulated in their relation to the land, to others, to themselves, to the dead – the different elements of the relational ontology sketched by Arendt. Democracy and equality do not stop, or even begin, with communication, free speech and discussion. They begin with a rejection of the differential distribution of precarity, a rejection of an order that privileges some bodies and lives, over others. Democratic politics challenges the forms of exclusivity that proper order introduces to our worlds.

NOTES

Chapter 1

1. Authors such as Cahan, Cohen and Althusser all in different ways insisted on the primacy of economic determination. In contrast Brenner, Offe and Meiskins-Wood and others aimed to develop more or less complex accounts of the relation between economic and political forces.
2. Marx developed his most sustained critique of representative democracy in a series of texts published in 1843 and 1844, responding to Hegel's *Philosophy of Right* and to Bauer's critique of the so called 'Jewish Question'.
3. For Marx, true universality would transcend the individual defined in terms of self-interest, and any system of political representation as conventionally understood. Representatives would be more like functionaries, equivalent to a shoe mender, who repairs your shoes but does not amend their size while doing so. In representative democracies the citizen is treated as if sovereign in the political realm, but her contingent existence constantly betrays this universality.
4. I do this work in Chapters 5 and 6, drawing in particular on recent interventions by Butler, Rancière and Balibar.
5. Rousseau is in fact summarising ongoing disputes about the origin of property, and the various legalistic and moralistic attempts to justify it.
6. See also Rancière on this: 'Man is not some future accomplishment beyond political representation. He is the truth hidden beneath this representation: man of civil society, the egotistical property owner matched by the non-property owner whose rights as a citizen are only there to mask radical non-right. The inability of citizenship to achieve man's true humanity becomes its capacity to serve, by masking them, the interests of man the property owner. Political "participation" is then just the mask of the allocation of lots. Politics is the lie about a reality that is called society. But, by the same token, the social is always ultimately reducible to the simple untruth of politics' (1999: 83). Rancière here echoes Marx's (1984) critique of liberal democracy in 'On the Jewish Question', but he stops short of thinking police orders as proprietorial orders.

7. Well-known as a theorist plagued by paradox, it is ironic that it is Rousseau who was most clear about this. His work vacillates between the argument that property is the source of all political evil, and his later attempt to legitimate it (Rousseau 1987b). The mythical history presented in Rousseau's second Discourse – which begins with a primitive condition in which there is little sense of the distinction between mine and thine; sees the emergence of society, families, the sexual division of labour, households and industry and results in what Rousseau termed *amour propre*; and finishes with the establishment of a civil order – tells a different story. The formation of civil society legitimates profound inequalities which arise in the articulation of private and *amour propre*: man's sense of self depends on the recognition of others, and property is one way in which this recognition might be achieved. Other authors have addressed the contradictions in Rousseau's account of property – contradictions which I do not propose to resolve. My point is instead a simple one: the paradoxes I talked about above arise because the founding of a political order is at the same time the founding of an order of property and propriety. The drawing of bounds around the appropriate demos is echoed within the bounds of a democratic regime, where properties are divided up and legitimated. The equality presupposed by democratic theory cannot be realised in an order which requires these forms of binding.

8. These arguments were developed in dialogue with Clare Woodford and will be published in an article 'Democratic theory: beyond the pale' (Woodford and Devenney forthcoming).

9. Habermas, for example, argues that the development of a social welfare paradigm within law recognised that legal freedoms were meaningless when actual freedom could not be exercised as a consequence of real inequalities. The transformation of bourgeois law in Western Europe thus resulted in a series of entitlements such as pensions, welfare provision and property. Both property law and contract law were, he notes, restricted to compensate for asymmetries in economic power. However, the social welfare model engenders a welfare state paternalism which impairs the individual autonomy it is supposed to encourage. The mistake with the social and the liberal paradigms of law is, he contends, that both focus on the question of how to ensure private autonomy. Neither sees the relationship between private and public autonomy as necessary, and thus both underplay the legitimacy derived from the forms of communication through which autonomy is expressed (Habermas 1996: 402–9). How might these basic rights be reconfigured within the deliberative framework? He argues that the welfare model views justice as distributive, while liberalism reduces justice to formal rights. The deliberative account of democracy recognises that 'the just distribution of social benefits is what results from the universalistic character of a law intended to guarantee the freedom and integrity of each' (Habermas 1996: 418). The extent to which these welfare benefits are required to meet the standards of autonomy, and thus of justice, is relative to specific situations and cannot be read off from an account of rights. Moreover, rights should be conceptualised as social relationships rather than as possessions, relationships which enable or constrain action.

While Habermas recognises that the consequences of material inequality are such as to damage the very possibility of participation as an equal, his critique of these legal paradigms does not ensue in a stronger account of the centrality of these economic rights. Indeed the promised analysis of these basic rights is barely realised in the last chapter of this text, and in later work he tends to treat problems of economic equality as issues to be resolved through deliberative procedures rather than as issues central to any account of the political. It is symptomatic of this shift from a balancing of the distributive and rights-based account of justice that in works published after *Between Facts and Norms* he never considers the living conditions that enable all to participate as equals.

Chapter 2

1. I have developed these arguments in many conversations with Clare Woodford about the differences between Laclau and Rancière.
2. The Latin word *passus* means step. The origin of the word trespass is to take a step into another's domain. However, there is another etymology for *passus*, as the perfect past participle of *patior*, meaning to suffer. This etymological uncertainty better captures what trespass in fact entails.
3. In 2015 Shell was found liable in the Hague court for oil spills in the Niger Delta. The case was brought by Friends of the Earth working with Nigerian activists against the oil companies.

Chapter 3

1. The only reference I can find to this work is in Davimes (2004).
2. Derrida writes: 'Yet if reading must not be content with doubling the text, it cannot legitimately transgress the text toward something other than it, toward a referent (a reality that is metaphysical, historical, psychobiographical, etc.) or toward a signified outside the text whose content could take place, could have taken place outside of language, that is to say, in the sense that we give here to that word, outside of writing in general. That is why the methodological considerations that we risk applying here to an example are closely dependent on general propositions that we have elaborated above; as regards the absence of the referent or the transcendental signified. There is nothing outside of the text [there is no outside-text; *il n'y a pas de hors-texte*].'
3. Josiah Ober (2008: 5) makes similar points, tracing the etymology and the uses of the term in Ancient Athens.

Chapter 5

1. Dahl suggested his own solution what he terms 'The Principle of Affected Interests' according to which '[e]veryone who is affected by the decisions of a government should have the right to participate in that government' (1970: 49).

2. I have recently written about this question with Clare Woodford (Woodford and Devenney forthcoming). I quote from our article here: 'A first set of theorists resolve the boundary problem on pragmatic, generally territorial, grounds. For them existing territorial or national boundaries (Saward 1998; Song 2012) express long standing cultures of democratic solidarity. For Song political solidarities are impossible unless the "demos" is bounded in terms of membership and territory. Territory is the focus for a "demos" constituted by a set of overlapping solidarities (Song 2012). Established democracies secure the rights and solidarities constitutive of democracy. She at no point considers the position of those outside the demos. Song also assumes that existing solidarities should be maintained, with no account of the violence intrinsic to most forms of solidarity . . . A second set of theorists accept that these contingent, often violent, histories have no necessary moral force. Rather, those affected by a decision, or subject to the coercive power of a state, constitute the appropriate demos . . . On this account "illegal" immigrants excluded by the actions of a state when securing its borders; those subject to imperial wars; or those affected by laws which regulate international trade regimes are members of the relevant demos. On both the coercion and the affected interests' accounts the boundaries of existing territorial regimes belie the fact that democratic claims exceed these boundaries. Instead they seek a general principle to guide us in delineating the appropriate demos. Their assumption is that democratic theory can discern a principle to demarcate legitimate from illegitimate manifestations of democratic power. Democracy is the means, not the end.
3. I have developed these arguments in an article with Clare Woodford titled 'Democratic theory: beyond the Pale' (Woodford and Devenney forthcoming).
4. See Woodford and Devenney forthcoming.
5. Demand is the basic unit of analysis in Laclau's theorisation of populism (Laclau 2005).
6. As I have noted in a previous chapter, Esposito traces the relation between persons and things back to Gaius' (1997) *Institutes*, a key to understanding the development of property law.
7. Marx developed his most sustained critique of representative democracy in a series of texts published in 1843 and 1844, responding to Hegel's *Philosophy of Right* and to Bauer's critique of the so called 'Jewish Question'.
8. For Marx, true universality would transcend the individual defined in terms of self-interest, and any system of political representation as conventionally understood. Representatives would be more like functionaries, equivalent to a shoe mender, who repairs your shoes but does not amend their size while doing so. In representative democracies the citizen is treated as if sovereign in the political realm, but her contingent existence constantly betrays this universality.
9. Clare Woodford and I have developed these arguments in an as yet unpublished article: 'Democratic theory: beyond the pale'.

Chapter 6

1. The concept of identification is most fully developed in Freud's second topography. It denotes two distinct processes: the first concerns identification as constitutive of the subject. Identity is built up through identifications with key figures, or parts of these figures, in the early years of a life. These primal identifications cast a spell over future identifications and are never simply forgotten with later identifications. They structure the form of those identifications without determining their form or content. Identification refers second to identifications of the self with another, part of another, or even an ideal, in later life. These identifications transform the subject who identifies an agency of the self with another and may incorporate this agency as part of the make-up of the self. Freud recognises that identifications constitutive of the subject are organised around an ultimately mobile cathexis. They are contingent because every child will have specific experiences of identification, and because such cathexes are never finally determinate of subjectivity. For the subject whose being is constituted on the basis of these primal identifications their exposure in the analytic situation is a wrenching of their being. It restores to these constitutive identifications their disorderly and conflictual nature, while never simply leaving the subject lost in this conflict. It is thus that Freud speaks of an ethics of the transference.
2. Mirowski (2013) studies the historical establishment, since the 1950s, of what he terms the neoliberal thought collective which in effect hegemonised economic thought, and established the boundaries within which public finance, taxation and investment could be conceptualised.
3. In this instance I conceptualise infinity in the terms outline by Badiou (2011) in *Being and Event*. However, for reasons that I hope this text has demonstrated I am dubious of any attempt to ontologise such a notion of multiplicity.

BIBLIOGRAPHY

Adorno, T. (1969) *Critical Models: Interventions and Catchwords*, New York: Columbia University Press.

Adorno, T. (1973) *Negative Dialectics*, New York: Seabird Press.

Adorno, T. W. and Horkheimer, M. (1985) *Dialectic of Enlightenment*, London: Verso.

Agamben, G. (1973) *Stanzas: Word and Phantasm in Western Culture*, Minneapolis: University of Minnesota Press.

Agamben, G. (1993) *The Coming Community*, trans. M. Hardt, Minneapolis: University of Minnesota Press.

Agamben, G. (1998) *Homo Sacer*, Stanford: Stanford University Press.

Agamben, G. (2009) *What is an Apparatus?*, New York: Stanford University Press.

Agamben, G. (2011) *The Kingdom and the Glory: For a Theological Genealogy of Economy and Government*, trans. L. Chiesa and with M. Mandarini, Stanford: Stanford University Press.

Agamben, G. (2014) 'What is a destituent power?', *Environment and Planning D: Society and Space*, 32, 65–74.

Agamben, G. (2015) *The Use of Bodies*, trans. A. Kotsko, Stanford: Stanford University Press.

Alaimo, S. (2010) 'The naked word: the trans-corporeal ethics of the protesting body', *Women & Performance*, 20: 1, 15–36.

Althusser, L. (1966) *For Marx*, London: Verso.

Althusser, L. (1969) 'Marxism and humanism', trans. B. Brewster in *For Marx*, London: Allen Lane.

Althusser, L. (1970) *Reading Capital*, London: Verso.

Althusser, L. (1971) *Lenin and Philosophy and Other Essays*, trans. B. Brewster, London: New Left Books.

Amnesty International Report (2016) 'Democratic Republic of Congo: "This is what we die for": Human rights abuses in the Democratic Republic of the Congo power the global trade in cobalt', <https://www.amnesty.org/en/documents/afr62/3183/2016/en/> (last accessed 24 June 2019).

Appiah, K. A. (2016) 'There is no such thing as Western civilisation', *The Guardian*, 9 November.

Arendt, H. (1981) *The Life of the Mind*, New York: Harcourt Publishers.

Aristotle (2000) *The Politics*, London: Penguin Classics.

Armitage, D. (2004) 'John Locke, Carolina and the Two Treatises of Government', *Political Theory*, 32: 5, 603–27.

Austin, J. (1962) *How To Do Things with Words*, Oxford: Clarendon.

Axelrad Cahan, J. (1994) 'The concept of property in Marx's theory of history: A defense of the autonomy of the socioeconomic base', *Science and Society*, 58: 43, 392–405.

Badiou, A. (2011) *Being and Event*, London: Continuum.

Badiou, A. (2018) *Greece and the Reinvention of Politics*, London: Verso.

Balibar, E. (2002) 'Possessive individualism reversed: From Locke to Derrida', *Constellations*, 9: 3, 299–317.

Balibar, E., Althusser, L., Establet, R., Macherey, P. and Rancière, J. (2017) *Reading Capital: The Complete Edition*, trans. B. Brewster and D. Fernbach, London: Verso.

Barkan, J. (2012) *Corporate Sovereignty: Law and Government under Capitalism*, Minneapolis: University of Minnesota Press.

Barkan, J. (2013) *Corporate Sovereignty: Law and Government under Capitalism*, Minneapolis: University of Minnesota Press.

Beard, M. (2016) *SPQR: A History of Ancient Rome*, London: Profile Books.

Bennington, G. (2016) *Scatter 1: The Politics of Politics in Foucault, Heidegger, and Derrida*, New York: Fordham University Press.

Bhandar, B. (2018) *Colonial Lives of Property*, Durham, NC: Duke University Press.

Bobbit, P. (2008) *Terror and Consent: The Wars for the Twenty-First Century*, London: Penguin Books.

Boucher, G. (2009) *The Charmed Circle of Ideology: A Critique of Laclau and Mouffe, Butler and Žižek*, Melbourne: Re-Press.

Brown, W. (2010) *Walled State, Waning Sovereignty*, New York: Zone Books.

Brown, W. (2015) *Undoing the Demos*, New York: Zone Books.

Brown, W. (2018) 'Neoliberalism's Frankenstein: authoritarian freedom in twenty-first century "democracies"', *Critical Times*, 1: 1, 60–79.

Burgis, T. (2015) *The Looting Machine: Warlords, Tycoons, Smugglers and the Systematic Theft of Africa's Wealth*, London: Harper Collins.

Butler, J. (1988a) *Gender Trouble: Feminism and the Subversion of Identity*, New York and London: Routledge.

Butler, J. (1993) *Bodies That Matter: On the Discursive Limits of 'Sex'*, New York and London: Routledge.

Butler, J. (1994) 'Against proper objects', *differences: A Journal of Feminist Cultural Studies*, 6: 2–3, 1–27.

Butler, J. (1997) *Excitable Speech: A Politics of the Performative*, New York and London: Routledge.

Butler, J. (1998) 'Left conservatism, II', *Theory and Event*, 2: 2.

Butler, J. (2004a) *Precarious Life: Powers of Violence and Mourning*, London: Verso.

Butler, J. (2004b) 'What is critique? An essay on Foucault's virtue', in S. Salih (ed.), *The Judith Butler Reader*, London: Basil Blackwell, pp. 302–22.

Butler, J. (2004c) *Undoing Gender*, New York: Routledge.

Butler, J. (2009a) 'Critique, dissent, disciplinarity', *Critical Inquiry*, 35: 4, 773–95.

Butler, J. (2009b) *Frames of War: When Is Life Grievable?* London: Verso.

Butler, J. (2010) 'Performative agency', *Journal of Cultural Economy*, 3: 2, 147–61.

Butler, J. (2015) *Notes toward a Performative Theory of Assembly*, Cambridge, MA: Harvard University Press.

Butler, J. and Athanasiou, A. (2013) *Dispossession: The Performative in the Political*. Cambridge: Polity Press.

Butler, J., Laclau, E. and Laddaga, R. (1997) 'The uses of equality', *Diacritics*, 27: 1, 2–12.

Butler, J., Laclau, E. and Žižek, S. (2000) *Contingency, Hegemony, Universality: Contemporary Dialogues on the Left*, London and New York: Verso.

Chambers, S. A. (2014) *Bearing Society in Mind: Theories and Politics of the Social Formation*, London: Rowman & Littlefield International.

Christophers, B. (2018) *The New Enclosure*, London: Verso.

Coetzee, J. M. (1999) *The Lives of Animals*, Princeton: Princeton University Press.

Cohen, G. A. (1995) *Self Ownership, Freedom, and Equality*, Cambridge: Cambridge University Press.

Collini, S. (2012) *What Are Universities For?* London: Penguin.

Cooper, M. (2017) *Family Values: Between Neoliberalism and the New Social Conservatism*, Cambridge, MA: Zone Books.

Copjec, J. (1996) *Read My Desire: Lacan against the Historicists*, Cambridge, MA: MIT Press.

Dahl, R. (1970) *After the Revolution? Authority in a Good Society*, New Haven and London: Yale University Press.

Dardot, P. and Laval, C. (2018) *Common: On Revolution in the 21st Century*, London: Bloomsbury Academic.

Davimes, S. (2004) 'Buffels and bullets', in S. Venter and C. Colart (eds), *Something to Write Home About*, Johannesburg: Jacana Books, pp. 94–6.

Dean, J. (2016) *Crowds and Party*, London: Verso.

Deleuze, G. (1988) *Foucault*, Minneapolis: University of Minnesota Press.

Deleuze, G. (1992) 'Postscript on the societies of control', *October*, 59, 3–7.

Deleuze, G. and Guattari, F. (1984) *Anti Oedipus*, London: Athlone.

Derrida, J. (1967) *Writing and Difference*, Chicago: Chicago University Press.

Derrida, J. (1976) *Of Grammatology*, trans. G. C. Spivak, Baltimore: Johns Hopkins University Press.

Derrida, J. (1978) *Writing and Difference*, Chicago: University of Chicago Press.

Derrida, J. (1994) *Specters of Marx*, London: Routledge.

Derrida, J. (1982) *Margins of Philosophy*, Chicago: Chicago University Press.

Derrida, J. (1985) 'Declarations of independence', *New Political Science*, 15, 7–15.

Derrida, J. (2002) 'Force of law: the "mystical foundation of authority"', in D. Cornell, M. Rosenfield and D. G. Carlson (eds), *Deconstruction and the Possibility of Justice*, London: Routledge.

Derrida, J. (2006) 'Performative powerlessness: a response to Simon Critchley', in L. Thomassen (ed.), *The Derrida Habermas Reader*, Chicago: University of Chicago Press.

Derrida, J. (2008) *The Animal That Therefore I Am*, New York: Fordham University Press.

Derrida, J. (2009) *The Beast and the Sovereign*, Chicago: Chicago University Press.

Devenney, M. (2004) *Ethics and Politics in Contemporary Theory*, London: Routledge.

Devenney, M. (2009) 'The limits of communicative rationality and deliberative democracy', *Journal of Power*, 2: 1, 137–54.

Devenney, M. (2011) 'Property, propriety and democracy', *Studies in Social Justice*, 5: 2, 149–65.

Devenney, M. (2019) 'The improper politics of representation', in L. Disch, M. van de Sande and N. Urbinati (eds), *The Constructivist Turn in Political Representation*, Edinburgh: Edinburgh University Press.

Disch, L. (2011) 'Toward a mobilization conception of democratic representation', *American Political Science Review*, 105: 1, 100–14.

Disch, L. (2015) 'The "constructivist turn" in democratic representation: a normative dead-end', *Constellations*, 22: 4, 487–99.

Easterling, K. (2014) *Extrastatecraft: The Power of Infrastructure Space*, London: Verso.

Ebila, F. and Tripp, A. M. (2017) 'Naked transgressions: gendered symbolism in Ugandan land protests', *Politics, Groups, and Identities*, 5: 1, 24–45.

Eileraas, K. (2014) 'Sex(t)ing revolution, femen-izing the public square: Aliaa Magda Elmahdy, nude protest, and transnational feminist body politics', *Signs*, 40: 1, 40–52.

Esposito, R. (2010) *Communitas: The Origin and Destiny of Community*, trans. T. C. Campbell, Stanford: Stanford University Press.

Esposito, R. (2015) *Persons and Things: From the Body's Point of View*, Cambridge: Polity.

Filmer, R. (2008) *Patriarcha; Or, the Natural Power of Kings*, London: Dodo Press.

Finkelman, P. (2012) 'Slavery in the United States: persons or property?' in J. Allain (ed.), *The Legal Understandings of Slavery*, Oxford: Oxford University Press.

Finley, M. (1953) 'Land, debt, and the man of property in classical Athens', *Political Science Quarterly*, 68: 2, 249–68.

Foley, D. (1983) 'On Marx's theory of money', *Social Concept*, 1: 1, 5–19.

Foucault, M. (1980) *Power-Knowledge*, Burlington: John Lutschak Books.

Fraser, N. (2000) 'Rethinking recognition', *New Left Review*, 3: 3, 107–18.

Friedman, M. (2002) *Capitalism and Freedom*, Chicago: University of Chicago Press.

Gaius (1997) *The Institutes of Gaius*, trans. W. M. Gordon and O. F. Robinson, London: Bloomsbury.

Glasman, M. (2014) 'The City of London's strange history: what the Romans did for London', *Financial Times*, 29 September, <https://www.ft.com/content/7c8f24fa-3aa5-11e4-bd08-00144feabdc> (last accessed 30 June 2018).

Gramsci, A. (2007) *Prison Notebooks*, London: Lawrence & Wishart.

Greer, A. (2012) 'Commons and enclosure in colonization of North America', *American Historical Review*, 117: 2, 365–86.

Gutmann, A. and Thompson, D. (2004) *Why Deliberative Democracy?*, Princeton: Princeton University Press.

Habermas, J. (1979) *Communication and the Evolution of Society*, London: Heinemann.

Habermas, J. (1996) *Between Facts and Norms: Contributions to a Discourse Theory of Law and Democracy*, trans. W. Rehg, Cambridge, MA: MIT Press.

Halberstam, J. (2018) *Trans**, Oakland: University of California Press.

Hardoon, D. (2017) 'An Economy for the 99%', Oxfam Briefing Paper, Oxford: Oxfam International.

Hardt, A. and Negri, M. (2000) *Empire*, Cambridge, MA: Harvard University Press.

Hardt, M. and Negri, A. (2009) *Commonwealth*, Cambridge, MA: Harvard University Press.

Hardt, M. (2010) 'The common in communism', *Rethinking Marxism*, 22: 3, 346–56.

Harris, C. (1993) 'Whiteness as property', *Harvard Law Review*, 106: 8, 1720–91.

Hayek, F. (1960) *The Constitution of Liberty*, Chicago: University of Chicago Press.

Honig, B. (2016) *Public Things: Democracy in Disrepair*, New York: Fordham University Press.

Keenan, S. (2014) *Subversive Property: Law and the Production of Spaces of Belonging*, London: Routledge.

Kioupkiolis, A. (2018) 'Commoning the political, politicizing the common: community and the political in Jean-Luc Nancy, Roberto Esposito and Giorgio Agamben', *Contemporary Political Theory*, 17: 3, 283–305.

Laclau, E. (1970) 'Argentina-imperialist strategy and the May crisis', *New Left Review*, 62, 3–21.

Laclau, E. (1977) *Politics and Ideology in Marxist Theory*, London: New Left Books.

Laclau, E. (1990) *New Reflections on the Revolution of Our Time*, London: Verso.

Laclau. E. (1993) 'Discourse', in R. A. Goodin and P. Pettit (eds), *The Blackwell Companion to Contemporary Political Philosophy*, London: Blackwell, pp. 431–7.

Laclau, E. (1994) 'Why do empty signifiers matter in politics?', in J. Weeks (ed.), *The Lesser Evil and the Greater Good*, London: River Oram Press.

Laclau, E. (2000) 'Identity and hegemony', in J. Butler, E. Laclau and S. Žižek (eds), *Contingency, Hegemony, Universality*, London: Verso, pp. 44–89.

Laclau, E. (2005) *On Populist Reason*, London: Verso.

Laclau, E. (2007) *Emancipation(s)*, London: Verso.

Laclau, E. (2014) *The Rhetorical Foundations of Society*, London: Verso.

Laclau, E. and Mouffe, C. (1985) *Hegemony and Socialist Strategy*, New York: Verso.

Lazzarato, M. (2012) *The Making of the Indebted Man*, Los Angeles: Semiotext(e).

Lazzarato, M. (2015) *Governing by Debt*, Los Angeles: Semiotexte.

Liberti, S. (2013) *Land Grabbing: Journeys in the New Colonialism*, London: Verso.

Livy (1960) *The Early History of Rome*, trans. A. de Selincourt, London: Penguin Classics

Locke, J. (1988) *Two Treatises on Government*, Cambridge: Cambridge University Press.

Lorey, I. (2015) *States of Insecurity*, London: Verso.

Losurdo, D. (2014) *Liberalism: A Counter-History*, London: Verso.

Macaskill, B. (1994) 'Coetzee's middle voice', *Contemporary Literature*, 35, 441–75.

MacDonald, L. (2009) *The Political Philosophy of Property Rights*, PhD thesis, University of Kent.

Malebranche [1680] (1992) *Treatise on Nature and Grace*, London: Clarendon Press.

Marchart, O. (2017) *Post-foundational Political Thought*, Edinburgh: Edinburgh University Press.

Marchart, O. (2018) *Thinking Antagonism: Political Ontology after Laclau*, Edinburgh: Edinburgh University Press.

Marx, K. (1956) *The Poverty of Philosophy*, London: Lawrence & Wishart.

Marx, K. (1975) 'Theses on Feuerbach', in *Early Writings: Marx*, London: Penguin Books, pp. 421–3.

Marx, K. (1976) *Capital: Volume 1*, trans. B. Fowkes, London. Penguin Harmondsworth.

Marx, K. [1844] (1984) 'On the Jewish question', in *Early Writings: Marx*, London: Penguin: pp. 211–41.

Marx, K. (2000) 'Preface to an introduction to the critique of political economy', in D. McLelland (ed.), *Karl Marx: Selected Writings*, London: Penguin, pp. 424–7.

Marx, K. and Engels, F. (1985) *The Communist Manifesto*, London: Penguin Classics.

Mbembe, A. (2003) 'Necropolitics', *Public Culture*, 15: 1, 11–40.

Mbembe, A. (2017) *Critique of Black Reason*, Durham, NC: Duke University Press.

Meintjes, S. (2007) 'Naked women's protest July 1990: we won't fuck for houses', in N. Gasa (ed.), *Women in South African History*, Johannesburg: HSRC Press, pp. 347–67.

Milios, J. (2009) 'Rethinking Marx's value-form analysis from an Althusserian perspective', *Rethinking Marxism*, 21: 2, 260–74.

Mirowski, P. (2013) *Never Let a Serious Crisis Go to Waste: How Neoliberalism Survived the Financial Meltdown*, London: Verso Books.

Mitchell, T. (2013) *Carbon Democracy*, London: Verso.

Montag, W. (2005) 'Necro-economics', *Radical Philosophy*, 134, 7–17.

Moseley, F. (2005) *Marx's Theory of Money: Modern Appraisals*, London: Palgrave Macmillan.

Mouffe, C. (2000) *The Democratic Paradox*, London: Verso.

Mouffe, C. (2005) *On the Political*, London: Routledge.

Mouffe, C. (2013) *Agonistics: Thinking the World Politically*, London: Verso.

Mouffe, C. (2018) *For a Left Populism*, London: Verso.

Munzer, S. (1990) *A Theory of Property*, New York: Cambridge University Press.

Norval, A. (2007) *Aversive Democracy*, Cambridge: Cambridge University Press.

Ober, J. (2008) 'The original meaning of "democracy": capacity to do things, not majority rule', *Constellations*, 15: 1, 3–9.

Ober, J. (2017) *Demopolis: Democracy Before Liberalism in Theory and Practice*, Cambridge: Cambridge University Press.

O'Connor, J. (2001) *Fiscal Crisis of the State*, Piscataway, NJ: Transaction Publishers.

Panagia, D. (2000) 'Dissenting words: a conversation with Jacques Rancière', *Diacritics*, 30: 2, 113–26.

Pierson, C. (2013a) *Just Property: A History in the Latin West. Volume 1 Wealth, Virtue and The Law*, Oxford: Oxford University Press.

Pierson, C. (2013b) 'Rousseau and the paradoxes of property', *European Journal of Political Theory*, 12: 4, 409–24.

Pierson, C. (2015) *Just Property: Volume Two: Enlightenment, Revolution, and History*, Oxford: Oxford University Press.

Plato (2007) *The Republic*, trans. D. Lee, London: Penguin Books.

Plato (2008) *Laws*, trans. B. Jowett, London: Clarendon Press.

Plutarch (1998) *Greek Lives*, Oxford: Oxford University Press.

Poulantzas, N. (1978) *Classes in Contemporary Capitalism*, London: Verso.

Primera, G. (2019) *The Political Ontology of Giorgio Agamben*, London: Bloomsbury.

Rancière, J. (1999) *Disagreement: Politics and Philosophy*, trans. J. Rose, Minneapolis: University of Minnesota Press.

Rancière, J. (2003) 'Comment and responses', *Theory and Event*, 6: 4, <http://muse.jhu.edu/journals/theory_and_event/v006/6.4ranciere.html> (last accessed 12 June 2018).

Rancière, J. (2004) *Philosophy and Its Poor*, Durham, NC: Duke University Press.

Rancière, J. (2007a) *Hatred of Democracy*, London, Verso.

Rancière, J. (2007b) *Dissensus: On Politics and Aesthetics*, London: Continuum.

Rancière, J. (2007c) *On the Shores of Politics*, London: Verso.

Rancière, J. (2010) 'Does democracy mean something?' in S. Corcoran (trans. and ed.), *Dissensus: On Politics and Aesthetics*, London and New York: Continuum.

Rancière, J. (2011) 'Democracies without democracy: an interview with Eric Hazan', in G. Agamben (ed.), trans. W. McCuaig, *Democracy in What State?* New York: Columbia University Press, pp. 76–81.

Renan, E. [1882] (1992) '*Qu'est-ce qu'une nation?*' (*What is a Nation?*), trans. E. Rundell, Paris: Presses-Pocket.

Repo, J. (2015) '"We're all princesses now": sex, class, and neoliberal governmentality in the rise of middle-class monarchy', *European Journal of Cultural Studies*, 18: 6, 741–60.

Rogan, E. (2009) *The Arabs: A History*, London: Penguin Press.

Rousseau, J.-J. (1987a) 'Discourse on the origins of inequality', trans. D. A. Cress, *The Basic Political Writings of Jean-Jacques Rousseau*, Indianapolis: Hackett Publishing Co., pp. 25–110.

Rousseau, J.-J. (1987b) 'On the social contract', trans. D. A. Cress, *The Basic Political Writings of Jean-Jacques Rousseau*, Indianapolis: Hackett Publishing Co., pp. 141–227.

Saramago, J. (1997) *All the Names*, New York: Mariner Books.

Sassen, S. (2014) *Expulsions: Brutality and Complexity in the Global Economy*, Cambridge, MA: Harvard University Press.

Saussure, F. (1995) *Course in General Linguistics*, London: Duckworth.

Savino, L. (2016) 'Landscapes of contrast: the neo-extractivist state and indigenous peoples in "post-neoliberal" Argentina', *The Extractive Industries and Society*, 3: 2, 404–15.

Saward, M. (1998) *The Terms of Democracy*, Cambridge: Polity Press.

Saward, M. (2006) 'The representative claim', *Contemporary Political Theory*, 5: 3, 297–318.

Saward, M. (2010) *The Representative Claim*, Cambridge: Cambridge University Press.

Saward, M. (2012) 'Claims and constructions', *Contemporary Political Theory*, 11: 1, 123–7.

Saward, M. (2016) 'Fragments of equality in representative politics', *Critical Review of International Social and Political Philosophy*, 19: 3, 245–62.

Schmitt, C. [1932] (1996) *Concept of the Political*, trans. G. Schwab, Chicago: Chicago University Press.

Schmitt, C. [1950] (2003) *Nomos of the Earth*, New York: Telos Press.

Searle, J (1989) 'How performatives work', *Linguistics and Philosophy*, 12, 535–58.

Shaxson, N. (2011) *Treasure Islands: Tax Havens and the Men Who Stole the World*, London: Bodley Head.

Sloterdijk, P. (1988) *Critique of Cynical Reason*, Minneapolis: University of Minnesota Press.

Song, S. (2012) 'The boundary problem in democratic theory: why the demos should be bounded by the state', *International Theory*, 4, 39–68.

Spengler, O. (1991) *The Decline of the West*, trans. C. F. Atkinson, Oxford: Oxford University Press.

Swift, L. (1979) 'Iustitia and ius privatum: Ambrose on private property', *American Journal of Philology*, 100: 1, 176–87.

Taylor, C. (1971) 'Interpretation and the sciences of man', *Review of Metaphysics*, 25: 1, 3–51.

Tyler, I. (2013) 'Naked protest: the maternal politics of citizenship and revolt', *Citizenship Studies*, 17: 2, 211–26.

Unger, R. M (2005) *What Should the Left Propose?* London: Verso.

Urbinati, N. (2006) *Representative Democracy: Principles and Genealogy*, London and Chicago: University of Chicago Press.

Urbinati, N, (2010) 'Unpolitical democracy', *Political Theory*, 38: 1, 65–92.

Urbinati, N. (2014) *Democracy Disfigured: Opinion, Truth, and the People*, Cambridge: Harvard University Press.

Vezovnik, A. (2013) 'Representational discourses on the erased of Slovenia: from human rights to humanitarian victimization', *Journal of Language and Politics*, 12: 2, 606–25.

Voltaire (2014) *Candide*, London: Millennium Publications.

Von Savigny, K. [1803] (2010) *Treatise on Possession, or, The Jus Possessionis of the Civil Law*, Detroit: Gale.

Waldron, J. (1988) *The Right to Private Property*, Oxford: Clarendon Press.

Weil, S. (2014) *On the Abolition of Political Parties*, New York: New York Review of Books.

Wittgenstein, L. (2009) *Philosophical Investigations*, 4th edition, trans. G. E. M. Anscombe, P. M. S. Hacker and J. Schulte, London: Basil Blackwell.

Wolin, S. (2016) *Fugitive Democracy and Other Essays*, Princeton: Princeton University Press.

Woodford, C. (2015) 'Modes of dreaming and doing – Jacques Rancière and strategies for a new left', *Philosophy and Social Criticism*, 41: 8, 811–36.

Woodford, C. (2017) *Disorienting Democracy: Politics of Emancipation*, London: Routledge.

Woodford, C. and Devenney, M. (forthcoming) 'Democratic theory: beyond the pale'.

Žižek, S. (1989) *The Sublime Object of Ideology*, London: Verso.

Žižek, S. (2004) *Iraq: The Borrowed Kettle*, London: Verso.

Žižek, S. (2006) *The Parallax View*, Cambridge, MA: MIT Press.

INDEX

Adorno, T., 23, 28, 31, 41, 50–1, 113
Agamben, G., 2, 25–9, 47–8, 60–2, 142
Althusser, L., 14–16, 42, 71, 150, 159
antagonism, 1, 10, 15, 32, 37–47, 86, 110, 149
Appiah, K., 48
Arendt, H., 76, 79–80, 158
Aristotle, 46, 109–10, 116
articulation, 2, 4, 10–11, 14–18, 20–1, 24–8, 36–7, 49–54, 81–2, 85–91, 97–9, 135–7, 142–9, 151–60

Badiou, A., 42, 160, 163
Balibar, E., 10, 15–16, 20, 119–22
Barkan, J., 21, 30
Bennington, G., 36, 43
Bhandar, B., 121
Brown, W., 17, 22, 85, 96–8, 113, 139–40
Butler, J., 69–82, 112

climate crisis, 1, 137, 151, 156
Coetzee, J. M., 55, 61
Cohen, G. A., 7, 55
colonial, 1–3, 7–10, 18–20, 29–31, 57–63, 67–8, 104–6, 118–22, 136
Congo, 6–7, 29–31
contingency, 3–4, 24–6, 42–4, 91–3, 148–50
Copjec, J., 47, 50

Dahl, R., 107
Dardot, P. and Laval, C., 62–3
Dean, J., 130–1
deconstruction, 8, 12, 14, 37, 47–9, 83, 90, 107
Deleuze, G., 46, 59, 96
democracy, 1–6, 28–31, 41–7, 77–80, 98–9, 103–35 141–5, 149, 153–7
Derrida, J., 37–8, 48–51, 55–6, 70–1, 75
Disch, L., 123–9

Easterling, K., 23, 85, 97
equality, 1–5, 12–14, 20–8, 43–7,
    64–6, 77–9, 104–10, 113–17,
    123–8, 139–42, 150–6
Esposito, R., 20–1, 51–2, 80

Foucault, M., 28, 46, 50, 112–13,
    157

Glasman, M., 35–6
Gramsci, A., 100, 115, 148

Habermas, J., 22, 70, 152, 160–1
Halberstam, J., 151
Hardt, M. and Negri, A., 3,
    52–5, 60
Harris, C., 21

improper, 1–5, 27–31, 33–67,
    72–3, 103–6, 107–14,
    116–19, 131–4, 137,
    156–8

Laclau, E., 10–11, 14–17, 38–47,
    72–3, 85–8, 99–100,
    142–51
Lazzarato, M., 85, 96, 118
Liberty, 17–18, 26, 36, 58, 65,
    119–22, 138–41
Livy, 141
Losurdo, D., 121

Marchart, O., 41, 44, 92, 149–50
Marx, K., 4, 8, 10–18, 41–7, 86–93,
    99, 124–6, 133–5
Mitchell, T., 29
Mouffe, C., 3–4, 14–18, 38–43,
    66, 85–8, 99–100, 138,
    154–5

neoliberalism, 17, 32, 62, 85, 99,
    138–40

Ober, J., 4, 108, 111–13, 161
occupation, 3, 9–12, 33–6, 52–3,
    57–9, 65–7, 76–82, 104–5,
    124–6
Ontology, 1–3, 10–12, 40–7, 50–2,
    60–3, 72–6, 146–50

performativity, 3, 69–81
Pierson, C., 8
Plato, 57, 114, 116–17
pluralism, 63, 107, 131, 152–4
Plutarch, 116
populism, 5–7, 87–8, 114, 118,
    135–57
possession, 2, 6, 9–13, 26–7, 30–1,
    74–6, 108–10, 120–1
Primera, G., 61
property, 6–33, 34–6, 45–9,
    51–66, 78–86, 115–22,
    137–42
propriety, 1–3, 18–23, 29–33,
    52, 66, 69, 80–1, 104–11,
    134–6

queer, 5, 137, 151–2, 156

Rancière, J., 20–4, 43–7, 61, 110,
    126–33, 142, 159
representation, 5, 123–9
Rousseau, J. J., 26, 108–9, 120,
    130, 160

Sassen, S., 5–8, 59, 74
Saward, M., 123–9
Schmitt, C., 8, 18–25, 27, 154
Song, S., 107, 143, 162

sovereignty, 12, 18, 20–2, 25–30, 31–4, 77–80, 110–15, 130–3, 138–41, 152–5

Transnational, 5, 104, 135–57
Tyler, I., 104

value, 4, 15, 39, 42, 54, 64, 86–101
violence, 1–3, 25–30, 50–2, 56–9, 67–9, 81–4, 143–5, 152–4

Woodford, C., 26, 46, 160–2

EU representative:
Easy Access System Europe
Mustamäe tee 50, 10621 Tallinn, Estonia
Gpsr.requests@easproject.com